GCSE 9–1
ENGLISH
LANGUAGE & LITERATURE
AQA
REVISION &
EXAM PRACTICE

Richard Durant
Jon Seal
Cindy Torn
Annabel Wall

Authors Richard Durant, Jon Seal, Cindy Torn, Annabel Wall
English series editor Richard Durant
Editorial team Haremi Ltd
Series designers emc design ltd
Typesetting Newgen KnowledgeWorks (P) Ltd, Chennai, India
Illustrations Newgen KnowledgeWorks (P) Ltd, Chennai, India
App development Hannah Barnett, Phil Crothers and Haremi Ltd

Designed using Adobe InDesign
Published by Scholastic Education, an imprint of Scholastic Ltd, Book End, Range Road, Witney, Oxfordshire, OX29 0YD
Registered office: Westfield Road, Southam, Warwickshire CV47 0RA
www.scholastic.co.uk

Printed by Bell & Bain Ltd, Glasgow
© 2017 Scholastic Ltd
1 2 3 4 5 6 7 8 9   7 8 9 0 1 2 3 4 5 6

British Library Cataloguing-in-Publication Data
A catalogue record for this book is available from the British Library.
ISBN 978-1407-16916-3

Note from the publisher
Please use this product in conjunction with the official specifications for AQA GCSE 9–1 English Language and AQA GCSE 9–1 English Literature and the sample assessment materials. Ask your teacher if you are unsure where to find them.

The mark schemes in this book are simplified versions of the AQA GCSE 9–1 English Language and AQA GCSE 9–1 English Literature mark schemes. See the AQA website for the official mark schemes.

Practice papers for English Literature and the answers for the practice papers are available online. Visit: www.scholastic.co.uk/gcse

How to use this book

Inside this book you'll find everything you need to help you succeed in the new GCSE 9–1 AQA English Language and English Literature specifications. It combines revision and exam practice in one handy solution. Broken down into papers and sections, it presents the information in a manageable format. Work through the revision material first or dip into the exam practice as you complete a section. This book gives you the flexibility to revise your way!

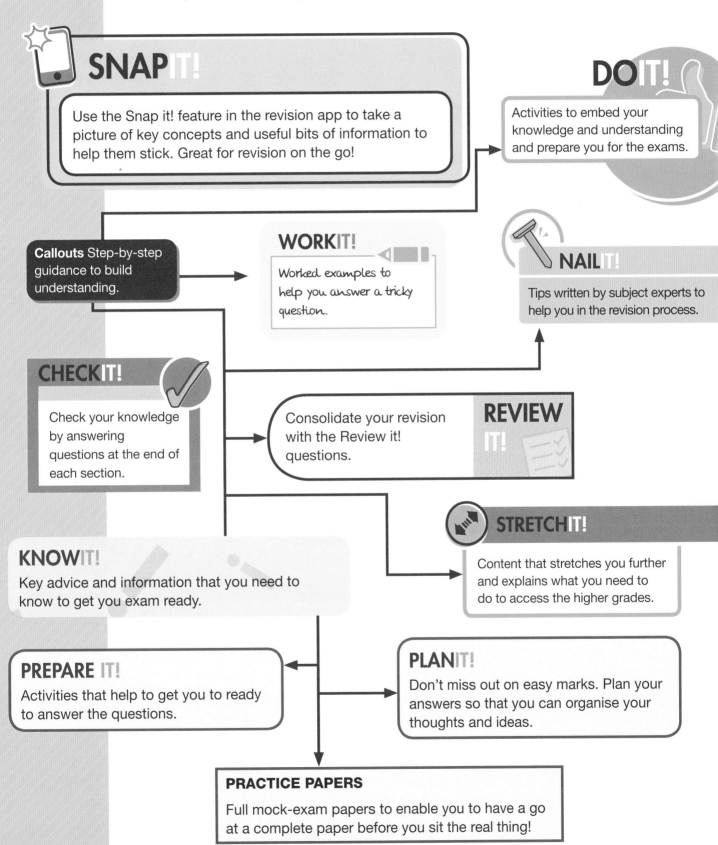

SNAPIT!

Use the Snap it! feature in the revision app to take a picture of key concepts and useful bits of information to help them stick. Great for revision on the go!

DOIT!

Activities to embed your knowledge and understanding and prepare you for the exams.

Callouts Step-by-step guidance to build understanding.

WORKIT!

Worked examples to help you answer a tricky question.

NAILIT!

Tips written by subject experts to help you in the revision process.

CHECKIT!

Check your knowledge by answering questions at the end of each section.

REVIEW IT!

Consolidate your revision with the Review it! questions.

KNOWIT!

Key advice and information that you need to know to get you exam ready.

STRETCHIT!

Content that stretches you further and explains what you need to do to access the higher grades.

PREPARE IT!

Activities that help to get you to ready to answer the questions.

PLANIT!

Don't miss out on easy marks. Plan your answers so that you can organise your thoughts and ideas.

PRACTICE PAPERS

Full mock-exam papers to enable you to have a go at a complete paper before you sit the real thing!

Revision Guide contents

Exam Practice contents

Acknowledgements

The publishers gratefully acknowledge permission to reproduce the following copyright material:

Text permissions
p.13: *Lord of the Flies*, William Golding, Faber & Faber, 1954; p.16: *Small Island*, Andrea Levy, Headline Review, 1996, p.337; p.22: *Atonement*, Ian McEwan, Vintage, 2002, pp.4–5; p.26: *Sons and Lovers*, DH Lawrence, Wordsworth, 1913; pp.31–2: *Brick Lane: A Novel*, Monica Ali, Scribner, 2003; p.50: *Tracks*, Louise Erdrich, Penguin Putnam, 1988; p.50: *Farenheit 451*, Ray Bradbury, Ballantine Books, 1953; p.50: *The Crow Road*, Iain Banks, Little, Brown, UK, 1992; p.50: *The Great Gatsby*, F Scott Fitzgerald, Scribner, 1925; p.50: *City of Glass*, Paul Auster, Sun & Moon Press, 1985; *Adventures of Huckleberry Finn*, Mark Twain, Chatto & Windus, 1885; p.50: *The Towers of Trebizond*, Rose Macaulay, Collins, 1956; p.50: *A Farewell to Arms*, Ernest Hemmingway, Scribner, 1929; p.51: *Never Let Me Go*, Kazuo Ishiguro, Faber & Faber Ltd, UK, 2005; p.59: 'Why it's time to let go of 'Let it Go'', by Rae Earl, theguardian.com, 17 December 2014, © Guardian News & Media Ltd 2016; p.61: *Travels in West Africa*, Mary Kingsley, 1897; p.61: 'Coroner issues warning after shocking crocodile attack', Oct 30, 2015. Used with permission of The Associated Press © 2016. All rights reserved; p.66: Letter to the President of the United States, 1852, attributed to Chief Seattle; p.71: *The Book of Household Management*, Mrs. Isabella Beeton, S. O. Beeton Publishing, London, 1861; p.72: Warm spiced cauliflower and chickpea salad with pomegranate seeds, from *Simply Nigella*, Nigella Lawson, Flatiron Books, 2015; pp.76–7: Letter to the President of the United States, 1852, attributed to Chief Seattle; p.96: *Never Let Me Go*, Kazuo Ishiguro, Faber & Faber Ltd, UK, 2005; p.112: *Macbeth*, William Shakespeare, Act 3 Scene 1, Cambridge School Shakespeare, Cambridge University Press; p.113: *Macbeth*, William Shakespeare, Act 3 Scene 1, Cambridge School Shakespeare, Cambridge University Press; p.120: *Strange Case of Dr Jekyll and Mr Hyde*, Robert Louis Stevenson, Longmans, Green & Co., UK, 1886; p.126: Department of Education, GCSE English Literature: subject content and assessment objectives © Crown Copyright 2013 Open Government Licence; p.128: *Lord of the Flies*, William Golding, Faber & Faber, 1954; p.129: *An Inspector Calls*, JB Priestley, 1945; p.130: *Lord of the Flies*, William Golding, Faber & Faber, 1954; p.130: *The Curious Incident of the Dog in the Night-Time*, Mark Haddon, Jonathan Cape, UK, 2003; p.131: *An Inspector Calls*, JB Priestley, 1945; p.132: *Lord of the Flies*, William Golding, Faber & Faber, 1954; p.140: 'War Photographer' from New Selected Poems by Carol Ann Duffy. Published by Picador, 2009. © Carol Ann Duffy. Reproduced by permission of the author c/o Rogers, Coleridge & White Ltd., 20 Powis Mews, London, W11 1JN; p.143: 'Neutral Tones', Thomas Hardy, 1867; p.146: 'Catrin', from Collected Poems, Gillian Clarke, Carcanet Press, 1997, © Carcanet Press Limited, Manchester, UK, reprinted by kind permission; p.151: 'A Memory', Lola Ridge, 1918; p.152: A Memory, Lola Ridge, 1918; pp.178, 179, 181: *Small Island*, Andrea Levy. Copyright © 2004 Andrea Levy. Reproduced by permission of Headline Publishing Group; p.206: Factory Media; p.207: *Travels with a Donkey in the Cevennes*, by Robert Louis Stevenson, 1879; pp.230, 232: *Macbeth*, William Shakespeare, Act 5 Scene 5, Cambridge School Shakespeare, Cambridge University Press; pp.237, 239: *A Christmas Carol*, Charles Dickens, Chapman & Hall, 1843; p.252: 'Mother, any distance greater than a single span', *Paper Aeroplane (Selected Poems)*, Simon Armitage, Faber and Faber Ltd; p.256: Your Dad Did What?, *Leaving and Leaving You*, Sophie Hannah, Carcanet Press, 1999, copyright Carcanet Press Limited, Manchester, UK, reprinted by kind permission; p.260: 'The Lesson' by Edward Lucie-Smith, from *101 Poems about Childhood*, ed. Michael Donaghy. Published by Faber & Faber, 2005. Copyright © Edward Lucie-Smith. Reproduced by permission of the author c/o Rogers, Coleridge & White Ltd., 20 Powis Mews, London,

W11 1JN; pp.262, 263, 256: *A Clergyman's Daughter* by George Orwell (Copyright © George Orwell, 1935). Reprinted by permission of Bill Hamilton as the Literary Executor of the Estate of the Late Sonia Brownell; p.270: Durham Advertiser, 17 Feb 1882. Throughout: mark schemes adapted from AQA GCSE English Language 8700 and English Literature 8702, AQA 2016.

Photo permissions
p.10: ibreakstock/Shutterstock; p.33: Vadim Ponomarenko/Shutterstock; p.35: matt_train/Shutterstock; p.38: mbuckley98@googlemail.com/Shutterstock; p.40: Cedric Weber/Shutterstock; p.45: Cedric Weber/Shutterstock; p.47: Heldinho/Shutterstock; p.48: Heldinho/Shutterstock; p.56: Marbury/Shutterstock; p.79: qvist/Shutterstock; p.110: Nadzeya Dzivakova/Shutterstock; p.111: Tharun 15/Shutterstock; p.119: lady-luck/Shutterstock; p.125: El Comondear/Shutterstock; p.136: Graeme Dawes/Shutterstock; p.145: Ionut Catalin Parvu/Shutterstock. p.192: Lisa S./Shutterstock.com; p.193: Angelo Giampiccolo/Shutterstock.com; p.197: Photo travel VlaD/Shutterstock.com; p.268: hraska/Shutterstock.com.

Every effort has been made to trace copyright holders for the works reproduced in this book, and the publishers apologise for any inadvertent omissions.

HOW TO REVISE!

PLAN YOUR REVISION

Get ahead by planning your revision!

Work out the **time** you have available for revising.

Think about when you work at your best. Are you a morning or an evening person?

Allocate **MORE TIME** for the topics you struggle with.

Revision works best in **SMALL BURSTS**, so keep sessions **SHORT AND SWEET**!

Remember to allow time to **PRACTISE** applying what you have revised.

Use your **revision app** to put together a revision timetable.

LOOK AFTER YOURSELF

Help your brain by looking after your whole body!

Take regular **breaks** from revising – your brain needs time to digest information in order to retain it.

HOTEL

Keep **hydrated** by drinking plenty of water – dehydration stops your brain from working at its full capacity.

Regular **exercise** helps stimulate the brain and will help you relax.

Get plenty of **sleep**, especially the night before an exam.

EAT WELL and limit unhealthy snacks – your brain needs fuel for memory and concentration.

Find methods of **relaxation** that work for you throughout the revision period.

BE PREPARED!

Limit potential stress on the day of an exam by getting everything you need ready the night before.

30

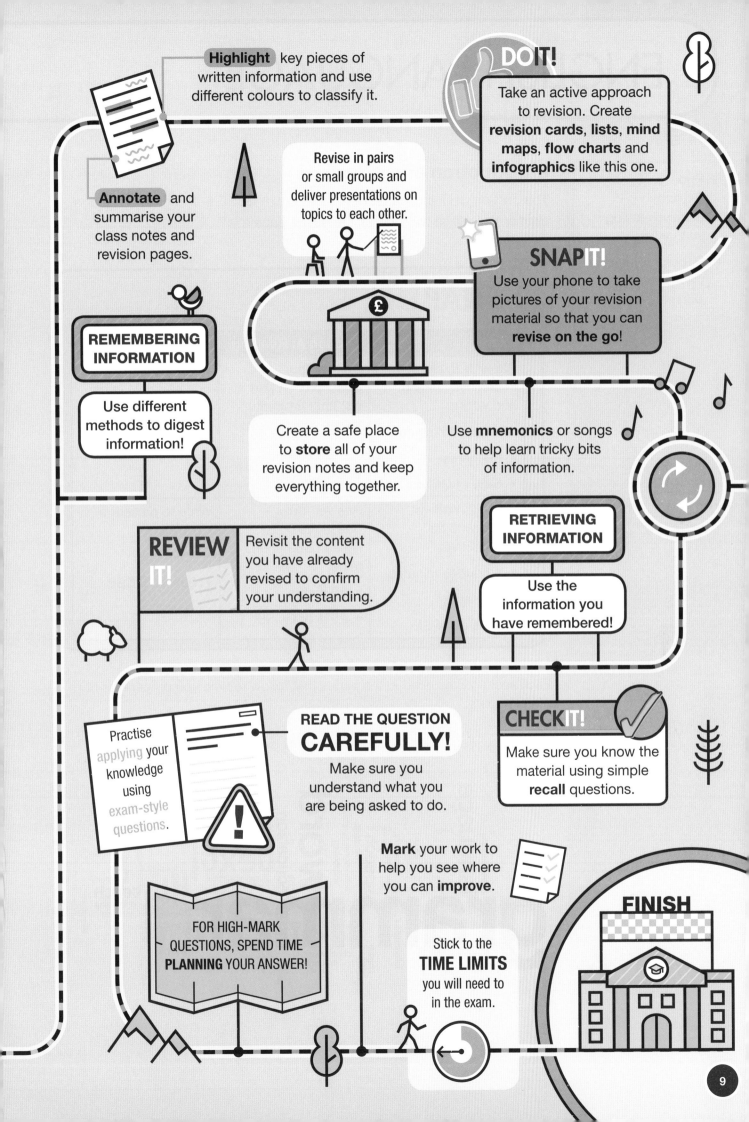

Highlight key pieces of written information and use different colours to classify it.

DO IT!
Take an active approach to revision. Create **revision cards**, **lists**, **mind maps**, **flow charts** and **infographics** like this one.

Annotate and summarise your class notes and revision pages.

Revise in pairs or small groups and deliver presentations on topics to each other.

SNAP IT!
Use your phone to take pictures of your revision material so that you can **revise on the go!**

REMEMBERING INFORMATION

Use different methods to digest information!

Create a safe place to **store** all of your revision notes and keep everything together.

Use **mnemonics** or songs to help learn tricky bits of information.

RETRIEVING INFORMATION

Use the information you have remembered!

REVIEW IT!
Revisit the content you have already revised to confirm your understanding.

Practise applying your knowledge using exam-style questions.

READ THE QUESTION CAREFULLY!
Make sure you understand what you are being asked to do.

CHECK IT!
Make sure you know the material using simple **recall** questions.

Mark your work to help you see where you can **improve**.

FOR HIGH-MARK QUESTIONS, SPEND TIME **PLANNING** YOUR ANSWER!

Stick to the **TIME LIMITS** you will need to in the exam.

FINISH

ENGLISH LANGUAGE

Introduction and advice

This section will help you prepare for the AQA GCSE 9–1 English Language exams. You will sit two English Language papers:

SNAPIT!

Exam	Section A: Reading	Section B: Writing
Paper 1: Explorations in creative reading and writing • 1 hour 45 minutes • 80 marks • 50% of GCSE	Answer four questions on part of a 20th/21st-century literary fiction text. • 40 marks • 25% of GCSE	Write a description or a narrative (story). • 40 marks • 25% of GCSE
Paper 2: Writers' viewpoints and perspectives • 1 hour 45 minutes • 80 marks • 50% of GCSE	Answer four questions on two linked non-fiction texts. • 40 marks • 25% of GCSE	Write to present a viewpoint. • 40 marks • 25% of GCSE

Each section is covered in the pages that follow to help you prepare for both of the papers.

Paper 1 Section A: Reading

Introduction and advice

You will be given an extract from a novel or story that was written after 1900. This extract will be referred to as a **source**.

You will have to answer four questions. The questions will help you think about how the writer tries to capture the interest of the reader.

When you open the paper, flick through it to find the four questions. Notice what the questions are asking. Knowing what the questions are asking will help you focus when you read the text. Spend 15 minutes reading the text carefully. As you read, mark bits of the text that might help you answer the questions.

Here is some important information about the four questions:

☞ Paper 1

☞ Section A: Reading

☞ Marks: 40

☞ Time: 60 minutes

DOIT!

Write down what you think are the four most important things to remember about doing this section of Paper 1. Make a list of bullet points.

SNAPIT!

Question number	You must show that you can...	Typical question stems...	Marks	Minutes to spend on question
1	Identify and interpret explicit and implicit information and ideas.	List four things that…	4	4
2	Show how writers use language to achieve effects and influence readers. Use relevant subject terminology to support your views.	How does the writer use language to…?	8	8
3	Show how writers use structure to achieve effects and influence readers. Use relevant subject terminology to support your views.	How has the writer structured the text to…?	8	8
4	Evaluate texts critically. Support this with appropriate textual references.	Someone has said that 'the writer makes the reader see the scene clearly in their mind'. To what extent do you agree?	20	20

STRETCHIT!

Section A of this paper will always be based on a piece of fiction written some time since 1900. To get the highest possible marks on Section A, Questions 2–4, you need to explain which techniques the writer has used and then explain the effect they have on the reader.

Question 1

Question 1 will ask you to find some information and ideas within the first few lines of the source you are given. Here is an example of a Question 1:

> List **four** things from this part of the text about Helen.   **[4 marks]**

Understanding the question

Question 1 will test whether you can find the information that is actually there in front of you. There are no marks for being clever and complicated: you just need to be clear, simple and accurate.

True statements from the text

Here is a sentence from a novel:

> As Amran crept through the darkened house, her heart was beating fast and she didn't dare to breathe.

What might we learn from this about how Amran is feeling?

A sensible answer would be: she was feeling scared. However, here is what one student wrote:

WORKIT!

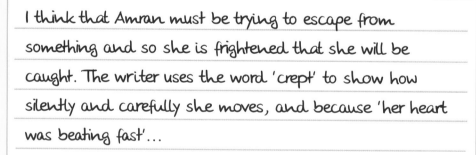

> I think that Amran must be trying to escape from something and so she is frightened that she will be caught. The writer uses the word 'crept' to show how silently and carefully she moves, and because 'her heart was beating fast'...

The exam markers want the answers to be 'true statements' of what is in the extract. This student is not answering the simple question and is wasting his time by making up possible explanations for how Amran is behaving.

NAILIT!

List four clear points that answer the question – don't waste time writing complicated answers or you risk losing time and marks.

NAILIT!

You should spend four minutes on this question.

NAILIT!

You must keep your answers to Question 1 simple and accurate. As you read the text, underline some short bits that are relevant to Question 1.

WORKIT!

Read the opening to the novel *Lord of the Flies* by William Golding.
List **four** things from this part of the text that show that the weather was hot.   **[4 marks]**

> The boy with fair hair lowered himself down the last few feet of rock and began to pick his way toward the lagoon. Though he had taken off his school sweater and trailed it now from one hand, his grey shirt stuck to him and his hair was plastered to his forehead. All round him the long scar smashed into the jungle was a bath of heat. He was clambering heavily among the creepers and broken trunks when a bird, a vision of red and yellow, flashed upwards with a witch-like cry; and this cry was echoed by another.

1   He had taken off his sweater.

2   He had fair hair.

3   There is so much here that makes me think of heat. For example, the word 'smashed' sounds angry and anger is often connected to heat. We sometimes say someone did something in the 'heat of anger', so smashed is angry and violent and therefore hot.

4   His hair is sticky with sweat.

> Only answers **1** and **4** are right. They would each get 1 mark.

Look again at the opening to *Lord of the Flies*. Some words and phrases that suggest the weather was hot are highlighted:

> The boy with fair hair lowered himself down the last few feet of rock and began to pick his way toward the lagoon. Though he had taken off his school sweater and trailed it now from one hand, his grey shirt stuck to him and his hair was plastered to his forehead. All round him the long scar smashed into the jungle was a bath of heat. He was clambering heavily among the creepers and broken trunks when a bird, a vision of red and yellow, flashed upwards with a witch-like cry; and this cry was echoed by another.

Inference: reading between the lines

Once you have chosen some words and phrases that show what the question has asked you, you must write your answers to the question.

There are two sorts of answer:

1   Things you can almost copy directly from the source.

2   Things that are implied in the source so that you have to draw a conclusion from the detail. For example, 'his hair was plastered to his forehead' does not actually tell you that the day is hot, but we can infer it – we can work it out for ourselves. If you are unsure of something you are inferring, then simply add some simple evidence from the source to back up your inference.

DOIT!

Imagine you are a teacher. Write a **short** note to the student who gave the four answers in the Work it! above. Explain why answers 2 and 3 are wrong and therefore get no marks.

NAILIT!

The answer booklet will have numbers 1–4 with space next to each number for your answers.

DO IT!

To explore the difference between knowing and inferring, find some pictures of people you don't know – perhaps in magazines or newspapers – and jot down things we can know about the person (for example, gender), and things we might infer about them from their picture (for example, they are angry).

Think about how our assumptions might affect our inferences. For example, if we don't like the look of a person, we might infer that they are untrustworthy. However, we would probably be wrong.

For example:

- He is feeling hot enough to remove his sweater.
- His hair is 'plastered to his forehead' – presumably with sweat.
- 'Clambering heavily' suggests that he is too hot to move easily.

Do not overdo the explanations: just add a few words of evidence if you are in doubt about your answer.

Here is a section from another novel:

> I left the 'welcome' desk and dragged my bags angrily for the next half hour up to my room. 'Just up the stairs,' I'd been assured. There were two flights of steep steps to negotiate before I could reach my assigned hovel on the third storey of the dilapidated building. Miguel was there already. Spread thinly across three-quarters of the cramped space were his pitiful belongings, and he was coughing extravagantly into the remaining quarter. My quarter.

When we read this extract, there are things we know and other things that we can only infer.

For example, things we **know**:

- It took him half an hour to get up to his room (although he might be exaggerating).
- His room is on the third storey.

Things we can **infer**:

- He is sarcastic.
- He is unhappy about the state of the building.

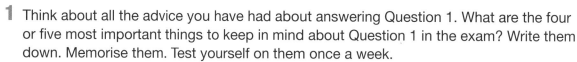

CHECK IT! ✓

1 Think about all the advice you have had about answering Question 1. What are the four or five most important things to keep in mind about Question 1 in the exam? Write them down. Memorise them. Test yourself on them once a week.

2 Here is a handy quiz on Question 1:

a How many minutes should you spend on Question 1?

b Should you explain and explore your answers to Question 1?

c How many pieces of information will you be asked to find?

d Will you be asked to find information from the whole source?

e What should you do as you read through the source?

f Which of the following things is being tested in Question 1?

- Evaluating the effect of the writing.
- Finding the information.
- Analysing the structure of the source.
- Exploring the writer's choice of language.

Question 2

This question will ask you to analyse how writers use language to achieve effects and influence readers. You will have to use relevant subject terminology to support your views.

Question 2 will ask you to comment on the effects of the writer's language choices in the next part of the source. For example:

> How does the writer use language here to describe the festival?
>
> You could include the writer's choice of:
>
> - words and phrases
> - language features and techniques
> - sentence forms.
>
> **[8 marks]**

NAIL IT!

You should spend eight minutes on this question.

Understanding the question

First, you need to be clear about what this question is testing. The question will ask you to suggest how a writer has chosen their language to have an effect on you. You must use subject terminology when you explain your views.

Here is what those key words mean:

SNAP IT!

Word	Explanation
Language	You need to think about words the writer has **chosen**. All of us express things in different ways: we make **choices**. We choose our words carefully so that we use the right ones for the effect we want to have. Writers choose *very* carefully. The writer's choice of words – and the writer's choice of sentence forms – is what we mean by the writer's **language**.
Effect	This is about how the reader responds to the writer's words: what does the reader think of/how does the reader **feel**? Writers choose their words to affect the reader in particular ways.
Your views	These are your beliefs about what the writer is trying to do and how they are trying to do it.
Evidence	These are the details from the text that you choose in order to support the views you put forward. Evidence can be in the form of quotations.
Subject terminology	These are technical words about language. English subject terminology includes words and phrases like sentence, verb, simile, rhetorical question.

Below is a short extract from the novel *Small Island* by Andrea Levy. Read the extract and the comments. The comments explain how Question 2 key words might be relevant to the extract.

Language: the second sentence is not a full sentence. It is not a complete statement. It has no verb. This is also true of sentences 4, 5 and 6.

The **effect** of these 'chopped up', incomplete sentences is that we get a sense of how surprised the **narrator** is. It is as though she cannot easily take in what has happened.

> I'd have recognised it anywhere, the back of Bernard's neck. Bony and scrawny like the back of a heel with his ears sticking out. Seeing me there on the pavement he came towards me. A hat. A white collar. A gaberdene mac* – every button done up and the belt too. He lifted his hat when he reached me, formal, courteous, as if this was a casual meeting. And I was collapsed, sitting on the pavement because my husband whom I hadn't seen for near five years had just approached me. And I said, 'Bernard. You've been away a long time.'
>
> And all he said was, 'Indeed.'
>
> Just that. In-bloody-deed.
>
> *Small Island*, Andrea Levy
>
> * A sort of raincoat

DO IT!

Read the *Small Island* text again. Look very carefully at the last line:

> Just that. In-bloody-deed.

How does the writer use language here to show the narrator's feelings? Write up to six lines to explain your ideas.

Use these rules:

- Explain your views, and use some evidence.
- Use some **subject terminology**.
- Analyse the effect of the writer's **choice** of language.

What is written in the comments is, of course, only a '**viewpoint**', but it is explained, and some details in the text – some **evidence** – is pointed out. 'Verb' and 'incomplete sentence' are examples of subject terminology.

Question 2 mark scheme

When the examiners mark your answers, they refer to **mark schemes**. These schemes are made up of 'band descriptors' rather like the ones below.

SNAP IT!

Mark scheme level	Band 2 descriptors (Roughly GCSE grades 2–3)	Band 3 descriptors (Roughly GCSE grades 4–6)	Band 4 descriptors (Roughly GCSE grades 7–9)
The student's answer...	• shows some appreciation of language choices	• shows clear appreciation of language choices	• examines language choices with insight and precision
	• comments on the effects of language choices	• explains the effects of some language choices	• closely analyses the effects of language choices
	• uses some relevant evidence, including quotations	• uses relevant evidence (including quotations) from different parts of the text	• carefully chooses a variety of evidence, including quotations
	• tries to use some subject terminology.	• uses helpful, relevant subject terminology.	• uses a range of precise and helpful subject terminology.

Look again at the ending to the short extract from the novel *Small Island* by Andrea Levy:

> Just that. In-bloody-deed.

How does the writer use language here to show the narrator's feelings?

You should have written your own answer in response to the activity on page 16. Here is another student's answer with some comments:

WORKIT!

Some accurate subject terminology – 'sentences', 'verbs', 'swearing'.

This answer would be placed low in Band 3.

Neither of these 'sentences' are real sentences. They don't contain verbs. They don't make sense really – not on their own. They sound more like someone talking than writing. The effect of that is that the words sound sarcastic and abrupt. They even sound rude and the swearing makes the rudeness even stronger.

Clear explanation of the effect of the writer's choice of words. No quotations, although details are pointed out.

Here are two more answers:

WORKIT!

Student answer A

The narrator uses a mild swear word – 'bloody' – to show that she is cross with Bernard. She keeps things short too. This might show that she is fed up.

Student answer B

Clearly the narrator is annoyed with Bernard. We get this impression because her made-up word, 'In-bloody-deed', contains a swear word and it echoes Bernard's words sarcastically. 'Just that' is an incomplete sentence – as though Bernard's ridiculous explanation doesn't deserve anything more.

Answer	How it compares with the mark scheme descriptors	Mark band
A	The student chooses one relevant quotation and gives a very brief explanation of what it tells us about the narrator, although nothing is said about how it affects the mood...	
B		
My answer		

DOIT!

Look back at the two student answers above, and at your own answer. Compare each answer with the band descriptors you've just looked at in the mark scheme. Would you give each answer a Band 2, 3 or 4? Explain your thinking.

Use a table like the one shown to analyse the three answers.

Sentence forms

One aspect of language choice that many students ignore is sentence forms. You will notice that one of the answers you have just looked at does begin to consider the **effect** of sentence styles: 'Just that' is an incomplete sentence – as though Bernard's ridiculous explanation doesn't deserve anything more.

All writers vary their word order and the lengths and sorts of sentence for effect. This is what the exam paper calls 'sentence forms'.

Here is the extract you read in the section on Question 1 on page 14. The writer is trying to use varied sentence forms to affect the way the reader responds to the narrator. The sentence forms help the narrator to show his feelings.

> I left the 'welcome' desk and dragged my bags angrily for the next half hour up to my room. 'Just up the stairs,' I'd been assured. There were two flights of steep steps to negotiate before I could reach my assigned hovel on the third storey of the dilapidated building. Miguel was there already. Spread thinly across three-quarters of the cramped space were his pitiful belongings, and he was coughing extravagantly into the remaining quarter. My quarter.

Below is what one student wrote about the extract:

WORKIT!

The first sentence has two clauses, separated by the word 'and'. The last ten words of the first sentence, consists of three adverbials giving more information about the verb 'dragged': 'angrily' (how); 'for the next half hour' (when) and 'up to my room' (where). This list of adverbials deliberately drags the sentence out and emphasises the physical dragging that the narrator is doing.

DOIT!

Collect together a number of well-written novels published in the last 100 years. In each novel, find an extract of around 100 words that makes reasonable sense on its own and is interesting to read. Analyse the sentence forms in each of those extracts.

DOIT!

Make some notes on the extract. Identify:

- different sorts of sentence (simple, compound, complex)
- varied lengths of sentence
- word order in sentences
- the effect of these.

STRETCHIT!

To gain the highest marks for Question 2 you need to:

- identify a range of language features and explore them in detail (write a lot about a little)
- explain the effect of the language features on the reader (what do they make you think of, how do they make you feel)
- use relevant subject terminology as part of your explanation
- choose the best quotes and embed them where you can.

NAILIT!

Don't just spot sentence features: explain how the chosen features convey meaning and effect.

Here is the first part of a Band 4 response to the *Small Island* extract:

WORKIT!

By the end of the extract the narrator's negative attitude towards Bernard is plain. Clearly the narrator is annoyed with Bernard. We get this impression because her made-up word, 'In-bloody-deed', contains a swear word and it echoes Bernard's words sarcastically. 'Just that' is an incomplete sentence – as though Bernard's ridiculous explanation doesn't deserve anything more. The incompleteness of the sentence also implies that the narrator can't be bothered either. You can imagine her turning to you and saying, 'Just that' as though they want you to notice that Bernard has just confirmed what the narrator has just been telling you about him. 'Just that' has an informal, oral quality. It's almost as though the narrator has said to the reader, 'there you go. Just like I was saying.' However, this weary, contemptuous attitude is present throughout the extract. Even at the beginning...

> This feature – use of an incomplete sentence – is explored in depth.

> Relevant subject terminology – oral, informal – is identified and its effect is explored.

> Impact on reader.

DOIT!

Add to the comments on this answer, and then finish off the answer. Try to:

- keep the same Band 4 quality
- use the bullet points in the Stretch it! on page 18 to guide you.

CHECKIT!

1 Look back over the advice in the last five pages about answering Question 2.

  a Without looking at this book, make a list of at least eight key words (or phrases) that are important in the typical wording of Question 2.

  b Next to each word (or phrase) explain why it is important.

    Here is an example of a key word and its explanation:

Word or phrase	Explanation and thoughts
Effect	The impact on the reader: how the chosen words make the reader feel or react. It is important to explain what the effect is (or effects are).

Question 3

NAILIT!

You should spend eight minutes on this question.

Question 3 will ask you to comment on the effects of the writer's structural choices in the whole of the source. For example:

> How has the writer structured the text to interest you as a reader?
>
> You could write about:
>
> * what the writer focuses your attention on at the beginning
> * how and why the writer changes the focus as the Source develops
> * any other structural features that interest you.   **[8 marks]**

Understanding the question

First, you need to be clear about what this question is testing. You will be asked to suggest how a writer has structured (organised) their writing to have an effect on you. You must use subject terminology when explaining your views.

The most important focus is on what are called structural features – the things that a writer uses to make their writing a **coherent** (or joined-up and understandable) whole. The structure of a piece of writing includes those features that hold it all together and make it work. Texts in this exam will typically be structured into a sequence of paragraphs which together exert an influence on the reader. Without structure, writing becomes random, hard to follow and ineffective. You must be able to identify structural features, and then explain their effects.

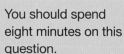

DOIT!

Write down some structural features for each of the following things:

a a bike

b a school

c a film

d an extract from a novel.

Before you review your understanding of structural features in writing, it is worth considering what we mean by the structure of a number of different things.

For example, if we dismantled a fridge and put all the bits in a bag, it would no longer be a fridge, even though every part was still there: it would no longer have the structure of a fridge.

Similarly, if we took an extract from a novel and jumbled up its words (or even its letters), we would no longer have an extract from a novel, even though it was still 'all there': the extract would no longer have a meaningful structure.

Here are some of the structural features of a fridge:

* door hinges to connect the door and allow it to open and close
* a motor in the right place and connected correctly
* a light that usefully comes on when the door opens
* right-angles at its corners.

Narrative fiction – like anything else – has features that hold it together, make it 'work', and make it recognisable as narrative fiction. There is no official list of these features, but some common structural features you might find in an extract from a novel include:

SNAPIT!

Structural feature	Explanation
Information put into a particular order (sequence)	For example, information about a character might be given to us in this order: appearance, behaviour, some background.
Dialogue to reveal character, move the narrative on, etc.	Writers often use direct speech (dialogue) so that we can 'hear' what characters sound like. It can bring them to life for us.
Narrative chronology	Most stories are told in the order they happened (their chronology). Some stories (and films) are structured around dramatic events, with shifts into the past and future to explain those events.
Narrative shifts	For example, from small, close-up details to larger and larger ones, or the opposite.
Repetition – of words, phrases, ideas, images, etc.	Repetition can be a sort of thread that connects parts of the text together.
Changing/ developing focus	For example, from description of view, to description of the immediate scene, to the thoughts of a character.
Extended images	A writer might describe a person or place in a certain way, and then develop this image over a few lines (or even chapters).
A particular style, tone or mood	A large part of a story (or all of it) might have a particular style, tone or mood: for example, humorous, sad, mocking, tense, and so on. Tone is the attitude of the writer or narrator towards what they are writing about.
Narrative voice and perspective	Often a story is told from one character's point of view – their perspective. Sometimes it is the author's 'voice' that we can almost hear.
Paragraphs	Changes of paragraph are often used to signal shifts: in time, place, topic, action, and so on. Topic sentences can be used to signal a changing or developing theme.
Summaries, introductions, conclusions	For example, an event or character might be introduced, developed, and some sort of conclusion reached.
Genre	Many stories fit a particular genre: horror, romance, science fiction, for example. The typical features of the genre may be part of the story's structure.

DOIT!

Think of all the structural features you have learned about during your English course. Write down a few, and give brief explanations for each one.

NAILIT!

Learn your list of structural features. Look out for examples of them in everything you read. Choose random parts of novels and stories and see if you can identify structural features in them.

Read this short extract from the novel *Atonement* by Ian McEwan. Here, a character called Briony is introduced to us. Notice how the writing is organised. Notice its tone, and other **structural features**, and how these give us a strong impression of Briony.

DO IT!

- What impression of Briony do you get?
- What other structural features has the writer used?
- How does each feature help to build the overall impression of Briony?

> She was one of those children possessed by a desire to have the world just so. Whereas her big sister's room was a stew of unclosed books, unfolded clothes, unmade bed, unemptied ashtrays, Briony's was a shrine to her controlling demon: the model farm spread across a deep window ledge consisted of the usual animals, but all facing one way – towards their owner – as if about to break into song, and even the farmyard hens were neatly corralled. In fact, Briony's was the only tidy upstairs room in the house. Her straight-backed dolls in their many-roomed mansion appeared to be under strict instructions not to touch the walls; the various thumb-sized figures to be found standing about her dressing table – cowboys, deep-sea divers, humanoid mice – suggested by their even ranks and spacing a citizen's army awaiting orders.
>
> *Atonement*, Ian McEwan

The overall impression we are given of Briony as a character (a person) is the overall structural feature of this extract.

Question 3 mark scheme

The mark scheme is similar to Question 2, except that the focus is on **structural features** rather than **language choices**. The answer must give evidence – not necessarily quotations – and use subject terminology accurately.

SNAP IT!

Mark scheme level	Band 2 descriptors (Roughly GCSE grades 2–3)	Band 3 descriptors (Roughly GCSE grades 4–6)	Band 4 descriptors (Roughly GCSE grades 7–9)
The student's answer...	• shows some appreciation of structural features • comments on the effects of structural features • uses some relevant evidence • tries to use some subject terminology.	• shows clear appreciation of relevant structural features • explains the effects of some relevant structural features • uses different forms of relevant evidence • uses helpful, relevant subject terminology.	• examines relevant structural features with insight and precision • closely analyses the effects of relevant structural features • carefully chooses a variety of evidence • uses a range of precise and helpful subject terminology.

DOIT!

Re-read the extract from *Atonement* (page 22) and look again at the mark scheme for Question 3.

Now read the answer extracts below. One of the answers is in Band 2, one is in Band 3, and one is in Band 4. Decide which is which, and write down why.

WORKIT!

> How has the writer structured the text to give a clear idea of Briony? **[8 marks]**

Student answer A

The writing is very persuasive for the reader. We aren't given any chance to see Briony unclearly: how she is, is very clear indeed. One way the writer does this is by using strong words about Briony's obsession right through the extract: she is 'possessed'; she has a 'controlling demon'; her dolls are 'under strict instructions'; her models are in 'ranks' awaiting 'orders'. All the words make us see Briony as an extreme controller. Also, the writer uses...

Student answer B

The writing is structured almost like a formal argument: it starts by asserting that Briony's strongest motivation is to 'have the world just so'. In other words, Briony wants to control and organise her world. The next few lines give examples of this to convince the reader that Briony has this 'controlling demon' inside her. Half-way through the extract, the phrase 'In fact' introduces an even more emphatic persuasion that Briony is a controller. This emphasis of Briony's controlling and ordering behaviour is strengthened by the use of contrast – with her sister's 'stew' of untidiness and everyone else's room being untidy as well. Another structural feature used by the writer in giving a clear picture of Briony is...

Student answer C

The writer keeps repeating words that have the same beginnings – un – unclosed, unfolded, and so on. This repeating seems to bang into the reader's mind this picture of the mess in Briony's sister's room, and of course Briony's room isn't like that at all. This repeating feature makes this picture very clear and strong. All the words about Briony's habits with her things are also very strong and that makes it really definite that Briony is a controller. You can't really disagree. So for example she 'coralls' her model animals, and her model people are in ranks and wait for orders.

Briony is also…

STRETCH IT!

To gain the highest marks for Question 3 you need to:

- identify a range of language features and explore them in detail (write a lot about a little)
- explain the effect of language features on the reader (What do they make you think of? How do they make you feel?)
- use relevant subject terminology as part of your explanation
- choose the best quotes and embed them where you can.

CHECK IT! ✓

1 Without looking at this book, make a list of at least ten structural features from memory. Write an explanation next to each feature.

2 Which one of the following three things could count as a structural feature?

    a spelling   **b** repetitions   **c** exclamation marks.

3 List three reasons for starting a new paragraph.

4 What image is being extended in the following sentence?

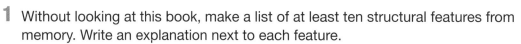

    'He quacked his way through the next song, flapping his arms helplessly, wishing he could float away unnoticed.

5 How many marks are available for Question 3?

6 What is meant by 'tone' in fiction?

7 How many minutes should you spend on Question 3?

8 What is meant by 'the structure of a fiction extract'?

Question 4

Question 4 will begin with a quoted reader reaction, and then ask you to write about the source in relation to that reaction. For example:

A student, having read this section of the text said: 'The writer creates a thrilling sense of tension in this extract. You are desperate to know what will happen.'

To what extent do you agree?

In your response, you could:

- write about your own impressions of what happens

- evaluate how the writer has created these impressions

- support your opinions with references to the text. **[20 marks]**

NAILIT!

You should spend 20 minutes on this question.

There are as many marks for Question 4 as there are for the first three questions altogether. Spend 20 minutes on this question, so that you can get as many of the 20 marks as possible.

Understanding the question

The question will ask you to consider how successful the writer has been in **engaging** the reader. Partly this is about giving a thoughtful **personal response**. Partly it is about choosing **evidence** from the text to support your response. You need to appreciate what the writer is trying to do, and how they are trying to do it. The golden rules for this question are:

- Read and understand the question carefully.

- Think about what impact or influence the writer is trying to have on you, the reader.

- Think about what is good (and perhaps less good) about the writing.

- Don't get carried away with your own feelings about the text: keep your distance.

- Use quotes from the text to support your thoughts.

- Use the bullet points in the question to help plan and structure your response.

DOIT!

Make a poster containing six frames – one for each of the golden rules. Write a rule in each box and draw a simple symbol or picture to help you remember each rule.

Responding to the text

Question 4 wants to know how you react to the text. You must show that you are sensitive to the meaning, tone and mood of the text.

For Question 4 you will write about part of the source (extract) you wrote about for the first three questions.

On page 26 there is a typical text extract for Question 4. The extract is taken from near the end of a novel by DH Lawrence, published in 1913. Paul is about to go away, but Miriam had been hoping he would stay.

> She stood before the mirror pinning on her hat. How bitter, how unutterably bitter, it made her that he rejected her sacrifice! Life ahead looked dead, as if the glow were gone out. She bowed her face over the flowers—the freesias so sweet and spring-like, the scarlet anemones flaunting over the table. It was like him to have those flowers.
>
> He moved about the room with a certain sureness of touch, swift and relentless and quiet. She knew she could not cope with him. He would escape like a weasel out of her hands. Yet without him her life would trail on lifeless. Brooding, she touched the flowers.
>
> 'Have them!' he said; and he took them out of the jar, dripping as they were, and went quickly into the kitchen. She waited for him, took the flowers, and they went out together, he talking, she feeling dead.
>
> She was going from him now. In her misery she leaned against him as they sat on the car. He was unresponsive.
>
> Where would he go? What would be the end of him? She could not bear it, the vacant feeling where he should be. He was so foolish, so wasteful, never at peace with himself. And now where would he go? And what did he care that he wasted her? He had no religion; it was all for the moment's attraction that he cared, nothing else, nothing deeper. Well, she would wait and see how it turned out with him. When he had had enough he would give in and come to her.
>
> *Sons and Lovers*, DH Lawrence

Question 4 requires you to give personal responses to the text, and explore the possible thoughts and feelings of the characters.

- Who do you like more – Miriam or Paul? Why?
- What are the differences between Miriam's and Paul's personalities?
- What does Miriam fear?
- What is important to Paul?
- What is Miriam's attitude towards Paul?

This sort of question requires you to 'enter' the text and to share the experiences of the characters.

Here is one reader's reaction to the extract from *Sons and Lovers*:

DOIT!

Think about the response questions and jot down your answers. Look carefully at the details in the text that influence your responses.

Then think of two or three other possible reactions to the text. Write them down. Decide which of these reactions you think are the most reasonable and explain why.

WORKIT!

The writer really makes you feel the depth of Miriam's distress. The writer takes you right inside her heart and mind.

26

Here is an example of a Question 4 on the *Sons and Lovers* extract on the previous page. Notice how it starts with a reader reaction statement:

A student, having read this section of the text said:

'The writer really makes you feel the depth of Miriam's distress. The writer takes you right inside her heart and mind.'

To what extent do you agree?

In your response you could:

- write about your own impression of Miriam's thoughts and feelings

- evaluate how the writer has created these thoughts and feelings

- support your opinions with references to the text.   **[20 marks]**

> Here is a reader reaction. You must use it as the focus for what you write about the extract.

> This is the actual question: how much do you agree with the reaction?

> These prompts are there to help you structure and develop your answer. The key ideas in these prompts are:
> 'your own impression'
> 'evaluate'
> 'references to the text'.

Key ideas in Question 4

Your own impression: you need to develop an impression – a response. Explore the **effect** of the writing as a reader – what does the extract make you think of? How does it make you feel?

Evaluate: to **evaluate** you need to decide how good (in other words how successful) the writing is. Explore **how** the writing makes you feel the way it does – how has the author been successful in making you feel this way?

References to the text: refer to the text to support the relevant points you make. Choose some very short quotations and explain how they are relevant and the effect they might have on a reader.

Look again at this extract from a novel:

> I left the 'welcome' desk and dragged my bags angrily for the next half hour up to my room. 'Just up the stairs,' I'd been assured. There were two flights of steep steps to negotiate before I could reach my assigned hovel on the third storey of the dilapidated building. Miguel was there already. Spread thinly across three-quarters of the cramped space were his pitiful belongings, and he was coughing extravagantly into the remaining quarter. My quarter.

Of course, the way that this extract has been written makes us have certain impressions of the narrator. It would be possible to rewrite the extract so that it contains roughly the same information in the same order, but gives a different impression of the narrator. For example, what if the extract began like this?

> Smiling, I turned from the welcome desk and carried my bags calmly up to my room.

We would probably get a different impression of the narrator: he or she seems calm and satisfied.

DO IT!

Answer the following two questions, making some references to the text:

- What impression do we get of the narrator and his feelings? (Your own impression.)
- What is good about the writing? (Evaluate.)

27

DOIT!

1 Try rewriting the whole extract on page 27 three times. Keep the same information but try to create three different impressions of the narrator:

• dangerous   • nervous   • confident.

2 Find short extracts in novels you have read. Decide what impression the reader gets about the character or the situation in the extract. Rewrite the extracts so that the reader gets different impressions.

By doing this you are experimenting with:

• how a writer creates impressions in the reader
• the quality of the writing
• how details in the text create particular impressions.

3 Now find an extract of about 350 words from another novel or story. Try to choose an extract that is interesting and makes reasonable sense on its own. Part of one of your English literature exam novels would be a good choice.

Write a typical Question 4 that is relevant to your chosen extract.

• Make sure you start with a reader reaction statement.
• Follow that with a 'To what extent do you agree…?' question.
• Try writing an answer for your own question.

Question 4 mark scheme

Here are the criteria ('descriptors') that exam markers will use when they mark Question 4.

SNAPIT!

Mark scheme level	Band 2 descriptors (Roughly GCSE grades 2–3)	Band 3 descriptors (Roughly GCSE grades 4–6)	Band 4 descriptors (Roughly GCSE grades 7–9)
The student's answer…	• tries to make some comments that evaluate the text • refers to a relevant example from the text • refers to some of the writer's techniques • uses a couple of helpful quotations.	• includes a clear evaluation • gives examples that support and clarify points • helpfully explains the effects of some of the writer's techniques • uses helpful quotations from different parts of the text.	• critically evaluates the text in a detailed way • gives examples from the text to explain views convincingly • analyses effects of a range of the writer's choices • justifies points with relevant quotations from different parts of the text.

Here is one student answer to the question on page 27, with some comments about how it might meet some of the descriptors.

WORKIT!

So the writer does keep saying how deep Miriam's despair and depression is – 'bitter', 'dead'...

> Choose some relevant quotations to support your views.

... but we also get this impression from the contrast with Paul's behaviour and attitude: he has 'a certain sureness of touch' and he is compared with a weasel that is impossible to hold onto because it is so lively. This contrast of characters makes the reader wonder whether this separation was inevitable.

Paul seems to be completely unaware as to how Miriam is feeling, making him seem shallow and uncaring in comparison to the depth of Miriam's 'brooding' unhappiness.

> Give examples from the text to convincingly explain these views.

This part of the answer seems to be in Band 3 (although the whole answer might be better or worse than Band 3).

 STRETCHIT!

To get to Band 4 of the mark scheme, you have to be a critical reader. You have to evaluate the text. This means being able to explain what you particularly notice, or like, about a text and why.

The Band 4 criteria are:
- critically evaluate the text in a detailed way
- give examples from the text to explain views convincingly
- analyse effects of a range of the writer's choices
- choose a range of relevant quotations to justify views.

1 Read the three answers in Check it! on page 30 – A, B and C.
2 Decide which answer is closest to Band 4.
3 Check the answer against the advice you have read in this Stretch it! section.
4 Improve the answer so that it is firmly within Band 4.

CHECKIT! ✓

1 Write down five important things you have already learned about how to answer a Question 4.

2 Below are parts of answers to the question on *Sons and Lovers* from page 27. Put these three answers into a rank order from best to worst. Within the answers, find examples of advice and rules for Question 4 being kept or broken.

Student answer A

It says 'brooding' and that shows she is thinking hard and a bit miserable about it. It's definite – we know just how she is feeling because the writer says it. We know she is deep in her thoughts. Later on it says 'misery' when she is leaning on him. Again we know exactly how deep she feels.

Student answer B

So the writer does keep saying how deep Miriam's despair and depression is – 'bitter', 'dead' – but we also get this impression from the contrast with Paul's behaviour and attitude: he has 'a certain sureness of touch' and he is compared with a weasel that is impossible to hold onto because it is so lively. This contrast of characters makes the reader wonder whether this separation was inevitable.

Student answer C

I don't really like this writing and I can't get into it because Miriam seems so hopeless and a bit pathetic. On the other hand, perhaps that means I am right inside Miriam's heart and mind. Although the author is telling the story (he is the narrator), we see things from Miriam's point of view, so we are sort of with her. For example, when it says 'It was like him to have those flowers' it doesn't say that the narrator says this: it's like Miriam has suddenly become the narrator!

3 Before moving on, make sure you have learned from all the essential advice and information about Question 4 on the last five pages. Test yourself on the questions below.

   a What percentage of the marks in the Paper 1 reading section come from Question 4?

   b How much time should you spend answering Question 4?

   c What are the golden rules for answering Question 4?

   d What is the importance of a reader reaction statement in Question 4?

The extracts in this section come from the beginning of Monica Ali's novel *Brick Lane*. Rupban is pregnant and plucking a chicken when she suddenly goes into labour. The local midwife arrives. The baby's name is Nazneen.

1 How many minutes should you spend reading the questions and the text extract (source)?

2 What should you do before you read and while you read the text?

3 What is the focus of Question 1? (What is it testing?)

4 How many minutes should you spend answering this question?

5

> Hamid ran from the latrine, although his business was unfinished. He ran across the vegetable plot, past the towers of rice stalk taller than the tallest building, over the dirt track that bounded the village, back to the compound and grabbed a club to kill the man who was killing his wife. He knew it was her. Who else could break glass with one screech? Rupban was in the sleeping quarters. The bed was unrolled, though she was still standing. With one hand she held Mumtaz's shoulder, with the other a half-plucked chicken.
>
> Mumtaz waved Hamid away. 'Go. Get Banesa. Are you waiting for a rickshaw? Go on, use your legs.'

List four things from this part of the text about urgency. **[4 marks]**

6 What is the focus of Question 2?

7 How many minutes should you spend answering Question 1?

8 Banesa arrives but pronounces the baby dead.

> 'See your daughter,' Banesa said to Rupban. 'Perfect everywhere. All she lacked was someone to ease her path to this world.' She looked at Cheepy-cheepy lying next to the bereaved mother and hollowed her cheeks; a hungry look widened her eyes slightly although they were practically buried in crinkles. It was many months since she had tasted meat, now that two young girls (she should have strangled them at birth) had set up in competition.
>
> 'Let me wash and dress her for the burial,' said Banesa. 'Of course I offer my service free. Maybe just that chicken there for my trouble. I see it is old and stringy.'

How does the writer use language to introduce Banesa?

You could include the writer's choice of:

- words and phrases
- language features and techniques
- sentence forms. **[8 marks]**

9 What is the focus of Question 3?

10 How many minutes should you spend answering Question 2?

11 Write down at least ten examples of structural features.

12 Now the baby comes back to life.

> Mumtaz took hold of Nazneen, who was still dangling by the ankle, and felt the small, slick torso slide through her fingers to plop with a yowl onto the bloodstained mattress. A yowl! A cry! Rupban scooped her up and named her before she could die nameless again.
>
> Banesa made little explosions with her lips. She used the corner of her yellowing sari to wipe some spittle from her chin. 'This is called a death-rattle,' she explained. The three women put their faces close to the child. Nazneen flailed her arms and yelled, as if she could see this terrifying sight. She began to lose the blueness and turned slowly to brown and purple. 'God has called her back to earth,' said Banesa, with a look of disgust.

You now need to think about all three extracts from *Brick Lane*.

How has the writer structured the text to interest you as a reader?

You could write about:

- what the writer focuses your attention on at the beginning
- how and why the writer changes this focus as the Source develops
- any other structural features that interest you.

[8 marks]

13 What is the focus of Question 4?

14 How many minutes should you spend answering Question 4?

15 Look back over all three extracts.

- How do you feel about one or more of the characters?
- How well do you think the writer has created the scene?
- How successful has the writer been in making the scene interesting?

Focus your answer on the second and third extracts from *Brick Lane*.

NAIL IT!

Create a plan for question 15 before you answer it.

16 A student, having read these extracts, said: 'Although what happens here could be very upsetting, it is in fact amusing.'

To what extent do you agree?

In your response, you could:

- write about your own reactions to the scene
- evaluate how the writer has prompted these reactions
- support your opinions with references to the text.

[8 marks]

Paper 1 Section B: Writing

Introduction and advice

The exam paper will ask you to write a description or a narrative. There will only be two tasks and you must choose **one** of them.

Here are examples of the sorts of writing task you might be asked to carry out:

☞ Paper 1

☞ Section B: Writing

☞ Marks: 40

☞ Time: 45 minutes

> Write the dramatic ending to a mystery story. **[40 marks]**

> Write a description of a place that is special to you. **[40 marks]**

> Write a description suggested by this picture. **[40 marks]**

> Describe an exciting day in your life. Focus on your thoughts and feelings at the time. **[40 marks]**

The writing task will appear as Section B on the paper. It is Question 5. (Questions 1–4 are in the reading section – Section A.)

The topic of the writing task will link to the text in the reading section of Paper 1.

Make sure you leave at least 45 minutes to do the writing task. In other words, don't spend more than an hour on Section A of the exam paper. You should aim to write at least two sides of average-sized handwriting – but remember the quality of your writing is more important than quantity.

STRETCH IT!

The best writing will tend to be more ambitious with its use of sentence variety and vocabulary. The focus of this paper is on creativity, and so high marks will go to writing that is accurate and well controlled, but also original.

Understanding the question

Question 5 comes after the reading section. It will always follow the same format:

- It will give you the context by telling you the audience (who you are writing for, such as fellow students, judges of a competition), the **form** (the type of writing: narrative or description) and the **purpose** (what it is for: the school website, a competition entry…).

- You must choose one of the two tasks.

- There will always be at least one picture and one written stimulus.

- It will focus on description, and/or narrative writing.

- It will always link to the theme of the reading stimulus in the reading paper.

The choice of task will change each year, so you need to be prepared to write both types of text:

- You could have a choice of a descriptive and a narrative task.

- You could have to choose between two descriptive tasks.

- You could have to choose between two narrative tasks.

Roughly speaking, the writing tasks will fall into five categories:

1 Descriptive writing with a visual image

2 Descriptive writing without a visual image

3 Narrative with a visual image

4 Narrative – writing the opening to a story

5 Narrative – writing a complete story

Here is an example of the choices you might be given for your exam writing task. The choice is between a description based on a picture, and a story opening without a picture stimulus.

> You are going to enter a creative writing competition.
>
> Your entry will be judged by a panel of people of your own age.
>
> **EITHER**: Write a description suggested by this picture:
>
>
>
> **OR**: Write the opening part of a story about a place by the sea. **[40 marks]**

These lines give the context: the purpose is to win a competition; the form is creative writing.

This is what you must actually do – the task itself. The audience - is people of your own age.

There will be a given context for the tasks, with a definite audience, purpose and form for your writing. You will notice that the context is the same for both tasks. The sea is the topic that is common to both tasks, so the reading text in Section A of this exam paper must have featured the sea as a main topic.

Although the context, topic and mark scheme will be the same for descriptive and for narrative writing, it is important that you write in the correct form. Some students start to write a description and then they shift into narrative part-way through. This is a risk, particularly when you are asked to describe an event.

Of course, good narrative writing will always include descriptions, and descriptions of events will have to include some element of narrative. However, it is worth being clear about the typical key features of each of these two forms.

Narrative	Descriptive
• written in the past tense	• written in the present tense
• action important	• action not important
• fiction	• non-fiction

NAILIT!

In the exam, write narrative in the past tense. Write descriptions of places in the present tense. (Descriptions of past events will have to be written in the past tense.)

DO IT!

Read the three pieces of writing. Which one is fiction narrative? How do you know?

These are **typical** features, but the two forms can overlap. For example, descriptive writing can include descriptions of actions, and just occasionally fiction narratives are written in the present tense.

> **A**
>
> Nestling among rich green pine groves and backed by the spectacular snow-capped San Antonio mountains, Sudorno Hotel is a jewel in the island's crown. At night it gleams like a diamond as it catches the moonlight over the tranquil bay.

> **B**
>
> She caught a glimpse of the hotel through the fading light. It shone like a jewel. She crouched into the cover of the thick undergrowth and stealthily made her way towards her target. It was certainly a perfect, tranquil place, but no guest would get much sleep that night.

> **C**
>
> On the best day of my life I was excited from the moment I woke up. The moment I opened my eyes I almost gasped with the thrill of knowing where I would be going that day. I flung back my bed covers and flipped myself out of my top bunk, landing perfectly on my feet before I leaped into the bathroom.

There are 40 marks for the writing task:

- 24 marks for content and organisation
- 16 marks for accuracy.

Content is about your ideas and how you express yourself so that you 'connect' with your reader (audience). You should communicate clearly, effectively and imaginatively and use tone, style and register that are appropriate for the given form, purpose and audience.

Organisation is about how you structure your content, for example, with paragraphs, discourse markers, openings and closings. You should organise information and ideas, using structural and grammatical features to support coherence and cohesion.

Technical accuracy is about spelling, punctuation and grammar, and about using effective sentence length and structure and vocabulary. Use a range of vocabulary and sentence structures for clarity, purpose and effect with accurate spelling and punctuation. You can lose a lot of marks for being inaccurate, so be careful. (See Technical accuracy section on page 95.)

Question 5 mark scheme

Whatever category the writing task belongs to, it is meant to help you to write creatively. The skills involved in writing the task are always the same, and every task will be marked against the same mark scheme. On page 37 is a simplified version of the mark scheme for you to refer to as you revise.

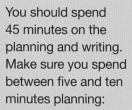

NAIL IT!

You should spend 45 minutes on the planning and writing. Make sure you spend between five and ten minutes planning:

- your ideas
- how your ideas will be organised
- the sort of words and phrases that will be effective and appropriate.

SNAPIT!

Mark scheme level	Band 2 descriptors (Roughly GCSE grades 2–3)	Band 3 descriptors (Roughly GCSE grades 4–6)	Band 4 descriptors (Roughly GCSE grades 7–9)
Content	• is mainly clear in expression • keeps trying to match register to purpose, form and audience • chooses words with some care • uses some linguistic devices.	• is clear, effective and engaging throughout • mainly matches register to purpose, form and audience • precisely chooses words and phrases for deliberate effect • uses varied linguistic devices for impact.	• wins the reader over and holds their interest throughout • precisely matches register to purpose, form and audience • uses a wide and adventurous vocabulary • carefully chooses linguistic devices for effect throughout.
Organisation	• uses suitable ideas that have some variety and sometimes link together • uses some paragraphs and discourse markers • uses some other structural features (for example, deliberate repetition, topic sentences).	• uses varied ideas, linking them well • carefully organises paragraphs around well-chosen discourse markers • uses structural features for deliberate impact.	• is highly structured and developed around a range of dynamic and complex ideas • is highly coherent and fluent in organisation, incorporating discourse markers in a natural way • uses a range of structural features skilfully and creatively.

DOIT!

Look at the mark scheme and decide which areas you will need to concentrate on to move your writing towards the next band up. Write these down as personal targets for improvement.

✓ CHECKIT!

1 How many marks are available for the writing section of Paper 1?

2 How many marks are available for content and organisation?

3 How many writing tasks will be on the paper for you to choose from?

4 How is the writing task linked to the texts in the reading section?

5 You will be given a context for your writing. What is meant by context?

6 Which two sorts of writing will you have to choose from in this writing exam?

Question type 1: descriptive writing with a visual stimulus

A typical descriptive question for this part of the exam paper could be:

> You are going to enter a creative writing competition.
>
> Your entry will be judged by a panel of people of your own age.
>
> Write a description suggested by this picture:
>
>
>
> [40 marks]

Planning and generating ideas

The question tells us that the purpose for the writing is a competition entry and the audience is a group of people your age. However, as they are going to judge this entry you need to impress them. In the exam instructions on the front of the paper you are instructed to 'write in full sentences'. This tells you that you should write in Standard English (no text-speak or emojis) and you must make sure that your sentences are formed and punctuated correctly.

Look at the picture above.

One method of planning and structuring your description is to think of yourself looking at the scene. Imagine yourself to be a camera, one that can record what is seen and heard – but can also include other senses too. As you observe this scene, you can break it down into **five phases**:

1. **Set the scene**. This is where you create a wide-angled shot which gives a sense of the whole picture.

2. **Draw in other senses**. Sounds might work especially well here, but you could also describe smell or touch.

3. **Zoom in on one part of the scene**. Describe it in close detail.

4. **Find a contrast within the picture**. If it is a busy street, is there part of the picture where it is quiet?

5. **Back to the big picture.** Decide how you will return to the whole picture. How has the scene changed since the opening section? Has time moved on?

You should plan your ideas in response to the picture using a table like the one below, which relates to the example exam question on page 38. The prompts are there to help your thinking as you begin to generate your ideas. You should add questions that you find helpful as you use this method. Remember the prompts are sections of your description and sections may be one or more paragraphs each.

Phase	Notes – ideas and language
Phase 1: **Set the scene** • Where is it? or What is it? • What are the key colours? • Where are your eyes drawn to first of all? • What is the mood and atmosphere of this scene?	relaxing colourful rainbow foreground like a photo from a tourist brochure brooding background of cliff like a monster/evil whale?
Phase 2: **Draw in other senses** • What can you add to the plan here? • Smell? Sound?	
Phase 3: **Zoom in on one part of the scene** • What is the mood or atmosphere within the detail? • What is it that makes it interesting? Does it change the mood of the picture? (For example, a child crying on a sunny beach, someone walking alone along a crowded street.) • What realistic details can you add?	
Phase 4: **Find a contrast within the picture** • What can you add to the plan here? • What contrasting mood is suggested?	
Phase 5: **Back to the big picture** • How will you end your description? With the contrast or will you return to the whole picture? What changes will have taken place since the first section? • What realistic details can you add?	

Complete the rest of this table referring to the photo on page 38.

Find an interesting photograph in a magazine or online. Stick it on a sheet of paper and then prepare a description of it filling in a table like the one here.

Linguistic devices: figurative language

The mark scheme for this question measures your ability to use a range of linguistic devices. Figurative devices (or imagery) are part of this group and can help you to write successful, descriptive pieces of writing.

- Simile: when two things are compared using **as** or **like** (for example, he fought **like** a lion).

- Metaphor: a figure of speech in which two things are compared, usually by saying one thing is another (for example, he **was** a lion in battle, or he **roared** with anger).

- Personification: describing non-human objects using human characteristics: actions, body parts, emotions, and so on (for example, the hail hammered **angrily** against the **terrified** window).

Look at the picture of the castle below and read one student's description:

WORKIT!

Exhausted by many lifetimes of cold and wind, the castle rests solidly in its landscape. Over the decades, it has crept towards the moat, desperate to paddle its stone and turrets. Glorious sunsets hide its ageing battlements as they silhouette in perfection, like a warrior against the horizon. But like those tourists who have been coming back year-by-year to soak up the sun, its skin has become cracked and worn by a weathered existence.

> Notice how the student has repeated ideas and images. This is an extended metaphor. The student suggests that the castle is like an ageing warrior who is aching to rest its elderly structure.

Here are some relevant descriptors that exam markers would use to judge the quality of writing. Look in particular at the final bullet point in each column.

Mark scheme level	Band 2 descriptors (Roughly GCSE grades 2–3)	Band 3 descriptors (Roughly GCSE grades 4–6)	Band 4 descriptors (Roughly GCSE grades 7–9)
Content	• is mainly clear in expression • keeps trying to match register to purpose, form and audience • chooses words with some care • uses some linguistic devices.	• is clear, effective and engaging • mainly matches register to purpose, form and audience • chooses increasingly sophisticated words and phrases for effect • uses a range of appropriate linguistic devices.	• is convincing and compelling throughout • assuredly matches register to purpose, form and audience • manipulates the reader in subtle ways • uses a wide, ambitious vocabulary • uses carefully crafted linguistic devices throughout.

Here is what an exam marker wrote about the castle description on page 40:

This is an ambitious and confident description. It engages the reader throughout. Its extended metaphor – of the castle as an exhausted warrior – is well handled and very believable. The simile that compares the weathered castle to sunburn is also original (although perhaps it goes too far).

CHECKIT!

1 Write a few sentences to describe details from the castle scene on page 40. Use three types of imagery: simile, metaphor, personification.

2 In your sentences, are there images/ideas that are repeated or extended?

3 If not, which one is your favourite (strongest, most powerful) image/idea?

4 What would/could your extended metaphor be? How will this improve your writing?

Question type 2: descriptive writing without a visual stimulus

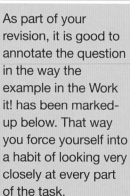

NAILIT!

As part of your revision, it is good to annotate the question in the way the example in the Work it! has been marked-up below. That way you force yourself into a habit of looking very closely at every part of the task.

You may be asked to write without a visual stimulus. Look at the question below.

Your school or college is asking students to contribute some creative writing for its website.

Describe an occasion when you faced a personal challenge. Focus on the thoughts and feelings you had at that time. **[40 marks]**

Planning

The **audience** here is the school community (students and teachers) but, as it is for the website, it will also have a wider audience of adults and even young people outside the school.

The **form** is creative writing for a school website.

The **purpose** is to describe an occasion, and – by implication – to show the school in a good light.

Preparing the question is always very important, and it is especially important for questions without a picture stimulus. Preparing the question means making sure you understand exactly what it is telling you to do, and making sure you have taken note of all the information in the question.

Here is how one student identified the key words in the question and planned their response:

WORKIT!

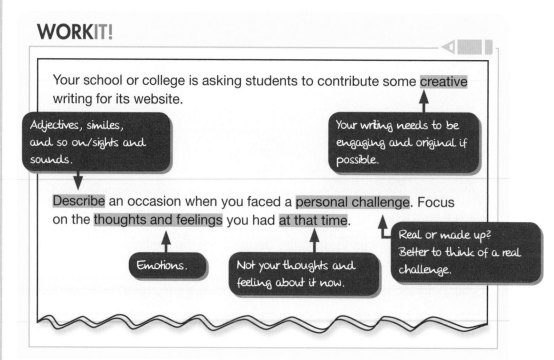

This question is asking you to write about a personal challenge. However, it is asking you to describe your **thoughts** and **feelings**. Don't fall into the trap of just telling the story. This student has prepared the task very well by considering all its parts.

Below is the student's plan for the question. They have used **before**, **during** and **after** planning categories, and identified thoughts and feelings for each. This is a good example of producing a plan after having worked out exactly what the question is asking of you.

WORKIT!

Personal challenge – my first day at a new school		
Before	**Thoughts:** Watching children in the playground – thinking that they look as if they belong there. Knowing that I will have to make new friends. Wishing that I didn't have to go. Thinking that if I ran away no-one would ever be able to find me.	**Feelings:** Missing the comfort of my old friends. Feeling nervous, apprehensive. Feeling as if my legs will not hold me. Feeling that it's all too noisy.
During	**Thoughts:** Walking into the classroom thinking that everyone is looking at me. Trying to remember names but knowing that I would forget and then they would all hate me. Thinking that the teachers seem different, more terrifying than my old school.	**Feelings:** Feeling out of control as if I'm on a rollercoaster. Getting an answer right and worrying that I would make a fool of myself.
After	**Thoughts:** It's over... It's over... It's over! Trying to think that it wasn't that bad – but really thinking it was. Thinking that I have to convince my mum that I am fine and happy.	**Feelings:** Feeling relieved but angry that I had to leave everyone I knew. Feeling happy that it was over but feeling dread that I had to go back. Understanding that it would get better. That I had started to make friends.

Here is another example question:

> A leading breakfast cereal maker is offering a prize for the best description of the perfect breakfast. The judging panel will be made up of young employees of the company.
>
> Write a description of your perfect breakfast. This could be a breakfast you have had, or one you would like to have.
>
> **[40 marks]**

DOIT!

Prepare the question and then write a plan. You could (but you don't have to) use a before, during and after structure as shown above. You will need this plan later in this section of the book.

DO IT!

Write the opening paragraph of the 'perfect breakfast' task that you were given on page 43.

NAIL IT!

- Engage your reader appropriately at the start.
- Use your plan and your annotations.
- Use the mark scheme to make sure your writing is as sophisticated as it can be.
- Avoid incomplete sentences.

DO IT!

Look at answers A and B.

- Which answer is better?
- What makes it better?

Now look again at the mark scheme on page 37. Find elements of each answer (A and B) that match that mark scheme.

Starting your writing

Your writing needs to:

- communicate clearly, effectively and imaginatively
- use tone, style and register that are appropriate for the given form, purpose and audience.

If you engage your reader effectively and in an appropriate way at the start of the writing, then the exam marker will have immediate confidence in you.

Look back at the 'personal challenge' task in Work it! on page 42. How might you begin your description? Look at these different opening paragraphs about a personal challenge:

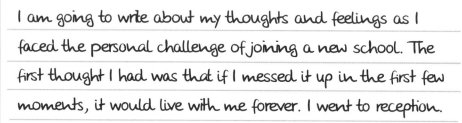

WORKIT!

Student answer A

I am going to write about my thoughts and feelings as I faced the personal challenge of joining a new school. The first thought I had was that if I messed it up in the first few moments, it would live with me forever. I went to reception.

Student answer B

As I stood watching the whirling children, I knew that the first introductions would shape the rest of my days in this school. Thoughts scattering with dread, I slowly opened the gate and walked into reception. My heart pounded.

Here is what an exam marker wrote about each answer:

Student answer A

This answer is working at a low Band 2. It is mainly clear in expression and some words are chosen with care (for example, 'it would live with me forever'). However, the content does not match the purpose of a piece of descriptive writing at the start ('I am going to write about my thoughts and feelings as I faced the personal challenge of joining a new school').

Student answer B

This answer is working at Band 4. It is convincing and compelling and assuredly matches register to purpose, form and audience. There is evidence of wide vocabulary – for example, 'scattering with dread'.

One common trap that students fall into when writing descriptions is to use incomplete sentences. This is especially true when students just copy phrases from their plans straight into their writing. It is as though the student is **writing** a series of captions for a scene rather than a proper description. Here are some incomplete sentences (captions) that could go with the castle picture you have already worked with:

- Squatting on the lake
- Sandy brown in the mid-afternoon light
- An access bridge like an outstretched tongue

Here is the first incomplete sentence turned into a full sentence:

The castle squats on the lake.

Sometimes incomplete sentences can be joined together into one flowing sentence. For example:

Sandy brown in the mid-afternoon light, the castle squats on the lake with its access bridge stretched out like a tongue.

DO IT!

Turn the other two incomplete sentences into full sentences.

Look at an extract from a student's writing about a frosty morning:

> Snow and ice everywhere on the paths and roads. People's footsteps showing the route they had taken, engraved deep and easy to see. Frost on the branches slowly turning to ice as another layer started to grow.

Now look at the corrected extract below:

> Snow and ice are everywhere on the paths and roads. People's footsteps are showing the routes they have taken and are engraved deep and easy to see. Frost on the branches is slowly turning to ice as another layer starts to grow.

CHECK IT! ✓

1 What is meant by 'annotating the question'?

2 What is involved in planning an answer?

3 What is important about the opening of your writing?

4 Which is the better opening below, and why?

   a Cradled in the blue-green waters of the Indian Ocean, the beach shimmers gently like a dream of paradise.

   b The sea is a sort of bluey-green, and the beach is lovely and bright and hot. It is just perfect for me.

5 Which of the following are incomplete sentences?

   a The sky grazed the white-capped waves at the horizon.

   b My heart thumped with nerves.

   c Heart thumping with nerves.

   d Next to the bacon was the shiniest, roundest fried egg I'd ever seen.

   e The plumpest sausage I'd ever tasted.

Question type 3: narrative with a visual stimulus

A local travel agent is planning a display of story openings with beach settings. Your English teacher has asked you to write for the display.

Write the opening of a story suggested by this picture:

[40 marks]

Preparation and planning

You should approach writing a story based on a picture in the same way that you would approach any other narrative writing:

- plan your ideas and some of the language you will use

- engage your reader at the start of your writing

- don't forget the mark scheme.

Writing tasks will ask you only to base your writing on the picture. It should therefore be a platform, a starting point for your own ideas.

When answering this type of question you should:

- make notes around the picture stimulus

- ask yourself questions in your notes

- think in terms of narrative events rather than just describing what is there

- use the picture as a starting point: literally think outside the box.

Spend a few minutes studying the picture and asking yourself questions about it.

Below are the notes that one student made on the picture.

WORKIT!

Perhaps they are all watching something happening at sea? Perhaps a fleet of speed boats is approaching the beach?

What is just outside the picture on this side? What if it is high fences and armed guards? Perhaps this is a beach being guarded from terrorist attack.

The picture is taken from a high angle. Is someone watching the beach through binoculars, perhaps on a hotel balcony?

Perhaps someone has just realised that he cannot see his wife and one of his children. Lost? Kidnapped? Running away from him?

What is interesting about this student's notes is that they are definitely seeing the picture as a source for a story, not a description. That is important: a picture stimulus for a story risks getting purely descriptive responses from students.

Here is the opening of a student's writing about the beach picture:

WORKIT!

From his observation tower on the promenade, Marcus scoured the beach with his binoculars. In his dark grey, ill-fitting uniform, he felt uncomfortable under the merciless midday sun. His watch bleeped the fifteen-minute signal, and he briefly lowered his binoculars to give the compulsory 'all ok' wave to his comrades in the neighbouring towers. 'Don't ignore the bleep,' their fat, useless commander always warned them. 'It's the bleep of life. Dead men ignore the bleep.' Marcus raised the glasses again, and sweat mingled with a rising sense of resentment as his magnified gaze swept across the lucky bodies on the beach.

> Suddenly, his attention was caught by two details:
> Firstly, a sun-burnt man standing on tip-toe, shading
> his eyes and peering into the distance, and then -
> almost immediately afterwards - a roaring sound that
> grew louder with every second. He swung his binoculars
> in the direction of this noise and was alarmed to see
> a whole fleet of large speed boats racing towards the
> shore, their prows raised on waves of white froth.

DO IT!

Compare this writing with the descriptors in the mark scheme on page 37.

Notice how this student has used their notes on the picture. Notice too how they have tried to use two typical elements of narrative fiction: action and character. This has helped them to avoid writing purely descriptively.

This writing is firmly in the top band of the mark scheme: Band 4. This is what one exam marker said about this student's writing:

> This is a compelling opening that immediately creates
> a very believable character in Marcus: we seem to get
> to know him straight away. We assume he is some sort
> of security guard but the low-quality, impractical
> uniform hints that he works for a company that is
> not very professional. This impression is confirmed by
> the description of the 'commander'. The student uses
> ambitious and creative vocabulary to keep the atmosphere
> alive: 'magnified gaze', 'scoured' and 'merciless'. On
> the other hand, the student also uses simple language
> choices when he wants to speed up the action. Although
> the writing is in the third person - 'he', 'Marcus' - we
> get the sense that we are getting Marcus' view of events
> and this helps the reader to sympathise with Marcus.

DO IT!

Find a variety of interesting pictures. Make notes around each picture. Think beyond the frame of the picture.

✓ CHECKIT!

1 What does 'thinking outside the box' mean for picture stimulus questions?

2 Action is one main element of narrative fiction that makes it different from description. Name one other element.

Question type 4: narrative – writing the opening to a story

A typical narrative question for this part of the exam paper could be:

You are going to enter a creative writing competition.

Your entry will be judged by a panel of people of your own age.

Write the opening part of a story about a place that has been damaged by a storm.

[40 marks]

Preparation and planning

It is important to note that this question only asks you to write the 'opening part' of the story, so it is important to engage your reader right from your first line.

Narrative hooks

It is possible to put story or novel openings into categories. These are often called **narrative hooks**. When you are generating your story ideas, it is helpful to know some of these categories or types of narrative hooks.

NAILIT!

Remember that the opening of a story should engage the reader's attention straight away.

Type of hook	Example
The hook that sets the mood and atmosphere	We started dying before the snow, and like the snow, we continued to fall. Louise Erdrich, *Tracks* (1988)
The hook that causes the reader to raise questions or surprises the reader	It was a pleasure to burn. Ray Bradbury, *Fahrenheit 451* (1953) It was the day my grandmother exploded. Iain Banks, *The Crow Road* (1992)
The hook that focuses on a character	In my younger and more vulnerable years my father gave me some advice that I've been turning over in my mind ever since. F Scott Fitzgerald, *The Great Gatsby* (1925)
The hook that starts with a key event or action	It was a wrong number that started it, the telephone ringing three times in the dead of night, and the voice on the other end asking for someone he was not. Paul Auster, *City of Glass* (1985)
The hook which addresses the reader directly	You don't know about me without you have read a book by the name of *The Adventures of Tom Sawyer*; but that ain't no matter. Mark Twain, *Adventures of Huckleberry Finn* (1885)
The hook that begins with dialogue	'Take my camel, dear,' said my Aunt Dot, as she climbed down from this animal on her return from High Mass. Rose Macaulay, *The Towers of Trebizond* (1956)
The hook that describes the setting	In the late summer of that year we lived in a house in a village that looked across the river and the plain to the mountains. Ernest Hemingway, *A Farewell to Arms* (1929)

Here are the first few lines of the novel *Never Let Me Go* by Kazuo Ishiguro and some thoughts by a student who had not read the rest of the book:

WORKIT!

Very direct opening. It sounds like she is talking to me.

Not really descriptive – more factual.

'waste of space' is unusually informal for a narrative. That sort of language is usually only used in speech in stories.

The style sounds more like talking than writing. I feel like I know Kathy and we're having a conversation.

I feel uneasy now: why would a donor not be expected to do well? Why would anyone be a repeat donor? What would they be donating? She's a carer so they must be donating body parts!

> My name is Kathy H. I'm thirty-one years old, and I've been a carer now for over eleven years. That sounds long enough, I know, but actually they want me to go on for another eight months, until the end of this year. That'll make it almost exactly twelve years. Now I know my being a carer so long isn't necessarily because they think I'm fantastic at what I do. There are some really good carers who've been told to stop after just two or three years. And I can think of one carer at least who went on for all of fourteen years despite being a complete waste of space. So I'm not trying to boast. But then I do know for a fact they've been pleased with my work, and by and large, I have too. My donors have always tended to do much better than expected. Their recovery times have been impressive, and hardly any of them have been classified as 'agitated,' even before fourth donation.

DOIT!

1 Find seven different novels or stories written for adults. Try not to spend too long thinking about your choices. A good way of doing this activity is to go to your school library or local library fiction section and simply take seven novels off the shelves at random.
   Read the first page of each novel in turn. Don't turn the first page – even if the page stops in mid-sentence. Now answer these questions:

   • How is the writer trying to hook me into the story?
   • Does the first page have characters, descriptions, dialogue?
   • What sort of story is this? (Horror? Real-life drama? Romance?)
   • What will happen in the story?
   • What clues on the first page suggest what might happen?

2 Do the same exercise for the first page of a modern novel you have studied on your GCSE course. Try to forget that you have read the whole novel. Try to re-read the first page 'for the first time'.

3 Find another novel. Turn straight to the second page. Read up to page ten or to the end of the chapter – whichever comes first. Now try to write the 'missing' first page. Finally, compare your version with the real first page.

DO IT!

1 Look at the three openings below written by students. Decide which narrative hook each student has used.

Student answer A

The sea surged against the rocks as the storm continued its war on the village. Gates swung from hinges that could barely hold on. In Devon this was nothing new, but the villagers were still afraid.

Student answer B

I need to tell you something right from the start. Storms are different here. You think you have seen it all on the Geographic channel? You're wrong.

Student answer C

'Move away from that window!' she screamed as the torrent of water simultaneously flooded through the door and the windows. The baby woke and began to wail as chaos swirled in with the water.

2 Which do you think is most successful?

3 Try out three different types of hook for your opening to a story about a place that is damaged by a storm.

4 Write three or four sentences for each type of hook listed in the table on page 50.

DO IT!

Describe each of the events below to show what is happening, rather than telling your reader what is happening.

- A man got his car stuck in mud. He was angry.
- A boy fell over and cut his hand.
- The dog was excited by the snow.

Show don't tell

When you are writing either a narrative (story) or a description, it is important to show your reader details rather than to tell them. For example, if your character is cold in your story, it is better to show that they are cold by the way they speak and behave rather than just to tell your reader 'they were cold'. Look at the example below:

Tell	Show
She was cold	Shoulders hunched against the wind, she pushed her hands further into her coat pockets. Her scarf whipped against her face as she moved stubbornly down the street.

CHECK IT! ✓

1 Seven different narrative hooks have been explained in this section. Each of the openings below uses at least one of these seven hooks. Which hooks are used by each opening?

  a She caught a glimpse of the hotel through the fading light. It shone like a jewel. She crouched into the cover of the thick undergrowth and stealthily made her way towards her target. It was certainly a perfect, tranquil place, but no guest would get much sleep that night.

  b When she had finally finished swimming, she carefully put her leg back on.

  c You know how it's always just when you're about to do something that your parents ask you if you've done it yet? Well, that's what makes me mad.

2 Rewrite the following sentence so that it shows, rather than tells: *He was clumsy.*

3 Name five things you should try to include in the first page of your story in order to engage the reader.

Question type 5: narrative – writing a complete story

NAILIT!

For this type of question, you will be asked to write a **whole** story, whereas in the fourth question type (on page 50) you will be asked to write only **the opening** to a story.

A typical narrative question for this part of the exam paper could be:

> You have been invited to produce a piece of creative writing for a local newspaper.
>
> Write a story about a celebration or party that goes badly wrong.
>
> **[40 marks]**

Preparation and planning

You are writing a whole story, so you need to keep the plot manageable. You also need to make sure that the story is believable.

- Keep your storyline simple – the events, characters and settings only matter if you portray them in exciting ways.

- You are better opting for an exciting 'single-event story' with one or two characters and telling it well, rather than planning a complicated story and running out of time.

- Keep your storyline simple by keeping to personal experience. You will write more convincingly about situations you know or understand.

- Use a simple structure to help you shape your ideas. Here is a simple four-part structure that can be used in a story you will have only 45 minutes to plan and write:

  1 Normality

  2 Disruption/problem

  3 Climax/crisis

  4 Return to normality/result

- Never use clichéd endings '… and then I woke up and it was all a dream…' '… and they lived happily ever after.'

- Don't over-use dialogue, as this can get out of control and make your writing difficult to follow.

Look at the table on page 54, showing a four-part structure for creative writing. It is an example of a student's planning notes for a story about a celebration or party that goes badly wrong.

DOIT!

Using the plan in the table, write the opening paragraph to this story.

WORKIT!

Normality	1st person narrative
	Going to an 18th birthday party
	Lots of fun and noise
Disruption/problem	Lots of dancing and drinking
	Everyone having lots of fun, but risks are becoming clear (drunkenness)
Climax/crisis	Someone suggests setting off the fireworks
	Description of the fireworks
	One firework doesn't go off... disaster
Return to normality/result	After the party in hospital
	A new version of normality

Here is one student's writing using the plan:

WORKIT!

Everyone said you should never return. Why didn't I listen?

It was the 18th birthday of the year and the focal party for our group where we all thought about reaching adulthood. We had started the evening by ordering takeaway, and as I phoned the order through, Chris got the party started.

'Food shouldn't be long,' I said as we walked into the living room to just give it one last check.

After months of planning, we had everything we needed to host the perfect party. We had food. We had drink and we had entertainment. By planning down to the last detail, we knew we had thought of everything. The music was good and loud. We had researched loads of drinking games and best of all – we had fireworks.

As people arrived and the atmosphere livened up, the drink went down faster and faster.

Everybody was dancing round and Chris skittered past me, wearing a badge saying '18 today'. As I made my way through the living room, my feet were unsteady beneath me. I realised that I'd had too much to drink. Chris and Mel were in the corner, drinking shots of vodka one after the other. The bottle was almost empty. 'Time for the fireworks?' he asked. 'I think so,' I agreed.

We picked up the bag of fireworks from the kitchen where we had left it, and made our way up the garden path. The night was cold and dark and the only noise to be heard was the music coming from the house. As we lit the first fuse, a glowing orange rocket shot upward, exploding into a flower of silver and blue crackles. People crowded by the door to see. Cheers and whoops of joy surrounded us. One by one the rockets set off, until we came to the very last one - the big one.

As I lit the fuse I was full of anticipation, waiting to be amazed by a huge display of sounds and sights - but they didn't come. I looked back at the fuse. It wasn't lit. Everyone said you should never go back, but I didn't listen. Unsteadily I bent down towards the fuse...

I lay in bed, and touched my face. I felt a bandage and in my heart I knew that I should have listened. Everyone said you should never return.

DO IT!

1 Try to apply the four-part story structure to this story. Find the points where each of the four parts begins.
2 Use the mark scheme on page 37 to assess this student's writing.
   a Decide on the band.
   b Find three descriptors from the mark scheme to support why you have placed the writing in that band.

✓ CHECK IT!

1 Why is personal experience often good material for a story in the exam?

2 What four-part structure could be used for a story?

3 Name two things that can ruin a story.

1   How many writing tasks will be offered in Question 5?

2   What two sorts of writing can be set in the writing tasks?

3   What percentage of the marks for the writing task are given to technical accuracy?

4   How does Section B (writing) link to Section A (reading) on Paper 1?

5   Name three typical features of narrative.

6   How much time should you leave on Paper 1 for Section B: Writing?

7   How much time should you spend planning the writing task?

8   Name three types of figurative language.

9   What metaphor has been extended in the following text?

> " Sally glanced back at her pursuer, who kept closing the gap, never deviating from the invisible track he seemed to be gliding along. His face had a metallic gleam in the sunlight and the pistons of his arms and legs never faltered for a moment. "

10   Name a trap to avoid when doing descriptive writing.

11   For which sort of writing task is 'before, during and after' a useful planning structure?

12   Which of the following sentences is incomplete?

   a   A delicious aroma of chocolate.   b   As I had promised to do it, I did.   c   She ran.

13   What is the most important thing to remember about the opening of a story?

14   Name three common narrative hooks that can be used at the start of a story.

15   What is the difference between showing and telling?

16   Rewrite this sentence so that it shows rather than tells:
     She was selfish.

17   Name a simple four-phase story structure that you could use in the exam.

18   When planning a narrative task based on a visual image, what does 'thinking outside the box' mean?

19   You have been invited to produce a piece of creative writing about fears and superstitions.

   Write a story set in or near a deserted house as suggested by this picture:

   [40 marks]

Paper 2 Section A: Reading

Introduction and advice

You have one hour to do this part of the paper, including 15 minutes for reading and planning. You will be given **two** non-fiction texts. One of these will have been written before 1900. The other will have been written after 1900. They will be linked by topic.

You will have to answer four questions. The questions will ask you about what the writer is telling you, and about how the writer is trying to influence you. Here are the types of question you will be asked, and the marks you can get:

☞ Paper 2
☞ Section A: Reading
☞ Marks: 40
☞ Time: 60 minutes

SNAP IT!

Question number	You must show that you can...	Typical question stems...	Marks	Minutes to spend on question
1	Identify and interpret explicit and implicit information and ideas.	Choose four statements that are true…	4	4
2	Select and synthesise evidence from different texts.	Write a summary of the differences between…	8	8
3	Explain, comment on and analyse how writers use language and structure to achieve effects and influence readers. Use relevant subject terminology to support your views.	How does the writer use language to influence…?	12	12
4	Compare writers' ideas and perspectives, as well as how these are conveyed, across two texts.	Compare how the two writers convey their different attitudes to…	16	16

When you open the paper, flick through it to find the four questions. Notice what the questions are asking. Knowing what the questions are asking will give you a sharp focus when you read the text.

Now spend a few minutes reading the texts carefully. As you read, mark bits of the text that might help you answer the questions.

STRETCH IT!

Identifying specific methods the writers use to influence you, and analysing the effects of these methods, will get you the top marks.

Question 1

NAILIT!

You should spend four minutes on this question.

Understanding the question

Question 1 will test whether you can find the information that is actually there in front of you. It will focus on the first of the two texts. You need to be accurate and read each statement carefully.

For example:

Read again the first part of **Source A** from **lines 1 to 15**.

Choose **four** statements below which are TRUE.

- Shade the boxes of the ones that you think are true.

- Choose a maximum of four statements.

A	There will be three non-fiction texts for you to answer questions about.	
B	One of the texts will have been written before 1900.	
C	There will be four questions.	
D	Question 2 will be about one of the texts.	
E	You shouldn't read the questions until you've read the texts.	
F	Question 3 will be about a writer's use of language.	
G	One central focus of the questions is on how writers influence readers.	
H	Another central focus is on how writers try to entertain readers.	

[4 marks]

You will be given statements that are true and statements that are false. You need to read them carefully.

The exam markers expect you to find 'true statements' from the extract. Remember that the statements may sound true – or may be true to you, but you need to **focus on what is in the extract**.

Inference: reading between the lines

NAILIT!

There are only four true statements. You will get one mark for each correct choice.

As with the first reading question on Paper 1, you will sometimes have to infer a piece of information in Question 1 on Paper 2. For example, in Work it! on the following page we **know** that statement A is correct because the writer uses the exact words in the suggested statement: 'I try to block it out'. For statement B, though, we have to infer that when the writer says that parents are 'being driven slowly insane' this **must** mean that they dislike the song, although the writer does not literally say that.

WORKIT!

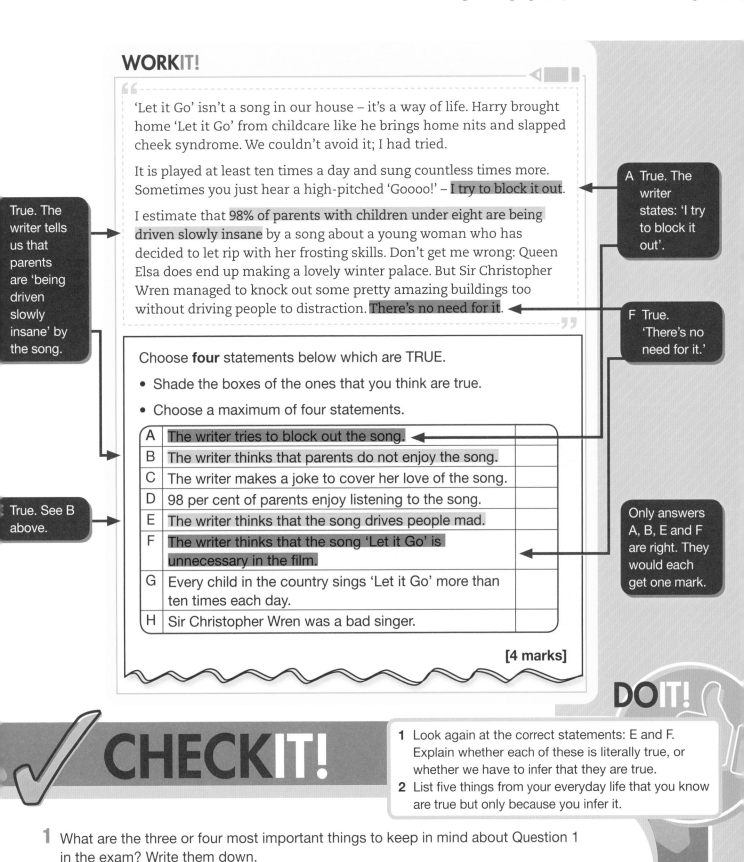

'Let it Go' isn't a song in our house – it's a way of life. Harry brought home 'Let it Go' from childcare like he brings home nits and slapped cheek syndrome. We couldn't avoid it; I had tried.

It is played at least ten times a day and sung countless times more. Sometimes you just hear a high-pitched 'Goooo!' – I try to block it out.

I estimate that 98% of parents with children under eight are being driven slowly insane by a song about a young woman who has decided to let rip with her frosting skills. Don't get me wrong: Queen Elsa does end up making a lovely winter palace. But Sir Christopher Wren managed to knock out some pretty amazing buildings too without driving people to distraction. There's no need for it.

True. The writer tells us that parents are 'being driven slowly insane' by the song.

A True. The writer states: 'I try to block it out'.

F True. 'There's no need for it.'

Choose **four** statements below which are TRUE.

- Shade the boxes of the ones that you think are true.
- Choose a maximum of four statements.

A	The writer tries to block out the song.	
B	The writer thinks that parents do not enjoy the song.	
C	The writer makes a joke to cover her love of the song.	
D	98 per cent of parents enjoy listening to the song.	
E	The writer thinks that the song drives people mad.	
F	The writer thinks that the song 'Let it Go' is unnecessary in the film.	
G	Every child in the country sings 'Let it Go' more than ten times each day.	
H	Sir Christopher Wren was a bad singer.	

[4 marks]

True. See B above.

Only answers A, B, E and F are right. They would each get one mark.

CHECKIT!

DOIT!

1 Look again at the correct statements: E and F. Explain whether each of these is literally true, or whether we have to infer that they are true.
2 List five things from your everyday life that you know are true but only because you infer it.

1 What are the three or four most important things to keep in mind about Question 1 in the exam? Write them down.

2 Read this extract:

I suppose it's understandable that 'Let It Go' is so popular. It's a tune about a moody adolescent yet it appeals strongly to very young children. Perhaps it's proof that kids are getting genetically stroppier earlier. As far as I can remember it's the first time pre-schoolers have adopted their own anthem with such passion. Either way it's a fantastic introduction to the world of pop where you can be in love with someone on Monday, spend too much time listening to them on Tuesday, and loathe them by Wednesday.

Write four **true** statements that could be used by exam markers for Question 1.

Question 2

Understanding the question

Question 2 will test whether you can find and interpret details from both of the texts on the paper. You need to show your understanding of what you have read in both texts.

For example:

> You need to refer to **Source A** and **Source B** for this question.
>
> Use details from **both** Sources. Write a summary of the similarities between hunting and fishing. **[8 marks]**

There are no marks for language analysis: you just need to focus on the details and show that you can infer information, as well as notice what the texts actually say. **Inferring** means reading between the lines.

We infer when we use information and clues to work something out for ourselves. Inferring always includes some degree of 'best guessing'.

Here is a sentence from a text:

> "
> Now, the reporters may not know it, but crocodiles, can also swim **under** water, and if that crocodile had wanted Sgt Jeff Tanswell, the boat wouldn't have stopped it.
> "

If you are asked what we learn here about crocodiles, we learn that:

- crocodiles can swim under water (factual detail)
- the boat wouldn't have stopped a crocodile attack (factual detail)
- the crocodile did not choose to attack at that moment (inference).

NAIL IT!

You should spend eight minutes on this question.

NAIL IT!

All the information you need will be in the two texts: you are not expected to use your own knowledge.

NAIL IT!

- Use short quotations to act as evidence for your findings.
- Do not analyse the writer's use of language for this question.

DO IT!

To explore the difference between knowing and inferring, find some pictures of people you don't know – perhaps in magazines or newspapers – and jot down things we can know (or see) about the person (for example, gender), and things we might infer about them from their picture (perhaps they look angry).

Think about how our assumptions might affect our inferences. For example, if we don't like the look of a person, we might infer that they are untrustworthy. However, we could be wrong.

Below is a example exam Question 2.

You need to refer to **Source A** and **Source B** for this question.

Use details from **both** Sources. Write a summary of the differences between what we are told about crocodiles and how people react to them.

[8 marks]

Source A – 19th century literary non-fiction

Mary Kingsley was a Victorian explorer. Here, she explains how she used to paddle into the swamps next to the main river in Africa, and the thrills and dangers that she then experienced.

> This is a fascinating pursuit. But it is a pleasure to be indulged in with caution; for one thing, you are certain to come across crocodiles. Now a crocodile drifting down in deep water, or lying asleep with its jaws open on a sand-bank in the sun, is a picturesque adornment to the landscape when you are on the deck of a steamer, and you can write home about it and frighten your relations; but when you are away among the swamps in a small dug-out canoe, and that crocodile and his relations are awake – a thing he makes a point of being at flood tide because of fish coming along – and when he has got his foot upon his native heath – that is to say, his tail within holding reach of his native mud – you may get frightened; for crocodiles can, and often do, in such places, grab at people in small canoes.

Source B – 21st century non-fiction

Coroner issues warning after shocking crocodile attack

> Family and friends watched in horror as a 15 foot, 7 inch crocodile leapt from a waterhole and clamped its jaws around the left shoulder and chest of Bill Scott as he stood in his 12-foot aluminium boat. The crocodile then flipped the 62-year-old man into the water and he was never seen again alive.
>
> Cavanagh said Scott might be the first person known to have been taken by a croc from a boat. But it was not the first time a croc had tried, Cavanagh said.
>
> Fisherman Jeff Bolitho had testified to the inquest that a 13-foot croc once leapt over the side of his boat, knocking Bolitho off his chair and leaving teeth marks in the back of his head and shoulder.
>
> Cavanagh recommended that the Northern Territory government add to its public crocodile warnings that: 'Saltwater crocodiles can attack people in boats and the smaller the boat, the greater the risk.'

NAIL IT!

Question 2 will always ask you to write a summary. Here, 'summary' just means concentrating on the essential information being asked for, and putting it into your own words (with brief quotations to support your points).

Here are some notes made by a student on the question on page 61. Their method of working is good. However, only three of the answers (A–E) in the final column are right.

WORKIT!

	Source A	Source B	What's different? What can I infer?
What we are told about crocodiles	• 'a picturesque adornment to the landscape' • 'lying asleep with its jaws open'	• 'a 15 foot, 7 inch. crocodile' • 'and clamped its jaws around the left shoulder and chest of Bill Scott'	A Source A suggests that the crocodile is beautiful. Source B suggests that it is a monster. B The word 'adornment' in Source A suggests that the crocodile is like a jewel worn by the landscape; nothing in Source B suggests a crocodile is beautiful. C 'clamped' is a violent word suggesting danger. This contrasts with the way the crocodile is always described as being calm and asleep. D In Source A we are introduced to crocodiles as calm, sleepy and harmless, whereas in Source B the crocodile is active and violent.
How people react to them	'and frighten your relations'	'Family and friends watched in horror'	E In Source A the friends and relations react with fear as they hear stories about the dangers crocodiles pose. In Source B family and friends also react in 'horror' as they are actually witnessing the attack.

DOIT!

Imagine you are a teacher. Write a short note to the student to explain why answers C and E in the Work it! above are wrong and therefore get no marks.

Preparing your answer

Take a four-step approach to Question 2.

1 Underline the focus for the question to make sure you keep on track.

2 Find details in the texts relating to these key words. Underline and annotate the texts.

3 As you work, ask yourself, 'What can I work out (infer) from this relevant detail?'

4 Bring relevant details and inferences from both texts together in your own answer.

Look again at a section from Source A. Words that tell us about crocodiles are highlighted:

> ... but when you are away among the swamps in a small dug-out canoe, and that crocodile and his relations are awake – a thing he makes a point of being at flood tide because of fish coming along – and when he has got his foot upon his native heath – that is to say, his tail within holding reach of his native mud – you may get frightened; for crocodiles can, and often do, in such places, grab at people in small canoes.

Crocodiles are awake at flood tide.

Mud is a crocodile's native habitat.

Writing your answer

You can write your answer to Question 2 in two ways:

1 Write about both sources at once by merging your ideas into one paragraph.

2 Write two linked paragraphs where you talk about each source in turn, using comparing (and/or contrasting) words to make links as you go (for example, 'however' and 'similarly'). These words are sometimes called discourse markers or connectives.

Read the two different versions below of part of an answer to Question 2. Which is the merged style of response and which is the linked paragraphs style of response? Decide which method seems to work better – especially for you.

DO IT!

Make a list of words and phrases that could help you to interpret, and to compare and contrast in this question.

WORKIT!

Student answer A

Both extracts tell us about crocodiles. In Source A the crocodiles are first shown as 'a picturesque adornment to the landscape', suggesting that they are beautiful and to be admired. However, in Source B the crocodile is first shown in terms of its size, '15 foot, 7 inch', and from this I can infer that it is a creature to be scared of. This difference continues as in Source A the crocodiles are shown as 'lying asleep with its jaws open' as opposed to the jaws of the crocodile in Source B being 'clamped' around a man's shoulder and neck. This movement in Source B contrasts with the crocodile's stillness in Source A, making it seem far more aggressive and fierce.

Student answer B

In Source A the crocodiles are first shown as 'a picturesque adornment to the landscape', suggesting that they are beautiful and to be admired. The crocodiles are then shown 'lying asleep with its jaws open' which suggests that they are peaceful and are at rest.

However, in Source B the crocodile is first shown in terms of its size, '15 foot, 7 inch', and from this I can infer that it is a huge creature and something to be scared of. This source goes on to tell me that the jaws of the crocodile in Source B were 'clamped' around a man's shoulder and neck. This suggests that the jaws are huge and I can infer that this creature is aggressive and fierce.

The exam markers will reward the quality of your response rather than how many items you choose to write about. They will use a mark scheme like this:

SNAPIT!

Mark scheme level	Band 2 descriptors (Roughly GCSE grades 2–3)	Band 3 descriptors (Roughly GCSE grades 4–6)	Band 4 descriptors (Roughly GCSE grades 7–9)
The student writes about...	... at least one of the texts, and: • interprets • tries to infer • chooses some appropriate detail • points out some relevant similarities and/or difference(s).	... both texts, and: • clearly synthesises and interprets • makes clear inferences • chooses clear, relevant details • points out clear, relevant similarities and/or differences between texts.	... both texts, and: • perceptively synthesises and interprets • makes perceptive inferences • chooses very precise, relevant details • explores perceptive, relevant similarities and/or differences between texts.

Here is what an exam marker said about student answer A on page 63:

> This part of the answer points out very clearly relevant differences between the presentations of crocodiles in the two texts. Information from the two texts is brought together neatly, and sometimes revealingly – as when the student uses inference to note that the crocodile is beautiful in one text, but huge and thus terrifying in the other. A number of simple, clear, relevant details are chosen here. These strengths lift the answer just into the top band.

CHECKIT! ✓

1 What, for you, are the four or five most important things to keep in mind about Question 2 in the exam? Write them down.

2 "He was sweating all over."

From this statement do we know he is hot, or do we have to infer it?

3 Which is the highest band you could reach for Question 2 if you only write about one of the texts?

4 Write down at least two words used to compare or contrast.

Question 3

Understanding the question

Question 3 will test your understanding of how writers use language to influence the reader. You will also be expected to use appropriate subject terminology and quotations to support your points.

For example:

> You need to refer **only** to **Source B**, the journal of Mildred Thomas.
>
> How does Thomas use language to convince us that she made the right decision? **[12 marks]**

The question offers 12 marks, and so a lengthy answer is needed.

The key focuses for this question are:

- words
- phrases
- language features
- language techniques.

NAILIT!

You should spend 12 minutes on this question.

NAILIT!

Question 3 will tell you to just focus on one text.

SNAPIT!

Key focus	Explanation
Words	You need to think about the words – the vocabulary – the writer has chosen. All of us express things in different ways: we make choices. We choose our words carefully so that we use the right ones for the effect we want to have. Writers choose very carefully. Sometimes paying attention to individual words can be revealing for a reader.
Phrases	When words are joined into phrases, sometimes the phrase is more powerful than the individual words. Look at how words are combined for effect.
Language features and techniques	These are specific devices used by the writer: such as, similes, metaphors, rhetorical questions, and so on. Never just spot these devices: write about their effect on the reader.
Sentence forms	Writers can say the same thing in different ways to different effects. They achieve this partly by varying the lengths of sentences and the order of information in them. Look out for sentence variety.
Effect	This is about how the reader responds to the writer's words: what does it make them think of? How does it make them feel?
Your views	These are your beliefs about what the writer is trying to do and how they are trying to do it.
Evidence	These are the details from the text that you choose in order to support the views you put forward. Evidence can be in the form of quotations, especially in this answer.
Subject terminology	These are technical words about language. English subject terminology includes words and phrases like sentence, verb, simile, rhetorical question.

Below is a short extract from a letter to the President of the United States in 1852. It is not certain who wrote the letter, but many believe the author was Chief Seattle, a Native American leader.

> The President in Washington sends word that he wishes to buy our land. But how can you buy or sell the sky? The land? The idea is strange to us. If we do not own the freshness of the air and the sparkle of the water, how can you sell them? Every part of this earth is sacred to my people. Every shining pine needle, every humming insect. All are holy in the memory and experience of my people. We know the sap which courses through the trees as we know the blood that courses through our veins. We are part of the earth and it is part of us. The perfumed flowers are our sisters. The bear, the deer, the great eagle, these are our brothers. The rocky crests, the juices in the meadow, the body heat of a pony, and man, all belong to the same family. The shining water that moves in the streams and rivers is not just water, but the blood of our ancestors. If we sell you our land, you must remember that it is sacred. Each ghostly reflection in the clear waters of the lakes tells of events and memories in the life of my people. The waters murmur in the voice of my father's father. The rivers are our brothers. They quench our thirst. They carry our canoes and feed our children. So you must give to the river the kindness you would give any brother.

A typical Question 3 using this extract would be:

How does Chief Seattle use language to influence the President of the United States?

Read part of a student's answer, dealing with the purpose and audience of the extract:

Firstly, think about the purpose of the text and its audience. What is written in this letter – the content – should match the purpose (why it was written) and the audience (the intended reader).

WORKIT!

View and evidence

The purpose of this text is to influence the thinking of the President of America. Chief Seattle is responding to a request to buy land. His first purpose is to challenge the president's thinking about the land and this request. He begins by posing questions 'how can you buy or sell the sky? The land?' Within our society we understand the concept of selling land. However,

Subject terminology

Analyse the effect of the writer's choice of language.

the idea of selling the sky is as 'strange' to us as it is to Chief Seattle. The word 'strange' has the effect of challenging and surprising the reader – as it would also challenge the President of the United States. The tone is formal and measured. It does not attack but by raising these seemingly simple questions he challenges what we understand by ownership of the land.

Now, let's look carefully at the effect of language. Read the short extract from Chief Seattle's letter again (page 66). Look very carefully at references to family. To help us answer the example question on page 66, we could consider how Chief Seattle uses references to family to influence the president.

1 Write up to six lines about how Chief Seattle uses references to family to influence the president using the three rules in the Nail it!

2 When you have written your answer, compare it with the two below from the other students. Decide which of the three answers is best, and why.

3 Think about which answer makes best use of the three rules.

4 Find examples of those rules being used in the two answers below **and** the answer in the Work it! on page 66.

NAIL IT!

Make sure you stick to these rules:

- Explain your views, and use some evidence.
- Use some subject terminology.
- Analyse the effect of the writer's choice of language.

WORKIT!

Student answer A

Chief Seattle uses references to family to show that we are 'part of the earth' just like family. He uses lists to show that there are lots of things that we are part of.

Student answer B

Chief Seattle links the 'sap' that courses through trees with the 'blood' that runs through our veins. This metaphor of life-blood is linked to the idea of family blood lines. To Chief Seattle, all living things are connected to the earth. He lists different elements of the planet – 'the bear, the deer, the great eagle' – as well as listing family links: 'brother', 'grandfather'. The effect of this listing makes it sound like a prayer. This effect links to the 'sacred' earth that contains the blood of his ancestors.

Question 3 mark scheme

SNAPIT!

Mark scheme level	Band 2 descriptors (Roughly GCSE grades 2–3)	Band 3 descriptors (Roughly GCSE grades 4–6)	Band 4 descriptors (Roughly GCSE grades 7–9)
The student's answer...	• shows some understanding of language • attempts to comment on the effect of language • uses some appropriate textual detail • makes some use of subject terminology, mainly appropriately.	• shows clear understanding of language • explains clearly the effects of the writer's choices of language • uses a range of relevant textual detail • makes clear and accurate use of subject terminology.	• shows detailed and perceptive understanding of language • analyses the effects of the writer's choices of language • uses a range of precisely chosen textual detail • makes sophisticated and accurate use of subject terminology.

Here is student answer B with some marker's comments in the margin:

WORKIT!

> Chief Seattle links the 'sap' that courses through trees with the 'blood' that runs through our veins. This metaphor of life-blood is linked to the idea of family blood lines. To Chief Seattle, all living things are connected to the earth. He lists different elements of the planet – 'the bear, the deer, the great eagle' – as well as listing family links: 'brother', 'grandfather'. The effect of this listing makes it sound like a prayer. This effect links to the 'sacred' earth that contains the blood of his ancestors.

Makes some use of subject terminology, mainly appropriately. Although this isn't strictly a metaphor, it makes a useful comparison between 'sap' and 'blood'.

Uses a range of relevant textual detail.

Shows detailed and perceptive understanding of language.

You will see that this snippet from an answer is strong in some places, weaker in others.

DOIT!

1 Look carefully through your own answer (that you wrote for the Do it! on page 67). Find examples of descriptors from the mark scheme in your answer. Compare the mark scheme with student answer A on page 67.
2 Reconsider your rank order for student answers A and B, and the answer in the Work it! on page 66.

CHECKIT! ✓

1 What are the four or five most important things to keep in mind about Question 3 in the exam? Write them down.

2 What is the main focus of Question 3?

3 In his letter to the president, Chief Seattle uses rhetorical questions. Write down at least two other specific language techniques that he uses. Give examples.

4 What are the effects of these techniques on the reader?

Question 4

Understanding the question

NAILIT!

You should spend 16 minutes on this question.

Question 4 asks you to compare writers' ideas and perspectives (their points of view), and how they use language to convey their ideas. For example:

For this question, you need to refer to the **whole of Source A**, together with **Source B**.

Compare how the two writers convey their different ideas and perspectives of the events that they describe.

In your answer, you could:

- compare their different ideas and perspectives

- compare the methods they use to convey their ideas and perspectives

- support your response with references to both texts.   **[16 marks]**

The question will always mention the writers. This is important, as this is what makes it different from Question 2. You need to show your understanding of **what** you have read in both texts and **how** the texts are written in order to convey the writers' attitudes.

Here is what the key words in the question mean:

SNAPIT!

Key word	Meaning
Compare	The word 'compare' asks you to identify and analyse the main similarities and differences between the texts. Remember the texts will have been carefully selected to allow you to be able to do this.
Methods	The word 'method' asks you to write about form, structure and language. • Form is the format or text type, such as a letter, diary, article, etc. • Structure is the way the content and ideas are organised. • Language is the choice of words that the writer has chosen to use. It is 'how' a writer creates the text.
Convey	The word 'convey' in the question literally means to 'communicate' or 'send'. In the exam it means that you must write about the effects of the language used as well as tone, imagery, emphasis or bias. It's important to think about what we are told in each text and what has been left out.
Support	The use of the word 'support' here means that you must use quotations, from both texts, to act as evidence for your points.
Ideas and perspectives	These are the writers' thoughts, viewpoints, impressions and attitudes.

DOIT!

Look back over the advice about key words in Question 4.

1 Without looking at this book, make a list of key words that are important in the typical wording of Question 4.
2 Next to each word (or phrase) explain why it is important.
3 You could make these into flashcards to help you to remember them.

DOIT!

1 Look at the student's notes.
   a Which points do you agree with most strongly?
   b Can you improve some of the others?
   c Can you add any further ideas?
2 Write three or four sentences to compare the language used in the titles of the two cookery texts by Mrs Beeton and Nigella Lawson.
3 Now you need to expand your response. Look at the question in the exam question on page 71. What else do you need to answer the question?

For this question it is also important to remember that exam markers are looking for **detailed** responses – you must make sure that you write enough. The fact that this question equals 16 marks will give you a clue that this needs to be a sustained answer. You should aim to write four detailed points/paragraphs.

As for Question 2, you can **interweave** your ideas from both texts, or write about each text, making occasional relevant comparisons.

We are going to compare two texts from cookery books. The first text is from *The Book of Household Management* which appeared in 1861 and was written by Mrs Beeton. The second text is by Nigella Lawson, a popular cook, journalist and TV personality. The text appeared on her website.

Read the titles of the two texts. Notice the tone of each of them and the differences in the language used.

> BOILED CAULIFLOWERS
>
> Mrs Beeton

> Warm spiced cauliflower and chickpea salad with pomegranate seeds
>
> Nigella Lawson

Read one student's notes in response to these titles:

WORKIT!

Mrs Beeton

We know the key ingredient – cauliflower – but we don't know anything else.

The adjective 'boiled' provides a straightforward description of what will be happening to the cauliflower.

The word 'boiled' sounds plain and not very comforting.

The tone is practical – no nonsense.

Nigella Lawson

We are given almost a complete list of the ingredients.

The adjective 'Warm' makes us think of comfort and 'spiced' makes us think of exotic locations. This also links to 'chickpea' and 'pomegranate'.

'Spiced' also suggests warmth.

The tone is sumptuous and comforting.

Here is a typical exam question:

For this question, you need to refer to the **whole of Source A**, together with **Source B**.

Compare how the writers convey their different ideas and perspectives of how to cook cauliflower.

In your answer, you could:

- compare their different ideas and perspectives
- compare the methods they use to convey their ideas and perspectives
- support your response with references to both texts.   **[16 marks]**

NAIL IT!

Read the question before you read (or re-read) the two texts.

Source A

BOILED CAULIFLOWERS.

INGREDIENTS. – To each ½ gallon of water allow 1 heaped tablespoonful of salt.

Mode. – Choose cauliflowers that are close and white; trim off the decayed outside leaves, and cut the stalk off flat at the bottom. Open the flower a little in places to remove the insects, which generally are found about the stalk, and let the cauliflowers lie in salt and water for an hour previous to dressing them, with their head downwards: this will effectually draw out all the vermin. Then put them into fast-boiling water, with the addition of salt in the above proportion, and let them boil briskly over a good fire, keeping the sauce-pan uncovered. The water should be well skimmed and, when the cauliflowers are tender, take them up with a slice, let them drain, and, if large enough, place them upright in the dish. Serve with plain melted butter, a little of which may be poured over the flower.

Time. – Small cauliflower, 12 to 15 minutes, large one, 20 to 25 minutes, after the water boils.

Average cost, for large cauliflowers, *6d.* each.

Sufficient. – Allow 1 large cauliflower for 3 persons.

71

Source B

Warm spiced cauliflower and chickpea salad with pomegranate seeds

This is one of my favourite suppers, although there's nothing that says you can't serve this as a vegetable side as part of a more conventional meal. And you could also bolster it further by crumbling in some feta. But for me, it is perfect just as it is: the tomatoes almost ooze into a dressing in the oven, and the cauliflower softens, but not soggily.

And this is also very, very good cold, so if you have some left over, it makes a fabulous packed lunch, or provides instant gratification on those days you have to eat fridgeside, with your coat still on, you're so hungry.

Method

1 Preheat the oven to 220°C /gas mark 7/425°F. Trim the cauliflower and divide into small florets. Pour the oil into a large bowl, add the cinnamon and cumin seeds, and stir or whisk to help the spices disperse. Tip in the prepared cauliflower and toss to coat. Pour the contents of the bowl into a small oven tray (I mostly use a disposable foil baking tray measuring 30 × 20cm/12 × 8 inches) and place in the oven for 15 minutes. Don't wash out the bowl you've been using just yet.

2 Add the chickpeas to this bowl, and add the harissa, tasting it first to see if you want both tablespoonfuls, and, at the risk of being repetitive, toss to coat. Quarter the tomatoes and add them to the bowl, and shake or stir to mix. When the cauliflower has had its 15 minutes, remove the tray, quickly tip the chickpeas and tomatoes over the cauliflower, and toss to combine before returning to the oven for a further 15 minutes until the cauliflower is tender.

3 When it's ready, remove from the oven and sprinkle the salt over the vegetables, then (and this isn't the last time) toss to combine with half of the pomegranate seeds before dividing between 2 bowls. Divide the parsley leaves – without chopping them – between the 2 bowls and toss to mix. Scatter with the remaining pomegranate seeds.

Look at the question on page 71 again. The first bullet point states: compare their different ideas and perspectives. Although this is a suggestion, 'you could...' it is always wise to follow that suggestion.

Some elements you could consider are:

• their ideas

• the impressions we are given about the subject – how do the writers present it?

• what we are told and what is left out

• the tone

• the purpose of this text – what is most important to the writer?

Look at the notes made by a student below:

WORKIT!

Ideas and perspectives

Source A	Source B
Does not say whether this is a side dish or a main dish 'Allow 1 large cauliflower for 3 persons'.	States clearly that this could be used as a 'side' dish or a main dish.
Gives detailed, step-by-step instructions, 'Choose cauliflowers that are close and white'.	Gives detailed step-by-step instructions, 'Preheat the oven...', but also adds personal details, 'you have to eat fridgeside, with your coat still on, you're so hungry'.
The tone is practical and instructional: 'Allow', 'Choose'. The tone is detached from the reader.	The tone changes. At first the tone is indulgent and comforting, 'And you could also bolster it further', but then becomes more practical and instructional in the method: 'Pour', 'Divide'. The tone is conversational with the reader with some humour 'eat fridgeside'.
We do not know whether the writer likes cauliflower. This information has been left out.	Provides opinions 'But for me, it is perfect just as it is' and 'provides instant gratification'.
The writer seems to favour 'plain' cooking. The cauliflower is cooked whole with nothing added other than 'plain melted butter'.	The writer seems to favour comforting food with lots of 'oil', 'spices' and 'feta'.
The writer seems to see cauliflower as containing lots of insects, which she describes as 'vermin'.	The writer seems to see cauliflower as a 'favourite' providing 'instant gratification'.

Look carefully at how this student's method has allowed her to compare relevant aspects of the texts.

- Could you improve any of her notes?
- See if you can find any more points of comparison.

Look again at the exam question on page 71.

The second bullet point states:

> - compare the methods they use to convey their ideas and perspectives

Again, although this is a suggestion, **always** follow that suggestion.

Some elements you could write about here are:

- What is the form of the writing (the text type)?
- How are the ideas organised?
- What are the key features of the language?
- Word choices.
- Sentence structures.

DOIT!

Use the notes here and your own ideas to compare the ideas and perspectives in the two texts. Write at least two detailed paragraphs.

Here are the thoughts that one student had about the texts' language and methods:

WORKIT!

Method	Source A	Source B
Form	The form is a recipe. It gives step-by-step instructions on how to cook cauliflower. At the end of the recipe it gives additional information about cost, 'Average cost, for large cauliflowers, 6d. each', and how many people an average sized cauliflower would feed.	The form is a recipe. It gives step-by-step instructions on how to cook a dish using cauliflower. However, at the start there is a section where the writer gives her opinion of the dish, 'This is one of my favourite suppers,' and puts herself in the place of the reader, 'you're so hungry'.
Structure	The recipe uses imperatives to begin each instruction. This is what we would expect for a recipe: 'Allow', 'Choose'.	The recipe section also uses imperatives to begin each instruction. Again, this is what we would expect for a recipe: 'Add', 'Remove', 'Divide'.
Language	Some language will surprise the reader as it has negative associations. We are told to remove 'decayed outside leaves'. We need to 'remove the insects', using salt water to 'draw out all the vermin'. These are words that we would not expect to find in a recipe.	Language used is positive. Cauliflower is a 'favourite' and is 'perfect'. Sensual language: 'ooze', 'tender'.

Question 4 mark scheme

Here is an example of a mark scheme for Question 4:

SNAPIT!

Mark scheme level	Band 2 descriptors (Roughly GCSE grades 2–3)	Band 3 descriptors (Roughly GCSE grades 4–6)	Band 4 descriptors (Roughly GCSE grades 7–9)
The student's answer...	• tries to compare ideas and perspectives • makes some comments on how writers' methods are used • chooses some appropriate textual detail/references, not always supporting from one or both texts • identifies some different ideas and perspectives.	• compares ideas and perspectives in a clear and relevant way • explains clearly how writers' methods are used • selects relevant detail to support from both texts • shows a clear understanding of the different ideas and perspectives in both texts.	• compares ideas and perspectives in a perceptive way • analyses how writers' methods are used • selects a range of judicious supporting detail from both texts • shows a detailed understanding of the different ideas and perspectives in both texts.

Read the extract from a student's response to the question on page 71 below, then look at the mark scheme for this question:

WORKIT!

Nigella Lawson writes in an informal tone about food, which matches her relaxed and more modern approach to cookery. She talks about cauliflower using positive language telling the reader that the recipe is one of her 'favourites' that provides 'instant gratification'. She also jokes all the way through her recipe about the number of times the ingredients need to be tossed. Mrs Beeton uses a much more formal tone with her choice of language, 'Choose cauliflowers that are close and white', which reflects the language of the time the recipe was written. Mrs Beeton's instructions are easy to understand and seem to be full of plain common sense. Her recipes are simple using only 'water' and 'salt' with the cauliflower. At the end she suggests that it can be served with 'melted butter' but she adds that this should be 'plain'. Nigella Lawson, however, uses very sensual language to describe her dish.

Here are some exam marker's comments on this student's answer.

This extract from an answer indicates that the full response would achieve Band 3. It compares ideas in a clear and relevant way and is starting to explain clearly how the writers' methods are used. This would need to be developed to secure Band 3. It selects relevant detail from both texts and shows understanding of the perspectives in both texts.

DOIT!

Write at least two detailed paragraphs comparing the methods the two cookery texts use to convey their ideas and perspectives. Use the student notes from the table on page 74 to help you. Use the mark scheme and bullet points in the question to guide your writing.

STRETCHIT!

Often, a writer's point of view is only fully appreciated across a whole text, rather than just in individual words, phrases and sentences: structure does influence readers. For example, the introduction in Source B (page 72) – Nigella Lawson's recipe – is consistent in style and tone: it is warm, almost conspiratorial throughout – a personal relationship is built between Lawson and her readers. Her language is consistently sensual: 'ooze', 'soggily', and 'fabulous'. Looking at language patterns across a whole text is one way to boost your answer into the top band.

These patterns create a consistent tone, which in turn conveys the writer's perspective.

Always ask yourself these questions when taking on Question 4:

- Is the information in the two texts placed in a particular order? For example:

  - Does the text give just one opinion?

  - Does it offer a balanced point of view?

  - Does it change at any point in the text?

- Are there any words or phrases that are repeated throughout the text? (Such as: family language, violent images, extended metaphors.)

- What is the tone of the text? (For example, is it sombre, upbeat, ironic or enthusiastic?)

- Are there any links or changes between the first and the last paragraphs of the text?

CHECK IT! ✓

1 How many texts will you need to write about in Question 4?

2 Question 3 focuses on the writers' use of language. What is the main focus of Question 4?

3 How much should you write for your answer to Question 4?

4 When you read a whole text, one way of analysing and tracking the development of its ideas and perspective is to label each paragraph with a word or short phrase, summing up what the paragraph is about.

Look at the full text of Chief Seattle's speech that you studied part of earlier. Use a word or short phrase to sum up the key purpose of each paragraph. The first one is done for you.

When you have identified the purposes of each paragraph, you will be in a better position to meet some of the top band criteria. In particular, you will be better placed to compare ideas and perspectives in a perceptive way.

"

The President in Washington sends word that he wishes to buy our land. But how can you buy or sell the sky? The land? The idea is strange to us. If we do not own the freshness of the air and the sparkle of the water, how can you sell them? Every part of this earth is sacred to my people. Every shining pine needle, every humming insect. All are holy in the memory and experience of my people.

No one owns the land.

We know the sap which courses through the trees as we know the blood that courses through our veins. We are part of the earth and it is part of us. The perfumed flowers are our sisters. The bear, the deer, the great eagle, these are our brothers. The rocky crests, the juices in the meadow, the body heat of a pony, and man, all belong to the same family.

CHECK**IT!**

The shining water that moves in the streams and rivers is not just water, but the blood of our ancestors. If we sell you our land, you must remember that it is sacred. Each ghostly reflection in the clear waters of the lakes tells of events and memories in the life of my people. The waters murmur in the voice of my father's father. The rivers are our brothers. They quench our thirst. They carry our canoes and feed our children. So you must give to the river the kindness you would give any brother.

If we sell you our land, remember that the air is precious to us, that the air shares its spirit with all the life it supports. The wind that gave our grandfather his first breath also receives his last sigh. The wind also gives our children the spirit of life. So if we sell you our land, you must keep it apart and sacred, as a place where man can go to taste the wind that is sweetened by the meadow flowers.

Will you teach your children what we have taught our children? That the earth is our Mother? What befalls the earth befalls all the sons of the earth.

This we know: The earth does not belong to man, man belongs to the earth. All things are connected like the blood that unites us all. Man did not weave the web of life; he is merely a strand of it. Whatever he does to the web, he does to himself.

One thing we know: Our God is your God. The earth is precious to him and to harm the earth is to heap contempt on its Creator. Your destiny is a mystery to us. What will happen when the buffalo are all slaughtered? The wild horses tamed? What will happen when the secret corners of the forest are heavy with the scent of many men and the view of the ripe hills is blotted by talking wires? Where will the thicket be? Gone! Where will the eagle be? Gone! And what is it to say goodbye to the swift pony and the hunt? The end of living and the beginning of survival.

When the last red man has vanished with his wilderness, and his memory is only the shadow of a cloud moving across the prairie, will these shores and forests still be here? Will there be any of the spirit of my people left? We love this earth as a newborn loves its mother's heartbeat. So if we sell you our land, love it as we have loved it. Care for it as we have cared for it. Hold in your mind the memory of the land as it is when you receive it. Preserve the land for all children and love it, as God loves us all.

As we are a part of the land, you too are part of the land. This earth is precious to us. It is also precious to you. One thing we know: There is only one God. No man, be he Red Man or White Man, can be apart. We are all brothers.

Chief Seattle

Paper 2 Section A: Reading

1   How long should you spend on Section A, including reading and planning?

2   How many of the texts on the paper will have been written before 1900?

3   Which of the following is the main focus of the questions on this paper?

   a   The information the writers give me.

   b   The attitudes of the writers and how they try to influence me.

   c   How much I agree with the writers.

4   In which of the statements below do we have to infer that the writer hates the music?

   a   I hated that tune.

   b   The music left me with a sense of loathing.

   c   Whenever I heard that song I put my hands over my ears and screamed.

5   In Question 1 of the exam, how many true pieces of information must you find?

6   How many minutes should you spend on Question 2?

7   In Question 2, how carefully should you analyse the writer's use of language?

8   What does 'summary' mean in Question 2?

9   In Question 2, are marks awarded

   a   for the number of the points you make, or

   b   for the quality and relevance of your answer?

10   Write down seven useful words and phrases that help you to compare or contrast.

11   How many texts will you be asked about in Question 3?

12   Which of the following is the main focus of Question 3?

   a   Information   c   Language devices

   b   Text structure   d   The effects of language choices

13   In the following student's answer, find an example of evidence, and an example of subject terminology.

> To strengthen his argument by appealing to our emotions, Chief Seattle uses a sequence of personal pronouns: 'my', 'our', 'you'. Not only does this...

14   How long should you spend answering Question 4?

15   What is the main focus of Question 4?

16   What does 'convey' mean in Question 4?

17   Read the following text and choose which word best fits the writer's perspective on car drivers:

> Do they really need to keep jumping in their cars to satisfy every whim? Is burning up precious fossil fuel and polluting the planet a reasonable alternative to making the effort to walk round to the local shop?

   a   love   c   disapproval

   b   dislike   d   approval

18   In the text used in Question 17 above, what persuasive technique is used twice? What effect does this have on the reader?

Paper 2 Section B: Writing

Introduction and advice

The writing task appears on the paper as Question 5. It comes straight after the reading questions in Section A.

Unlike in Paper 1, there will be just one writing task: you will not have a choice. The exam paper will ask you to express your own personal viewpoint on a topic. That topic will link to the texts in the reading section of Paper 2.

Here is a example exam writing task:

> 'Teenagers nowadays spend far too long on social media. Not only does this waste their time, but it also leaves them open to stress and abuse.'
>
> Write the text of a leaflet for parents, advising them on how they can help their teenage children use social media sensibly.   **[40 marks]**

Understanding the question

The task will tell you the context for your writing. The context is the audience, purpose and form. You will also be given a strong statement about the topic. This will help you to develop your own strong point of view.

The audience will always require you to write formally, and for one of these purposes:

- to explain
- to instruct or advise
- to argue
- to persuade.

The form could be:

- a letter
- an article (for example, for a newspaper)
- the text for a leaflet
- a speech
- an essay.

In the task above:

- the **audience** is parents
- the **purpose** is to advise
- the **form** is the text of a leaflet.

NAIL IT!

Spend 45 minutes on planning, writing and checking your writing:

- Planning: 5 minutes.
- Writing: 35 minutes.
- Checking, correcting and improving: 5 minutes.

79

Here is another example Question 5 (writing task):

> 'The modern world has no need for a classroom. Students could easily learn sitting at home using the latest technologies.'
>
> Write an article for a broadsheet newspaper in which you explain your point of view on this statement. **[40 marks]**

DO IT!

Identify the audience, purpose and form in this example question.

You need to plan your writing, and its style, so that it is just right for the given audience, purpose and form.

There are 40 marks for the writing task:

- 24 marks for content and organisation
- 16 marks for technical accuracy.

DO IT!

On a sticky note, write seven bullet points summing up the essential dos and don'ts for being successful in this task. Stick the note somewhere you will often see it.

Content is about your ideas and how you express yourself so that you 'connect' with your reader (audience).

Organisation is about how you structure your content: paragraphs, sections, openings and closings, and so on.

Technical accuracy is about spelling, punctuation and grammar, and about using effective sentences and vocabulary. (See Technical accuracy section on page 95.)

The mark scheme for writing on Paper 2 is the same as the mark scheme for Paper 1 on page 37.

CHECK IT! ✓

1 How many marks are available for the writing section of Paper 2?

2 How many marks are available for technical accuracy?

3 How many writing tasks will be on the paper for you to choose from?

4 How is the writing task linked to the texts in the reading section?

5 What are the four purposes that could be in the writing task?

6 Which of the following three forms will not be in the writing task?

- speech
- article
- story

Language

The writing section of Paper 2 tests how effectively you can communicate your own personal view in a formal way. Therefore, you will need to organise your writing well and use formal language and tone.

Here are two versions of the same leaflet. One of them is written in an appropriate register; the other one is not.

WORKIT!

Student answer A

Welcome to this unique and treasured private garden, tucked serenely into a secret corner of our beautiful countryside.

Student answer B

Hey! Come on in! We're just loving our private garden that's quiet and all in this corner of our countryside.

DOIT!

1 The sentences below have been written for a head teacher (the 'audience').

My mates and me get loads of homework. That's not right cause it makes us stressed. We already have enough stuff to do in school :C :C We don't want no more homework being set by teachers.

Rewrite these sentences in Standard English – formal English.

2 Find some non-fiction texts and try rewriting parts of them so that they contain the same information but use inappropriate tone and language. This is a useful way of showing yourself how important it is to get the register right.

Preparation

Read Question 5 of the exam paper (the writing task) very carefully. Spend a minute preparing the question and making sure you fully understand it.

Here is another example Question 5:

An environmental charity has launched an essay writing competition on the following issue:

'The earth does not belong to us: we belong to the earth.'

Write an essay explaining your viewpoints about humans' relationship with the planet. **[40 marks]**

NAILIT!

Preparing the question must be quick, which is why it is worth practising.

That way you will get quicker at it.

The question starts with a statement designed to stir up strong opinions. The actual task is printed below the statement. Make sure that you identify the specific audience, purpose and form for the writing. In this task they are:

- audience (reader/s): judges of a writing competition

- purpose: to explain (your points of view)

- form: an essay.

There is another layer to preparing a question though: you also need to jot down some of your own thoughts, questions and useful vocabulary.

Here is how one student annotated the question:

> *Are the people who think we are ruining the earth experts?*

> *Adult judges?*

> *What does this mean? Do I agree? Is this about how people use the planet's resources?*

An environmental charity has launched an essay writing competition on the following issue:

'The earth does not belong to us: we belong to the earth.'

Write an essay explaining your viewpoints about humans' relationship with the planet.

> *Outlining opinions with explanation, examples, arguments, beliefs and values.*

DO IT!

Write down some synonyms for these two words:

- relationship
- belong.

This student marked up the question as a form of one-minute preparation. You will notice that as part of their preparation, this student has written down words they think will be useful. Many of these are synonyms for key words in the question. Synonyms are words that mean roughly the same thing: for example, big/large; violence/force; woman/female.

Here is another typical Question 5:

DO IT!

1 Copy out the question and prepare it as above.
2 Identify the audience, the purpose and the form in this writing task.

'School uniform is important because it allows students to focus on their work rather than on fashion.'

Write a letter to the governors at your school, arguing for or against this statement. **[40 marks]**

CHECKIT! ✓

1 What is Standard English?

2 How long should you spend preparing the question?

3 What is a synonym and why are synonyms important when preparing the question?

Planning

You should spend five minutes planning the content, structure and tone for your writing. It is necessary to spend this long as **good planning supports well-organised, clear and relevant ideas**.

Think back over all the advice you have received about planning during your GCSE course. Also look at any planning you have done. This process will help you work out the best ways to plan, and those areas where you have weaknesses and have not been effective enough in the past.

One good way to appreciate the importance of planning is to take a published text and then 'back plan' from it. To do this you should identify where the different sections of the text begin and then try to decide what the key purpose of that section is. When a text is in paragraphs, it is easy to spot the sections as they begin where paragraphs begin.

Here are two paragraphs from a non-fiction text:

> However delicious, burgers are certainly not without their downside. Most notable is their typical nutritional content. Quite frankly, the average burger's fat and calorie levels should make even the most dedicated junk-food lover have second thoughts about eating them. For example, one well-known brand's burger-with-cheese combo throbs with nearly 765 calories and 46 grams of fat, placing it well above the competition's burgers. Personally that makes me feel sick, and if an early heart attack is on your wish list, then I'd go ahead and order the double with cheese. This feast contains a staggering 1024 calories, 71 grams of fat, and 177 milligrams of cholesterol! Keep a paramedic handy for that one.
>
> So what's on offer if you're hankering after low-fat fast food? Well, not much. The only items reasonably low in calories and fat tend to be chicken sandwiches – as long as you do without the mayonnaise. Of course, you could order your beef burger without the cheese. This could cut the calories to 505 and the fat to 19 grams, which isn't too bad. However, I'd hesitate to recommend a burger without the cheese or mayonnaise. It really wouldn't taste of much.

We could sum up the topic of the first paragraph with the words 'nutritional content'. It's worth noting in passing something else about the structure of the text these two paragraphs are from: the first paragraph above seems to begin with a link to the previous paragraph, and that paragraph was presumably about 'burgers' taste'.

DOIT!

1 What is the topic of the second paragraph in the extract on page 83? Use no more than three words.
2 Gather together a variety of non-fiction texts (such as leaflets, articles, advice sheets) and back plan them. Spot and label the topic of each of their sections, and note any connections between the sections. Why have the sections been put together in the order that they are?
3 Below is one way to plan any non-fiction text in which you are going to state and develop a point of view. This example is one student's six-paragraph plan for a letter to the governors about school uniform. It is not complete. Copy it out and add detail to it.

WORKIT!

Introduction:

Explain which side I'm on. Show respect for the opposite view...

Dear Governors... I would like to put forward my views on... while I realise that...

Point 1:

Uniform is uncomfortable... It gets in the way of concentration...

Point 2:

Choice of clothes is an expression of identity... Creativity... Individuality

Point 3:

Point 4:

Acknowledge other side just to reject it. 'I know that some people say that...' However... Despite that... Use rhetorical question... If it's really true that... then why...?

Conclusion:

Thank you for reading... Giving me your time and attention... I do hope that...

Yours faithfully...

The opening

The first paragraph of your writing is crucial. You will need to reassure the exam marker that you can get your style, tone and vocabulary right for the task you have been given. In the opening, you must think carefully about your audience, purpose and form, and make sure your language is right for them.

DO IT!

Below are three different students' opening lines for the school uniform task on page 82. Read the three versions, and, as you read, think about how well the writing fits the advice you have already read. Try to put these three openings in order from best to worst. Write down your reasons for this order.

WORKIT!

Student answer A

Governors, you might like to wear fuddy old clothes but we do not. I've seen you wandering round the school like confused old crows, but there's no need to make us be the same as you. You're probably just jealous anyway. Cut us some slack! That's what I say, and now I'm gonna argue about it for you. By the time I've finished my argument you are going to think you've been stupid all these years you've made us wear the horrible stuff.

Student answer B

Dear governors,

I know that you have carefully debated the school uniform issue and have decided to keep it. I quite agree with you: I like wearing my own kit out of school but having to choose what to wear every day at school would be a total nightmare. I think that wearing school uniform means one less thing to worry about in the mornings, and that means there is more space in our minds for learning. Who in their right mind would want to do anything that crowds out learning? So, yes – let's keep school uniform: let's carry on concentrating on what really matters. Why would we want it any other way?

Student answer C

Dear Governors,

I realise that you believe that school uniform is important because it allows us all to focus on our work rather than on fashion and other matters that many adults would consider trivial. I understand where you are coming from: I know that you really do have our best interests at heart, and you sincerely want us to succeed and go on to lead happy and successful lives. However, I would like to put forward arguments for why all those great aims could be achieved even by students who attend lessons in their own clothes. In fact, I am going to suggest that this freedom of expression might even boost achievement.

Question 5 mark scheme

Below is part of one student's school uniform letter. A few relevant descriptors from the mark scheme have been pointed out in the margin.

WORKIT!

> Bourton Valley School
> West Bourton
> RL13 2CC
> 1st of July 2017
>
> Dear Chair of Governors,
>
> After reading about your proposed review of the school's uniform policy, I am writing to share my viewpoint, which I feel is mirrored by the majority of students at our school. Although some might argue that a school uniform helps us focus on our work, I would argue that wearing our own choice of attire would allow for greater concentration in class.
>
> Despite many adults' concerns, most teenagers are not obsessed with fashion and it is perhaps patronising to assume so. Moreover, the majority of teenagers dress for comfort rather than fashion in their spare time. Comfort is an essential requirement when focusing on our work; I would argue that most school uniform is uncomfortable. For instance, school ties are restrictive around the neck and shirts are often a tight fit. As a result, many companies have relaxed the need for such clothing in the workplace: employees can now relax and focus on their work. Conversely, many schools still insist upon this outdated mode of dress. Surely student focus is more important than old-fashioned notions of 'smart' clothing?
>
> The world has changed and there is much more emphasis now on personal expression... [The rest of the letter has been cut out]...
>
> Yours faithfully
>
> Ms Mary Meadows (Year 11)

Margin notes:

- The letter is set out correctly: address, date, 'Dear...'
- Register reasonably well matched to purpose, form and audience.
- Sophisticated word choice – perhaps not entirely effective.
- Discourse markers integrated into the argument to help link and contrast ideas.
- Real-life examples make the writing engaging, with sustained use of linguistic devices.
- Letter signed off correctly.

DOIT!

Imagine you are marking this letter. Add a few helpful comments for the student to help them improve the writing. Use the mark scheme on page 37 to guide your comments.

CHECKIT! ✓

1 How long should you spend making your plan?

2 What are the benefits of planning?

Context

It's time to look more carefully at the three elements of the context of the writing task. The three elements are **audience**, **purpose and form**.

It's worth repeating that whatever combination of these appears in the exam question, the mark scheme is the same and your job will be to state, organise and develop an effective viewpoint.

You will have noticed that there are seven key elements of the mark scheme covering content and organisation. (The mark scheme for technical accuracy is covered on page 107.)

Those seven key elements are:

Content:

- clear and effective style
- using appropriate language choices
- effective vocabulary
- a range of linguistic devices used well.

Organisation:

- detailed and well-connected ideas
- well-organised paragraphs
- effective use of varied structural features.

Audience

Question 5 on Paper 2 – the writing task – will state an audience for the writing. The audience will almost certainly change from year to year. However, the exam board states that the audience will always require formal writing, and so the actual audience stated does not have an enormous significance for your own language choices. Here are three example tasks with the audience highlighted, and a brief explanation of why a formal style of writing would be needed.

> 1 Write the text of a speech for a debate at your school or college in which you persuade young people to become more involved in their local communities.

You might think that because the audience is young, you can use very informal language. That would be a mistake. The language should be formal because a school debate is formally organised. Your speech could include some words and phrases that might be expected to appeal strongly to that age group, but such words should be carefully chosen for effect and should be the exception, not the rule.

> 2 Write a letter to your local newspaper in which you argue for or against provision of a travellers' camp in your area.

Here, the audience is the readers of the local paper. They will tend to be adults, and almost all of them will be strangers to you. It would be rude and inappropriate to use informal language, and your arguments would sound less convincing.

3 Write an article for a national newspaper in which you explain your point of view about Britain's membership of the European Union.

Clearly, if you have been chosen to write an article for a national newspaper such as the *Daily Mail* or *The Times*, then you would be expected to use formal language. Again, it would be seen as inappropriate to use informal language.

Read the two different pieces of writing below. One is inappropriate and informal. The other is formal and much more interesting.

> **A**
>
> Get on down with the old folks in your area. You can help them with their rubbish computer skills, unwrap their manky sweets for them if they've got stiff fingers, and you could even chuck their rubbish out for them if they're too tired or lazy to do it for themselves.

> **B**
>
> There are many ways we could be helpful to old people living in our neighbourhood. Being helpful is not just about carrying out dull chores every week, such as making sure the rubbish is put outside for collection, and helping with a few routine jobs around the home. Being helpful can be about just reassuring them that they are not alone, and that they don't have to live out their lives in boredom and lonely isolation.

Purpose

The writing question will target one of four purposes:

1 to explain

2 to instruct or advise

3 to argue

4 to persuade

Whatever the purpose, you must give a clear point of view, with arguments and evidence, in language that is quite formal. However, it is worth considering some of the common features of each of these four purposes:

1 **Writing to explain (your point of view)**

- Start with a paragraph introducing your viewpoint.
- Give detailed reasons for your opinions.
- Give the reader information that supports your opinions (anecdotes, statistics, facts).
- Use a less passionate tone than if you were arguing or persuading.
- Sum up your key points at the end.

2 **Writing to instruct or advise (helping your reader)**

- Suggest things to the reader. (It would be a good idea to… You might want to…)
- Give some choices to the reader. (Alternatively, you could…)

- Share your opinions, but not too forcefully. (It's generally accepted that...)
- Use a tone that reassures the reader. (It's very common to feel...)
- Address the reader directly. (Use personal pronouns like 'you'.)
- Sum up your key points at the end. (Finally, the following points are important, remember to...)

3 Writing to argue (presenting a viewpoint with reasons)

- Present your opinions confidently.
- Keep your tone calm and polite – don't go on a rant.
- Use rhetorical devices to win your reader over (for example, rhetorical questions or repetition).
- Use connectives to link your ideas (however... similarly... although... as a result... in addition).
- Consider both sides of the argument (but stick to one side if the question tells you to do so).
- Use facts and statistics to support your points.
- Come to a conclusion after considering the facts (if you are considering both sides).

4 Writing to persuade (convincing your reader/changing your reader's mind)

If you are writing to persuade, you are aiming to convince the audience to agree with your viewpoint. Writing to argue and writing to persuade share many of the same features.

- Present your opinions strongly: aim to change your reader's opinion.
- Use rhetorical devices (like exaggeration, repetition, rhetorical questions).
- Criticise – and even mock – viewpoints that contradict your own.
- Use imperative verbs (do not believe; forget what others say...)
- Present opinions as facts. (The strongest evidence to support this is...)
- Use emotive language (words chosen for their emotional impact on the reader).

DO IT!

Below are four sentences. Each sentence is from a text with a different purpose. Read each sentence carefully and decide which one of the four purposes it best matches.

a Smoking is a silent killer, rotting your internal organs and poisoning those around you.

b As students, there are lots of ways to save money. You could use the discounts offered by many clothing shops, cinemas or leisure centres.

c The first reason I do not like social media is because it can waste a great deal of time.

d Recently, scientific studies have made us think again about the wisdom of using diesel fuel.

DO IT!

Here is the first paragraph from a student's persuasive writing:

If you think that wearing a uniform is a good idea, then you are crazy. School uniform is terrible. There are lots of reasons why it's terrible. For example, most people don't like it. I don't like it. If you think it's a good idea, then you're just wrong. I hate school uniform.

What makes this writing persuasive?

How could this persuasive writing be improved? (Look again at the mark scheme.)

DO IT!

Look back over your work from your English lessons. How many linguistic devices can you remember? List them in a table like the one opposite. Next to each device, write what it means and – if possible – give an example.

DO IT!

Think back over all the work you have done in English language, and then make a list of the key features of each form. Don't look at the suggestions on the next few pages until you have made your own list. The table below contains a few suggestions to start you off.

Linguistic devices

To make your writing interesting and engaging you must use a range of linguistic devices, just like any other author would do.

Device	Explanation	Example
Rhetorical question	A question is asked but no reply is needed.	'Do you think I'm stupid?'
Alliteration	Words near each other, deliberately starting with the same sound so that they stand out.	The most important question is why can't we all be kind and considerate enough not to kill each other?

Form

You will be told clearly what form to write. The form could be:

- a formal letter
- an article (for a newspaper, magazine or website)
- the text for a leaflet
- a speech
- an essay.

The exam marker should be able to recognise the form you are using, so it is important that you use some of the key features of the form you are given.

Form	Formal letter	Article	Leaflet	Speech	Essay
Typical features	Your address at the top	Engaging title	Subheadings	Direct address to listeners	Introduction
	Dear…	An opening paragraph to introduce the topic	Sections	Summing up	Different paragraphs for subtopics

Here are some of the features that the exam markers will want to see for each of the five forms:

SNAPIT!

Form	Features
Formal letter	• 'Dear…' • Paragraphs in an effective order • Addresses (e.g. yours and theirs) • Date • Yours sincerely or faithfully, as appropriate
Article	• An engaging title (e.g. to catch the reader's attention and introduce your point) • A strapline – a very short, snappy summary of the article under the title • An opening paragraph that provides an overview of the subject • Subheadings • An introductory paragraph • Paragraphs in an effective order
Leaflet	• A title that is clear, engaging and appropriate • Subheadings or boxes • Paragraphs or sections • Paragraphs in an effective order • Bullet points
Speech	• A clear address to the audience (e.g. Welcome, ladies and gentlemen, it is an honour to stand in front of you all today…) • A clear signing off (e.g. Thank you for sitting through these important ideas and I hope they will fill your thoughts on your way home.) • Rhetorical devices to engage the listener throughout • Sections/paragraphs in an effective order • A final address to the audience/summing up
Essay	• An introduction (i.e. your introduction would normally focus on the statement for discussion) • A conclusion (e.g. Finally… In conclusion… To conclude… In summary…) • Linked paragraphs in an effective order • An effective introduction and a convincing conclusion

DOIT!

1 Find some examples of each of the five forms. See how many of the features listed on page 91 you can find in the examples.
2 Note down any other common features you find for each form. Plan to use some of these in your own writing in the exam.
3 Create a revision poster for each form of writing. List the main features and include images and diagrams to remind you of the key ideas.

In the exam, whatever the form you are given in Question 5, don't waste any time drawing detailed images or diagrams, or making your title attractive with colours and special writing. You won't be given any marks for these fancy features.

CHECKIT! ✓

1 True or False?

   a You should spend time making the text look nice with special writing, fonts and colours.

   b Articles should contain a strapline.

   c You should start your speech with speech marks.

   d You can choose which form to use in the exam.

   e An essay should start with an introduction.

   f If you start a letter with 'Dear Madam' you should finish with 'Yours sincerely'.

2 Below are three tasks with different combinations of purpose, audience and form. For each of the three tasks, write the first 30–70 words, using language appropriate to the context.

   a A letter to your head teacher/principal explaining why you need a week off school/college.

   b A leaflet advising old people on how to stay fit and active.

   c An article in a free magazine persuading visitors of the advantages of your local area.

1   What number question is the writing task?

2   How long must you leave for the writing task?

3   How long should you leave for checking your writing at the end?

4   The writing task will include a context for your writing. What three things comprise the context?

5   Whatever the context of the writing task, the main focus is always the same. What is that focus?

6   What are the four possible purposes that the writing task covers?

7   What are the five possible forms that the writing task could take?

8   Identify the purpose and form in this exam question:

> Write an advice leaflet for the teachers of foreign students who will be visiting your local town to improve their English.

9   Content is one focus of the mark scheme. What are the other two focuses?

10   Explain which of the following two text extracts is more formal:

> **A**
>
> This is a very safe town, and there are very few precautions you will need to take. As long as your students follow a few simple rules and look after their belongings, then they will come to no harm.

> **B**
>
> This town is as safe as anything. The kids just need to behave themselves – no messing about – and they'll be ok.

11   What should you do when you prepare the question?

12   Write at least one synonym for each of the following words:
   - audience
   - purpose
   - form.

13   How many choices of task will you get in Question 5 of Paper 2?

14   Why might you acknowledge an opposing view in your writing?

15   Write down at least two benefits of planning.

16   Briefly explain what is good about this opening and how it might be improved:

> I hope your students will feel safe and happy in my town. I bet you will. There's really nothing much for you to worry about. In fact, it's a great place.

17   What should you bear in mind in the first paragraph of your writing?

18   What are the seven key elements of the mark scheme?

19 Which one of the four purposes is this writing for?

> Many parents worry about how closely they should supervise their children's leisure activities. On one hand, you want to be able to trust your children and give them the freedom to develop. On the other hand, you are responsible for their safety.

20 Which of the following questions is likely to be rhetorical? Explain why.

a Do you know when the bus is coming?

b Don't you just hate it when buses don't turn up?

c Which stop are you getting off at?

d Is this the right bus?

e Why does it always rain when I'm waiting for the bus?

21

'Prison is both cruel and pointless, and costs the rest of us a great deal of money. There are much better ways of dealing with people who are convicted of crimes.'

Write the text of a leaflet in which you persuade readers of your views on how we should deal with people found guilty of less serious crimes. **[40 marks]**

Writing: Technical accuracy

Introduction and advice

Technical accuracy covers a number of aspects including spelling, punctuation and grammar. Technical accuracy is extremely important as it accounts for a lot of marks. In the writing sections of Paper 1 and Paper 2, technical accuracy accounts for 40 per cent of the marks. Even in the English Literature exams some marks are given for spelling, punctuation and grammar (SPaG).

The six aspects of technical accuracy covered are:

1. Sentence demarcation
2. Punctuation
3. Sentences
4. Standard English
5. Spelling
6. Vocabulary

To get the most marks possible, you need to use all six aspects accurately, appropriately and effectively.

Sentence demarcation

Put simply, sentence demarcation is about using capital letters and full stops to mark the beginnings and ends of sentences. Sentences can also end with exclamation marks and question marks, where appropriate.

Below is some writing by a student. Five capital letters, three full stops, one question mark and one exclamation mark have been removed.

WORKIT!

> we cannot go on spoiling the planet we live on in just a few
> decades we have dug up and burnt the fossil fuels that nature took
> millions of years to create how much longer will we be able to carry
> on doing this we must stop it now our children and grandchildren
> will not thank us for using up all the planet's resources before they
> are even born

DOIT!

Copy out the writing and put in the sentence demarcations as you go.

On the following page are extracts from two different sorts of texts: a novel and an advertisement. In both cases, the capital letters and punctuation have been left out so that the beginning and end of the sentences are not shown.

DO IT!

Copy out each text, writing in the capital letters and ending the sentences with either a full stop, an exclamation mark or a question mark, as appropriate.

Novel extract

javad stretched and yawned he could hardly keep his eyes open how would he ever stay awake until morning and the safety of daylight he had promised to keep watch but now his will was weakening he edged a few inches away from the fire perhaps coldness would fight tiredness he knew that he and James would both rather be cold than dead

Advertisement extract

come alive with zingo fizz zingo fizz is the tingling new soft drink that will make you glad to be young if you're not young then zingo will make you think you are what could be wrong with that drink zingo it's good to be young even if you're not

DO IT!

Find a variety of texts: newspaper articles, leaflets, novels, and so on, and look carefully at how the beginnings and endings of sentences are marked. Note how sentences can be long, medium or even very short. Which sorts of text are most likely to use question marks or exclamation marks?

Punctuation

The exam marker is looking for a range of accurately used punctuation. This is because punctuation is one important way that a writer guides and controls the reader's reaction. Good writers use punctuation to make the reader pause, and to emphasise certain details for meaning and effect.

Punctuation is not just a matter of accuracy: it is also a matter of style and effect. In the exercise above, you probably found that punctuation is used in different ways for different purposes at different times. Writers use punctuation to help the reader. For example, sometimes writers use punctuation to make the reader pause so that they will notice an important detail.

Here is an extract from the novel *Never Let Me Go* by Kazuo Ishiguro:

Usually we just spread ourselves around the chairs and benches – there'd be five of us, six if Jenny B. came along – and had a good gossip. There was a kind of conversation that could only happen when you were hiding away in the pavilion; we might discuss something that was worrying us, or we might end up screaming with laughter, or in a furious row. Mostly, it was a way to unwind for a while with your closest friends.

In this one short paragraph the novelist, Ishiguro, has used:

- two dashes
- four commas
- four full stops
- one semicolon.

Here is an example of a student analysing one of Ishiguro's uses of punctuation:

WORKIT!

The writer, Ishiguro, uses a dash after 'benches'. This dash makes a pause as though the narrator is having a sudden extra thought, but pausing only very briefly. A full stop might have suggested that the narrator was calmer, less rushed.

Notice that Ishiguro writes some quite long stretches of words without any punctuation at all. The longest of these unpunctuated stretches is 18 words.

1 Read the extract from *Never Let Me Go* on page 96. Try to explain the purpose of each piece of punctuation.
2 Could Ishiguro have used any punctuation in those 18 words? If so, where, and why? Which works better: with punctuation or without? Why?
3 Now find short extracts (of about 50 words) from good examples of at least three of these different sorts of text:
   - fiction
   - a letter
   - an article from a newspaper, magazine or website
   - a leaflet
   - a speech
   - an essay.
   Underline all the punctuation marks in each short extract and explain the purpose of each one.
   Doing this research task will make you more aware of how punctuation is actually used. It will help you to understand that punctuation is not just used to obey rules: often it is used for deliberate effect.

Comma (,)

The comma is one of the most important pieces of punctuation. There are rules for where commas should be used. However, commas are actually used for three main purposes:

- To separate words in a list.
- To make the reader pause so that a detail can be emphasised.
- To make meaning clearer.

A comma must never be used instead of a full stop to end a statement; a complete statement is a sentence. It must end with a full stop.

- He walked over to his car, he got in. Wrong!
- He walked over to his car. He got in. Right!
- She was late, however no one minded. Wrong!
- She was late. However, no one minded. Right!
- He left the room, she followed. Wrong!
- He left the room. She followed. **Right!**

Look again at the different sorts of text you have gathered earlier in this section. Find a few commas in each text. Decide what each comma has been used for. You might find that it has more purposes than the three already listed in this section.

DOIT!

Each sentence below uses a comma for one of the three purposes. Decide which purpose is shown by the comma(s) in each sentence.

1 Having first tried to hide and control his panic, Imran finally decided to run.
2 It was going to be a long, boring, tiring and unpleasant day.
3 On Thursday it was sunny and bright, and rainy and cold was how Friday started out.

DO IT!

Which two of the following are punctuated correctly?

a It was a hot day, no one could be bothered to work.

b The dog ran, barked, jumped and then went still and quiet.

c I love chocolate. I'm going to buy some.

d We left the house, we never went back.

DO IT!

Go back over the different sorts of text you have gathered. Find examples of commas used to start sentences with non-essential detail.

Using a comma with fronted subordinate clauses and phrases

Sometimes we want to start a sentence with a non-essential detail, rather than with the main information. Often we do this for dramatic effect – to make the reader wait.

Here are some examples:

> Having arrived in plenty of time, I was annoyed that the party had already started.
>
> Outside the house, under the bright stars, Tom and Sarah were falling in love.
>
> Although she was older than her sister, she never seemed to get the best presents or the best room.

Exclamation mark (!)

Exclamation marks add emphasis to a statement – for example, shock or surprise. Do not overuse the exclamation mark in your writing. **Never** use double exclamation marks!

Semicolon (;)

You should not overuse the semicolon, but it can be very useful when used occasionally.

A semicolon can be used for two main purposes:

1 To separate multi-word items in a list. For example:

> I bought six juicy, ripe peaches; some expensive, but very mature cheddar cheese; a kilo of sausages; and some milk.
>
> There are many ways to use stationery to make your revision more exciting: you could use a mixture of highlighter pens; a range of different sized sticky notes; different coloured plain and lined paper; and a range of different cards to make flash cards.

2 To join two sentences that belong to each other in some way, perhaps by explaining each other. For example:

> He was not wearing his best jacket; he always looked scruffy.
>
> Revising is most effective when done in short bursts; research has shown that concentration wanders if you revise for long periods without a break.

In the second example above, the semicolon has been used instead of the word 'because'; the statement on one side of the semicolon explains the statement on the other side.

However, you will probably find that different texts and authors use semicolons for a variety of purposes – not just the two main purposes explained here.

Colon (:)

A colon is used for two main purposes:

1 To introduce some information – usually some sort of list.

2 To mean 'that is to say' or 'in other words'.

Apostrophe (')

Apostrophes are mainly used in two ways:

1 To show omission.

2 To show possession.

Omission means to leave something out: the apostrophe is used to replace letters in a word. For example:

- *Would not* becomes *wouldn't*.
- *I do not* becomes *I don't*.
- *You are* becomes *you're*.

Possession means showing that one thing belongs to another. For example:

> " Sarah's highlighter pen was missing. "

The apostrophe is always placed straight after the 'owner' (possessor). That means that if the owner is a plural ending in 's', then the apostrophe should appear after the 's'. For example:

> " The students' highlighter pens were missing. "

In this example, the apostrophe tells us that the missing pens were owned by more than one student. If the apostrophe came before the 's' then we would know that all the pens were owned by just one unfortunate student.

NAIL IT!

It's and *its* are special cases. We use the apostrophe if the word means '*it is*', but we do not use it if the word means '*of it*':

- It's a heavy kettle. (Omission: '*it's*' means '*it is*'.)
- He picked up the kettle by its handle. (Possession: the handle belongs to the kettle.)

DO IT!

Rewrite the following sentences, adding, moving or removing the apostrophes as necessary.

a We cant go to Nelums' party because we promised wed visit our nan's house.
b Its important to eat lots of vegetable's.
c The students ideas for raising money were very imaginative.
d Chanelles' idea for raising money was the most popular.

DO IT!

Look through the texts you gathered for the sentence demarcation section. Find every semicolon. Try to decide why each one has been used. You will probably find that different writers use semicolons for slightly different purposes. You might find some texts where they are never used.

Reviewing how you use (or don't use) punctuation is important: it allows you to spot which punctuation problems you should work on first.

Look at examples of your own writing.

- What sorts of punctuation do you most often leave out or use incorrectly?
- Do you currently use the full range of punctuation marks?
- Which punctuation marks do you avoid?
- Which do you overuse?

CHECKIT!

1 Punctuation should be used for accuracy. Name two other reasons for using punctuation.

2 What are the three purposes of a comma?

3 In which of the two sentences below should a comma have been used? Where should it have been used? Why?

a Leaping in the air Sadia neatly caught the ball.

b Sadia neatly caught the ball by leaping in the air.

4 One of the sentences below needs a colon. The other needs a semicolon. Write out the two sentences, putting in the correct punctuation. Explain why you have used the punctuation you have added in each sentence.

a He got up late he missed the bus.

b There was a reason he missed the bus he got up late.

5 In the following sentence two parents jointly own a car. Write out the sentence and put the apostrophe in the right place. Explain why you have placed the apostrophe where you have.

> I was shocked when I saw his parents car.

6 Copy out the text below and put the following pieces of punctuation in the right places.

- four full stops
- two commas
- one semicolon
- one colon

> Breathing heavily I came to a stop outside my destination the station I gasped for air my lungs were bursting although I had hardly got my breath back I forced my legs to take me onto the platform the train was coming in

Sentences

You need to craft your sentences so that your language has an impact on the reader. The exam marker will be looking for a **variety** of sentence forms used for effect. If you only use simple sentences, or compound sentences connected with the word 'and', you will get very few marks for technical accuracy.

Decide which of the following has a stronger impact on the reader:

> **A**
>
> Without a doubt, exercise is important. Eating healthily is important. Most crucially of all, we need to get enough sleep.

> **B**
>
> Exercise is really important and healthy eating is important and getting enough sleep is crucial.

Sentence variety is about using different types of sentence and the order of their parts to emphasise your main ideas and keep your writing interesting. In the examples above, the same information has been given in different ways. The first version is more engaging in terms of the types of sentence used and how they are organised.

Look at it again:

> Without a doubt, exercise is important.

This first sentence doesn't start with the main point, but with a dramatic emphasis, telling you that you can't disagree, even though you don't yet know what you **could** disagree with!

> Eating healthily is important.

This is a very short, assertive sentence.

> Most crucially of all, we need to get enough sleep.

Again, this final sentence does not start with the main point. 'Most crucially of all' creates a sort of dramatic pause that strengthens the main point when it arrives.

DO IT!

Here is something that a student wrote in an exam. Rewrite it so that its sentence variety is much more effective:

> He ran quickly. He got to the safety of the big rock. He looked back at the people and he couldn't see them and he felt relieved and he drank some water.

STRETCH IT!

Varying sentences is a key marker of a good writer. Variety not only keeps your ideas interesting: variety also gives you the opportunity to influence your reader and give your ideas persuasive power.

Look at the two extracts from exam answers below. They are similar in content, but the style of version B is much more varied and is likely to have a much more powerful effect on the reader.

WORKIT!

Student answer A

Seventeen-year-olds are too young to be driving. Many seventeen-year-olds can hardly walk in a straight line. It's not a good idea to let them drive cars. They can be really dangerous.

Student answer B

Barely able to walk in a straight line half the time, teenagers would be lethal behind the wheel of a car, and – however grown up they consider themselves to be – seventeen-year-olds are still only teenagers. Let them wait a year before they get the licence to kill.

NAILIT!

Connectives in the table starting with a capital letter are normally only used at the start of a sentence:

- I wanted to go. *However*, I didn't feel well enough.

- I wasn't feeling well. *Therefore* I didn't go.

Discourse markers

Discourse markers are words and phrases used to connect and sequence ideas and information. They help you to link paragraphs, sentences and even different parts of sentences. They are, therefore, essential to achieving sentence variety. Here is a table of one type of discourse markers – connectives – sorted into categories:

SNAPIT!

Cause and effect	Contrasting	Comparing	Time and sequence
because Therefore consequently so	In contrast whereas On the other hand Conversely However	Equally In comparison Likewise Similarly In the same way	while when since Next then Firstly
Adding	**Emphasising**	**Giving an example**	**Exceptions and conditions**
In addition Moreover Furthermore as well as What is more	Above all In particular especially	For example For instance as revealed by such as	although even though despite in spite of unless if

Standard English

In your English exams, you must write in Standard English. English is spoken in many versions (or 'dialects'). Because of this variety, there needs to be a standard version that everyone can understand. This is Standard English – a formal version of English that is used in business and all official circumstances. It is a polite form of language that should always be used between people who are not personal friends. Of course, it is not the form of English that is used between people who know each other well. Effective writers sometimes slip out of Standard English for effect. For example:

> Most people firmly believe that school uniform is crucial for the success of a school. It ain't necessarily so.

Here the writer has used the informal 'ain't' as a dramatic contrast with the previous very formal sentence.

Here, are some marking descriptors for sentences and Standard English.

Aspect	Band 2 descriptors (Roughly GCSE grades 2–3)	Band 3 descriptors (Roughly GCSE grades 4–6)	Band 4 descriptors (Roughly GCSE grades 7–9)
Sentences	The student's answer… • tries out different sentence forms	The student's answer… • varies sentences for effect	The student's answer… • uses a full range of appropriate sentence structures for effect
Standard English	• sometimes uses Standard English with some control of agreement.	• mostly uses Standard English appropriately and with controlled grammatical structures.	• always uses Standard English appropriately and with secure control of complex grammatical structures.

Here, is part of a student's letter to the governors to ask for the sports centre to be rebuilt. Some comments by an exam marker are also shown.

WORKIT!

The sports centre will be a fab and educational place for all ages and it will also provide a place where the community can get down and get fit, whilst having fun. The sports centre will have loads of activities that children and adults can get involved with - swimming, five-a-side football, squash, basketball, yoga, zumba and many stuff. These activities will become available as soon as the sports centre will be opened.

> Odd mix of informal and formal vocabulary.

> Sentences are fluent but the first two start in the same way.

> More correct to say 'is opened'?

NAILIT!

Be careful about using informal English. It really might not work. If in doubt, leave it out.

DOIT!

Which four of the following sentences use informal English?

a We were unable to go.
b Me and John went to the beach.
c He doesn't want to go shopping.
d She don't like curry.
e He was sat on the wall.
f We done it so badly.
g They did it well.

NAILIT!

Notice how the main changes to the student's writing are to do with:

• appropriate vocabulary

• sentence structure (how they are arranged)

• verb forms (for example, 'would' rather than 'will').

Leave some time at the end of your writing tasks in the exam so you can check through your work to correct any mistakes.

This student can use formal vocabulary and can sustain long sentences, but is not consistent in how they use and control these elements. There is some variety of sentence structure, and some control of register (formal English).

This writing would belong in the bottom of Band 3. The exam marker suggested this slight improvement in the writing to raise it to the top of Band 3:

WORKIT!

An enjoyable and educational place for all ages, a new sports centre would also provide a place where the community can get down and get fit, whilst having fun. The sports centre would have a wide variety of activities that children and adults could get involved with, such as swimming, 5-a-side football, squash, basketball, yoga and zumba. These activities would become available as soon as the sports centre is opened.

CHECKIT! ✓

1 Name two good reasons for varying your sentences.

2 Copy out the words below, completing them with two different discourse markers that make sense.

> "I was hungry I put two samosas in the oven"

3 Here are three pieces of students' writing. As you read through them, compare them with the descriptors for sentences and for Standard English on page 103. Decide which band each piece belongs in. They all belong to different bands: 2, 3 or 4. Which is which?

CHECKIT!

Student answer A

Advertising can be a right pain and get in the way of everything but overall it's a great thing. If there wasn't any adverts then companies can't make us aware of their great products and they wouldn't be able to grow into successful companies.

Student answer B

I realise that money is in short supply and there are so many worthy causes to be considered. However, overall our school is already very successful and up to date, and it is full of facilities that we can feel very proud of: a state-of-the-art recording studio; a bright and comfortable dining area; an all-weather playing surface – facilities that might even be considered to be luxuries. We need a new sports centre as well.

Student answer C

I know teenagers that are under pressure to start a relationship just to prove that they are mature. I know one who really don't know what she's doing. She just keeps getting hurt. I know many adults who wasn't very sensible when they was young either, although my aunt and uncle got married before they was twenty and they are glad they done it.

DO IT!

Make a list of your five most frequent incorrect spellings.

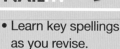

NAIL IT!

- Learn key spellings as you revise.
- Highlight the tricky section of words you misspell.
- Don't forget to include spellings from your other GCSE subjects.

NAIL IT!

Even during your revision weeks, make some time to read quality fiction and non-fiction. Look up and learn words you don't know. Write down these words and their meanings on sticky notes and post them in places where you will see them regularly.

Spelling

Most people are better spellers than they think. Never be ashamed of your spelling. It's worth remembering that:

- English is a difficult language to spell
- many great writers are not great spellers
- spelling actually accounts for very few marks. It is possible to get a mark for using a very good word even if you don't spell it correctly. However, students who are not confident about their spelling risk losing marks in other, related ways: they try to hide their spelling by using unclear handwriting or by using words that are too simple to be effective. Don't do that. Use the best word possible; write it clearly and spell it as well as you can.

Common mistake patterns

- Illogical spellings (such as, 'rember' instead of the correct 'remember').
- Homophone (same sound) mistakes (such as, 'their'/'there'/'they're' and 'new'/'knew').
- Combining words (such as, 'alot' instead of 'a lot').
- Contraction spelling mistakes (forgetting the apostrophe in 'don't' or 'I'll').
- Words that are missing a double letter (such as, 'finaly' instead of 'finally').
- Words given double letters by mistake (such as, 'untill' instead of 'until').
- A letter missed out by mistake (such as, 'belive' instead of 'believe').
- Letters reversed by mistake (such as, 'minuet' instead of 'minute').
- Using American spelling (such as, 'socialize' instead of 'socialise').
- Missing out silent letters (in words such as, 'parliament', 'government', 'Wednesday', 'science' and 'chocolate').

Spelling strategies

Here are some tricks to help you remember common spellings.

Necessary: a shirt has one **c**ollar and two **s**leeves (one c, two s).

Because: **b**ig **e**lephants **c**an **a**lways **u**nderstand **s**mall **e**lephants.

Vocabulary

The exam marker is looking for a range of vocabulary in your writing. The top marks in the exam will be given for 'wide and ambitious' vocabulary. However, it's important not to use complicated words if you're not sure of their meaning – being clear is more important.

- Avoid vague words (like 'big', 'ok', 'good' and 'nice').
- If it suits the form and purpose, use specialist words (like 'simile', 'environment' and 'identity').
- Try to choose words carefully to have an appropriate impact on the reader.

Mark scheme

The mark scheme for technical accuracy is the same for the writing tasks in both English Language papers. (There are no technical accuracy marks to be won or lost when you are answering the reading questions.)

SNAPIT!

Aspect	Band 2 descriptors (Roughly GCSE grades 2–3)	Band 3 descriptors (Roughly GCSE grades 4–6)	Band 4 descriptors (Roughly GCSE grades 7–9)
Sentence demarcation	The student's answer… • marks the beginnings and ends of most sentences	The student's answer… • marks the beginnings and ends of almost all sentences	The student's answer… • correctly marks the beginnings and ends of sentences
Punctuation	• often uses basic punctuation well	• uses a range of punctuation usually correctly	• uses a wide range of punctuation almost always correctly
Sentences	• tries out different sentence structures and types	• varies sentences for effect	• uses a wide range of sentence structures confidently and effectively
Standard English	• sometimes uses Standard English, perhaps with some mistakes over agreement or tense endings	• mainly uses Standard English with good control and flexibility	• uses appropriate Standard English with control and flexibility throughout
Spelling	• sometimes spells more complex words correctly (such as 'height', 'definite')	• makes few spelling mistakes – even complex and irregular words (such as 'accommodation', 'rhythmic', 'parallel')	• spells almost all words correctly, including adventurous vocabulary (such as 'combustible', 'opprobrium', 'machination')
Vocabulary	• varies vocabulary.	• chooses some precise and sophisticated vocabulary.	• uses a wide and adventurous vocabulary.

✓ CHECKIT!

1 What are homophones?

2 Here are three spellings. Which one is correct?

   a disappear   **b** dissapear   **c** dissappear

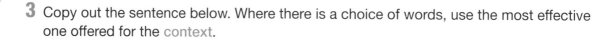

CHECKIT! ✓

3 Copy out the sentence below. Where there is a choice of words, use the most effective one offered for the context.

> She lay beneath the tree in <u>discomfort/pain/agony</u>, blood <u>dripping/oozing/coming</u> from the deep <u>wound/cut/gash</u> and soaking into the earth around her.

4 To get to know the mark scheme better, read the first part of a student's letter to the school governors about school uniform below. Here are some marker comments based on the mark scheme for technical accuracy:

- Correct layout for formal letter.
- The opening uses Standard English.
- Ambitious vocabulary is correctly spelled.
- Sentence structure is used for effect.
- A wide range of punctuation is used (semicolons and colons).

a In the letter, find examples of each of the five marker comments.

b Find examples in the letter of other descriptors from the mark scheme for technical accuracy.

> Welton Valley School
>
> West Bradley
>
> WS99 1BA
>
> 1st July 2019
>
> Dear Chair of Governors,
>
> After reading about your proposed review of the school's uniform policy, I am writing to share my viewpoint, which I feel is mirrored by the majority of students at our school. Although some might argue that a school uniform helps us focus on our work, I would argue that wearing our own choice of attire would allow for greater concentration in class.
>
> Despite many adults' concerns, most teenagers are not obsessed with fashion and it is perhaps patronising to assume so. Moreover, the majority of teenagers dress for comfort rather than fashion in their spare time. Comfort is an essential requirement when focusing on our work; I would argue that most school uniform is uncomfortable. For instance, school ties are restrictive around the neck and shirts are often a tight fit. As a result, many companies have relaxed the need for such clothing in the workplace: employees can now relax and focus on their work. Conversely, many schools still insist upon this outdated mode of dress. Surely student focus is more important than old-fashioned notions of 'smart' clothing?

5 Improve the letter by rewriting part of it and/or continuing it.

1 What percentage of the marks in the writing exams are accounted for by technical accuracy?

2 Is technical accuracy only about accuracy?

3 What are the six aspects of technical accuracy?

4 What are the three pieces of punctuation that can end a sentence?

5 Name seven different punctuation marks.

6 Why is punctuation important?

7 Which of the following sentences uses a comma incorrectly?

    a He wrote his story, but his teacher didn't like it.

    b The sports centre is fun, it also helps us get fit.

    c Although he was ill, he didn't go to bed.

    d He found a beautiful, quiet, sandy, beach.

8 In which sentence below is the semicolon not used correctly?

    a He woke up while it was still dark; he went downstairs.

    b It was raining; he put on his coat.

    c She realised all these things: she was excited, happy and impatient; her mother was angry, and her father wasn't going to help.

9 What are the two reasons for using a colon?

10 In which sentences below is the apostrophe not used correctly?

    a Sadiq's uncle bought some potatoe's.

    b Its hot today.

    c The childrens teacher couldn't be found anywhere.

    d I picked up the kettle by it's handle.

    e The river's flow was'nt fast enough.

11 What is meant by 'sentence variety'?

12 Discourse markers are words and phrases that make connections in texts. There are at least eight discourse markers in the text below. Find all of them.

> This tiredness stayed with Errol all week. He didn't seem to be able to get out of bed. Even when Hayley knocked on the door and called through the letter box, he just couldn't stir himself. Nights and days slowly passed through his stuffy room like silent visitors. They didn't trouble him though. His eyes were closed and he was elsewhere in his head. Because of his fever, he often didn't really know where he was.

13 Which one of the following sentences is not written in Standard English?

    a She waved to John and me.

    b Zanira and I went to the cinema.

    c We wasn't speaking to each other.

    d I did it well.

14 Which four of the following words are not spelled correctly?

definitely	independant	business	trouble	hopefull
neccessary	because	dissappear	disappoint	accommodation

ENGLISH LITERATURE

Introduction and advice

This section will help you prepare for the AQA GCSE English 9–1 Literature exams. Remember, English Language and English Literature are different subjects. They count as two different GCSEs – just like maths and physics. However, there are many skills you can transfer from English Language to English Literature and vice versa. Remember this as you work through your revision.

This is how the English Literature papers will be organised in the exams.

SNAP IT!

Exam title	Paper 1: Shakespeare and the 19th-century novel	Paper 2: Modern texts and poetry
Section A	**Shakespeare** One question about a Shakespeare play you have studied. You will be asked to write in detail about an extract and to write about the play as a whole.	**Modern texts** You will be asked to choose one of two questions about the modern play or novel you have studied. Your answer will be in the form of an essay.
Section B	**The 19th-century novel** One question about a 19th-century novel you have studied. You will be asked to write in detail about an extract and to write about the novel as a whole.	**Poetry** You will have studied either 'Love and relationships' or 'Power and conflict'. You will answer the question on the cluster you have studied.
Section C	No Section C for this paper	**Unseen poetry** You will be asked to answer two questions about two poems you have not seen before.

Each section in the rest of this guide will help you prepare for each of the different sections in both papers.

Paper 1 Section A: Shakespeare

Introduction and advice

Section A of the Paper 1 English Literature exam is the Shakespeare question.

You will have studied one Shakespeare play from this list.

- *Macbeth*
- *Romeo and Juliet*
- *The Tempest*
- *The Merchant of Venice*
- *Much Ado About Nothing*
- *Julius Caesar*

The exam paper will have questions on all the different Shakespeare plays. Don't be put off by this. You need to find the play you have studied and only answer that question.

☞ Paper 1
☞ Section A: Shakespeare
☞ Marks: 34
☞ Time: 55 minutes

DO IT!

Set a timer for three minutes. On a large piece of paper, make a spider diagram of everything you can remember about your Shakespeare play.

Understanding the question

Although there is only one question, you are asked to do two tasks:

1 For the first task, you will be given a short extract from a Shakespeare play you have studied. You will have to write about this in detail.

2 For the second task, you will have to write about the play as a whole.

However, you don't need to write about each task separately – you can combine them within your answer.

The question will ask you to look at theme or character or both.

The question on the paper will be like this.

Section A: Shakespeare

Answer one question from this section on your chosen text.

Macbeth

Read the following extract from Act 5 Scene 2 of *Macbeth* and then answer the question that follows.

At this point in the play Macbeth is speaking. He has just been told that his wife, Lady Macbeth, is dead.

> She should have died hereafter.
>
> There would have been a time for such a word.
>
> Tomorrow, and tomorrow, and tomorrow,
>
> Creeps in this petty pace from day to day
>
> 5   To the last syllable of recorded time,
>
> And all our yesterdays have lighted fools
>
> The way to dusty death. Out, out, brief candle!
>
> Life's but a walking shadow, a poor player
>
> That struts and frets his hour upon the stage
>
> 10   And then is heard no more. It is a tale
>
> Told by an idiot, full of sound and fury,
>
> Signifying nothing.

Starting with this speech, explain how far you think Shakespeare presents Macbeth as a desperate and changed man.

Write about:

• how Shakespeare presents Macbeth in this speech

• how Shakespeare presents Macbeth in the play as a whole.

[30 marks]
AO4 [4 marks]

Using the extract

Consider the first part of the question: **how does Shakespeare present the character in the speech?** The question will be about either a theme or character in the play. When writing about the extract it is helpful to think about language, structure and subject terminology.

Looking at language means thinking about the words that Shakespeare chooses to give his character.

You should read through the extract and pick out six interesting words or short phrases, making some annotations in the margin about language.

WORKIT!

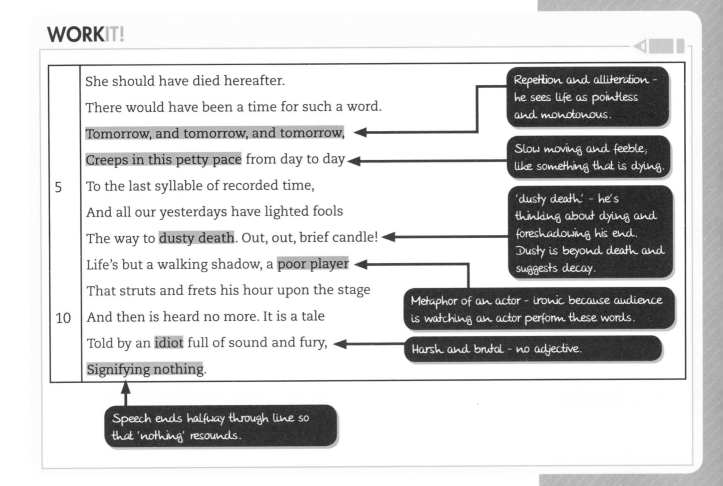

	She should have died hereafter.
	There would have been a time for such a word.
	Tomorrow, and tomorrow, and tomorrow,
	Creeps in this petty pace from day to day
5	To the last syllable of recorded time,
	And all our yesterdays have lighted fools
	The way to dusty death. Out, out, brief candle!
	Life's but a walking shadow, a poor player
	That struts and frets his hour upon the stage
10	And then is heard no more. It is a tale
	Told by an idiot full of sound and fury,
	Signifying nothing.

Annotations:
- Repetition and alliteration – he sees life as pointless and monotonous.
- Slow moving and feeble; like something that is dying.
- 'dusty death' – he's thinking about dying and foreshadowing his end. Dusty is beyond death and suggests decay.
- Metaphor of an actor – ironic because audience is watching an actor perform these words.
- Harsh and brutal – no adjective.
- Speech ends halfway through line so that 'nothing' resounds.

Next, consider the structure of the extract. This means the way it is built and put together. Use a different colour to highlight three words or phrases in your chosen extract. Make some more annotations, this time about structure. Think about the position of the words and phrases in the extract – why might Shakespeare have chosen to arrange them in this way?

Remember, you need to use subject terminology (specialist words or phrases that relate to the subject) such as metaphor, verb, image and alliteration. Write down all the specialist terms you can remember from your study of English Literature. Think about your work in poetry to help you. Start with rhythm, simile and onomatopoeia.

NAILIT!

Make sure that you always explain the terminology you use and back it up with examples. 'Macbeth uses an extended metaphor' on its own will get no marks in the exam. Instead, explain why that technique has been used, and its effect on the audience (both Elizabethan and modern).

DO IT!

Pick out two or three literary terms from the extract on page 112 and annotate them with notes explaining why you think Shakespeare chose to use them.

WORKIT!

'dusty death' – alliteration

'life's but a poor player' – metaphor

Throughout the speech, Macbeth uses the extended metaphor of an actor on the stage. Shakespeare does this to show that, even though life might be exciting at the time, ultimately it is short and meaningless.

DO IT!

Choose three of your annotations and write one or two sentences about each.

WORKIT!

The repetition of 'tomorrow' takes up a whole line, suggesting Shakespeare is instructing the actor to speak in a slow repetitive rhythm because Macbeth sees life as monotonous and hopeless.

The characters

In the second part of the question you are asked to look at how Shakespeare presents a character or theme in the whole play. In the example on page 112 the question asks you to look at Macbeth's character. This doesn't mean you have to write about **everything** he does or says. Instead, select particular moments, events and aspects of his character which best support your ideas.

You should organise your revision around theme and character, but to write about these you will need to think about characterisation (the way the character is constructed), **relationships**, **events**, **settings** and **context**. Refer to some key moments in the play and use quotations as evidence to back up what you say.

DO IT!

Write down five or six bullet points about the characterisation of each of the four main roles in the play you have studied. Back up each with an example from the text or from the play.

As an English Literature student, it is really important to write about the **characters** in a way that shows you know Shakespeare has made them up. Don't write about them as if they are real people. Above all, you will want to think about their motivation. What is it they want? Macbeth wants power, Juliet wants to be with Romeo and escape the shackles of the life her parents have chosen.

Shakespeare's plays are always about the **relationships** between characters. In *Romeo and Juliet*, Juliet's relationship with Romeo is obviously central to the play, but her relationships with her father, mother and the nurse are also important.

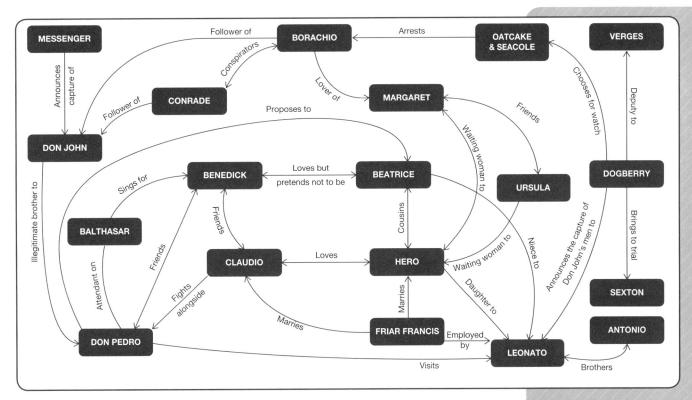

Relationship web for *Much Ado About Nothing*

DO IT!

A good writer ties their work together with themes – a group of ideas and images they keep referring back to, such as death, darkness, love, family and so on.

1   Make a theme web. Choose a theme from the play you have studied. Write the name of the theme on a piece of card and stick it to a large sheet of paper. Write events, ideas and quotations to do with that theme on pieces of card and arrange them on the paper. Put the most important events/ideas/quotations closest to the theme card. Repeat this for two or three themes.

- Macbeth - darkness.
- The murder of Duncan takes place at night.
- Just before murder of Banquo, Macbeth says; Nature seems dead and wicked dreams abuse curtained sleep.

2   Write a paragraph about the significance of one of your themes using ideas from your web. Make sure you back up your ideas with at least one quotation.

SNAP IT!

Make a diagram like the one above to show the relationships between the central characters in the play you have studied. Then take a photograph of it so that you can revisit it anywhere!

DO IT!

Reduce your play to the ten most important events. You could compare your ten key events with someone else. Discuss, argue and agree a combined list of ten.

Of course, you have to know the plot of the play but be careful; simply retelling the story won't get you any credit in the exam. You will need to interpret the **events** to make an informed personal analysis of the play.

Choose a particular scene from your play and write a sentence explaining how the setting informs what we understand about the characters.

The setting

When and where the whole play or scene or speech takes place can influence the audience's response to the characters and their actions. For example, most of the action in *Macbeth* takes place in a cold, dark and rather lonely castle or a bleak and desolate 'blasted heath'. You can refer to setting when answering both parts of the question.

WORKIT!

The events in 'The Tempest' take place on a fantasy island where Prospero can practise his magic, however, the island also suggests that he is self-centred and detached from the real world.

Context

It helps our understanding if we know something about the circumstances in which the play was written and how this might have influenced Shakespeare. This is called context. Context can also refer to the location where the play or scene takes place, the genre and the way different audiences might watch and understand the play. A student here talks about witches in the context of Shakespearean times:

WORKIT!

In Shakespeare's time, many women had been executed for supposed witchcraft. This meant the audience believed the witches had genuine supernatural power.

Read these two responses by students who were writing about context in a Shakespeare essay.

Student answer A

Shakespeare was born in 1564 and died in 1616, his father was a glove maker and he went to a school in Stratford-Upon-Avon.

Student answer B

Juliet is very young 'she hath not seen the change of fourteen years' and yet the friar sees it as appropriate for her to be married to Romeo. However, in Shakespeare's time it was not her young age that was unsuitable but the fact that the marriage had taken place in secret.

Which do you think is best and why? Write some feedback to each student.

Mark scheme

These improvement descriptors will help you to understand how to improve your answers.

SNAP IT!

Descriptors	Band 2	Band 3	Band 4	Band 5	Band 6
	The student's answer…	The student's answer…	The student's answer…	The student's answer…	The student's answer…
AO1 Read, understand and respond	• is relevant and backs up ideas with references to the text	• sometimes explains the text in relation to the task	• clearly explains the text in relation to the task	• thoughtfully explains the text in relation to the task	• critically explores the text in relation to the task
Use evidence	• makes some comments about these references	• refers to details in the text to back up points	• uses textual references effectively to back up points	• thoughtfully builds appropriate references into points	• chooses precise textual details to clinch points
AO2 Language, form and structure	• mentions some of the writer's methods	• comments on some of the writer's methods and their effects	• clearly explains the writer's key methods, and their effects	• thoughtfully explains the writer's key methods, and their effects	• analyses the writer's key methods, and *how* these influence the reader
Subject terminology	• uses some subject terminology	• uses some relevant terminology	• helpfully uses varied, relevant terminology	• makes thoughtful use of relevant terminology	• chooses subject terminology to make points precise and convincing
AO3 Contexts	• makes some simple inferences and shows some awareness of contexts.	• infers the writer's point of view and the significance of contexts.	• shows a clear appreciation of the writer's point of view and the significance of contexts.	• explores the writer's point of view and the influence of particular contexts.	• makes perceptive and revealing links between the text and relevant contexts.

Very good answers will explore how Shakespeare uses language and structure to create characters and their relationships. Very good answers connect what the characters say to the themes, ideas and the effects upon the reader.

Good answers will show a clear understanding of how Shakespeare develops characters and relationships using strong examples.

Weaker answers will only explain what happens to characters and relationships without using many examples. They will write about the characters as if they are real people and not acknowledge they are Shakespeare's constructs.

CHECKIT! ✓

1 How many marks are there for spelling, punctuation and grammar on the Shakespeare question?

2 There is one question, but it contains two tasks. What is the second task?

3 What two elements should your revision focus on?

4 Choose one of these areas you have revised: characterisation, relationships, events, settings, themes or context. Write a few paragraphs based on this question.

> How does Shakespeare use [characterisation/relationships/events/
> settings/themes/context] to present the character of [name of character]
> in [name of Shakespeare play you have studied]?

5 Choose a different extract taken from the play you have studied. It should be between 15 and 20 lines (you might find it helpful to print it out). Adapt the question below to fit your chosen Shakespeare play and extract:

> Explore how Shakespeare presents [name of character] in this extract
> and elsewhere in the play.

Paper 1 Section B: The 19th-century novel

Introduction and advice

You will have studied one of these 19th-century novels:

- *The Strange Case of Dr Jekyll and Mr Hyde* by Robert Louis Stevenson
- *A Christmas Carol* by Charles Dickens
- *Great Expectations* by Charles Dickens
- *Jane Eyre* by Charlotte Bronte
- *Frankenstein* by Mary Shelley
- *Pride and Prejudice* by Jane Austen
- *The Sign of Four* by Sir Arthur Conan Doyle

Just as with the Shakespeare section, the paper will have questions on all of these novels. Remember, you only need to answer the question on the novel you have studied. Once you have found your question, take some time to read through and understand it.

Understanding the question

The question will ask you to look at theme or character or both. To do this, you will need to show your understanding of these things in your answer:

- The characters and themes of the novel.
- The extract and the novel as a whole.
- How the writer uses language to make the novel interesting.
- The context of the novel, the time it was written and how it is still relevant today.
- Your own opinions and ideas.

You will need to back up your arguments with knowledge of the text, using evidence such as quotations.

- Paper 1
- Section B: The 19th-century novel
- Marks: 30
- Time: 50 minutes

DO IT!

Start by revising an overview of the novel. Decide on the ten most important events and summarise each in one sentence.

The question on the paper will look like this.

Robert Louis Stevenson: *The Strange Case of Dr Jekyll and Mr Hyde*

Read this extract from Chapter 2 and then answer the following question.

In this extract Mr Utterson meets Mr Hyde.

	The steps drew swiftly nearer, and swelled out suddenly louder as they turned the end of the street. The lawyer, looking forth from the entry, could soon see what manner of man he had to deal with. He was small and very plainly dressed and the look of him, even at that distance, went somehow strongly against the watcher's inclination. But he made
5	straight for the door, crossing the roadway to save time; and as he came, he drew a key from his pocket like one approaching home.
	Mr. Utterson stepped out and touched him on the shoulder as he passed. 'Mr. Hyde, I think?'
	Mr. Hyde shrank back with a hissing intake of the breath. But his fear was only momentary; and though he did not look the lawyer in the face, he answered coolly
10	enough: 'That is my name. What do you want?'
	'I see you are going in,' returned the lawyer. 'I am an old friend of Dr. Jekyll's–Mr. Utterson of Gaunt Street–you must have heard of my name; and meeting you so conveniently, I thought you might admit me.'
	'You will not find Dr. Jekyll; he is from home,' replied Mr. Hyde, blowing in the key. And
15	then suddenly, but still without looking up, 'How did you know me?' he asked.
	'On your side,' said Mr. Utterson 'will you do me a favour?'
	'With pleasure,' replied the other. 'What shall it be?'
	'Will you let me see your face?' asked the lawyer.
	Mr. Hyde appeared to hesitate, and then, as if upon some sudden reflection, fronted about
20	with an air of defiance; and the pair stared at each other pretty fixedly for a few seconds. 'Now I shall know you again,' said Mr. Utterson. 'It may be useful.'
	'Yes,' returned Mr. Hyde, 'lt is as well we have met; and apropos, you should have my address.' And he gave a number of a street in Soho.
	'Good God!' thought Mr. Utterson, 'can he, too, have been thinking of the will?' But he
25	kept his feelings to himself and only grunted in acknowledgment of the address.
	'And now,' said the other, 'how did you know me?'
	'By description,' was the reply.

Starting with this extract, how does Stevenson present Mr Utterson?

Write about:

• how Stevenson presents Mr Utterson in this extract

• explore how Stevenson presents Mr Utterson in the novel as a whole. **[30 marks]**

Using the extract

You will need to get used to dealing with extracts – short chunks of the novel. An extract is usually about 400 words long. It is helpful revision to create your own bank of likely extracts.

DOIT!

1 Choose one of your ten key events, from the activity on page 119. Find it in the novel and select an extract of about 400 words. Make a copy of your chosen extract, so that you can annotate it.

2 Re-read your extract, paying close attention to how the writer uses language. As you do so, underline interesting words and phrases and make annotations in the margins. Look at the language the writer uses. These questions will help you:
   • How does the writer use language to convey the setting or mood in the extract?
   • What effect does the language have? Consider: what does it make the reader think of? How does it make them feel?
   • If the writer uses dialogue, how do they make it interesting?
   • How do different characters speak?
   • How does the writer choose words for deliberate impact?
   • Which words or phrases tell you that this extract was written in the 19th century?

3 Read your extract and write one or two sentences for each of these questions:
   • Which characters appear and how are they presented?
   • How does the writer use a range of techniques in the extract to create a particular atmosphere?
   • Write down two other places in the novel that have similar ideas, language or details.
   • Write down two themes in the extract and find two other places in the novel where those themes are used.

Thinking about the novel as a whole

As well as the extract, the question will ask you to write about the novel as a whole, so you need to understand the complete book. These review activities will help you revise for this.

WORKIT!

'Great Expectations' starts in a very dramatic way. Pip is alone in the churchyard; suddenly the convict, Magwitch, attacks him. Dickens makes his central character vulnerable and right away the reader wants to know what happens to him. This vulnerability is echoed when he later goes go visit Miss Haversham. He is seen to be a small boy in a huge, frightening and semi-derelict house.

DOIT!

Find your list of the ten key events from the activity on page 119. Write each event on a separate card. Then add in five more events on new cards. Shuffle them and pin them up in the right order.

Write answers to these questions on the cards.
   • How do the events relate to each other?
   • Why do you think the writer has structured a particular event in that place in the novel?

You can organise your revision around character and theme because the questions will focus on these areas. To write about character and theme, you will need to think about characterisation (the way the character is constructed), relationships, events, setting and context.

SNAPIT!

To help you review characterisation, make a quick sketch for each of the four most important characters in the novel. Annotate each sketch with seven things you know about that character. Support them with quotes that you have learned. You can then take a picture of the sketches so you can look at them whenever you want!

Here is an example, with two examples of characterisation added:

Utterson in Jekyll and Hyde

→ Seems dreary but 'somehow lovable'.

→ Cold and embarrassed.

DOIT!

Make a table, like the one shown below, for the 19th-century novel you are studying.

In your chosen 19th-century novel, the writer will keep returning to central ideas (or themes), such as loneliness, becoming a gentleman, the danger of unrestrained science. It is helpful to connect these themes to specific and concrete events in the novel.

WORKIT!

Frankenstein			
Theme	Event	Quotation	How does this make the theme concrete?
Exploration	Walton's ship is freed from the ice and he returns home.	'It is past: I am returning to England. I have lost my hopes of utility and glory.'	Walton believes that his expedition has been a failure but he has not made the same mistakes as Frankenstein in pursuing his dream.
Creation			
Family			
The monstrous and the human			

Here is an example of an answer based on *A Christmas Carol*:

WORKIT!

> The language that Scrooge uses when he sees his younger
> self in the schoolroom juxtaposes with the language
> he uses when his nephew visits at the beginning of the
> novella.
> 'Why, it's Ali Baba!' Scrooge exclaimed in ecstasy. 'It's
> dear old honest Ali Baba! Yes, yes, I know.' Here he is
> enthusiastic and excited, as if he is a young boy again.
> This is significant because...

Context

Your understanding (and enjoyment) of the novel is greatly improved if you have some understanding of its context. It helps our understanding if we know something about the circumstances in which the novel was written and how this might have influenced the writer. Context can also refer to the location where the novel or scene takes place, the genre and the way different readers might understand the novel. For example, how does the context of the time in which you live influence your understanding of the novel?

Here is an example for Mary Shelley's *Frankenstein*:

WORKIT!

> In the early 19th century, people were fascinated by
> science and its possibilities. Mary Shelley explores this
> theme in her novel 'Frankenstein'. The novel becomes a
> warning about where uncontrolled science might lead.

Setting

The setting of the novel as a whole, or an individual scene, can help create tone and atmosphere. Setting tends to refer to the place, or places in which the novel takes place. The setting can influence the reader's response to the characters, their actions and the themes.

DOIT!

Look at the questions about language when you focused on the extract in the previous section (page 121). Connect this to the novel as a whole. Find two places in the novel where language is used in a similar way, and find two places in the novel where language is used in a very different way.

NAILIT!

Remember, context can refer to the location, the genre and the way different audiences might read and understand the text.

DOIT!

Use the internet or notes from your studies to research three things that were important at the time your chosen 19th-century novel was written. Write two or three sentences explaining how these ideas and attitudes might have influenced the writer.

WORKIT!

	Setting	Event	Chapter	Quotation	How is the setting used?
	A Christmas Carol				
1	Scrooge's counting house on Christmas Eve.	Scrooge's nephew visits to wish him 'Merry Christmas'.	(Stave) 1	'Scrooge had a very small fire, but the clerk's fire was so very much smaller that it looked like one coal.'	Scrooge is miserable and mean. Cold and unwelcoming. Opposite to the way Christmas should be.
2					
3					
4					

DOIT!

Create a table like the one shown above to identify four key settings in the 19th-century novel you have studied.

Mark scheme

The exam marker will be using the same mark scheme they used for the Shakespeare paper (see page 117).

Very good answers will explore the writer's craft. They will connect what the characters do and their relationships. They will explore how the writer communicates their ideas to the reader. They will give a personal response. They will use examples and quotations and explain them.

Good answers will show a clear understanding and use well-chosen examples.

Weaker answers will retell the story. They won't use examples to show knowledge of the novel and they won't say anything about the writer's craft.

DOIT!

Reduce your chosen novel to the six most important (key) quotations. You could use your ten key events to help you. Write them on separate cards and learn them.

CHECKIT! ✓

1 How many minutes should you leave to do the 19th-century novel question?

2 How long is the given extract likely to be?

3 What is meant by 'theme', and what are the central themes in the novel you have studied?

4 When you have revised these areas, it is a good idea to test your knowledge by doing some detailed essay plans and timed answers. There is nothing like putting yourself under this pressure to find out what you really know and can do.

Paper 2 Section A: Modern texts

Introduction and advice

Paper 2 is a large question paper. In Section A: Modern texts there are questions on 12 different novels and plays. Don't let this confuse you. You only have to answer **one** question on the play or novel you have studied.

You will have studied one modern novel from this list:

- *An Inspector Calls* by JB Priestley
- *Blood Brothers* by Willy Russell
- *The History Boys* by Alan Bennett
- *DNA* by Dennis Kelly
- *The Curious Incident of the Dog in the Night-Time* by Simon Stephens
- *A Taste of Honey* by Shelagh Delaney
- *Lord of the Flies* by William Golding
- *Telling Tales* by AQA Anthology
- *Animal Farm* by George Orwell
- *Never Let Me Go* by Kazuo Ishiguro
- *Anita and Me* by Meera Syal
- *Pigeon English* by Stephen Kelman

☞ Paper 2

☞ Section A: Modern texts

☞ Marks: 34

☞ Time: 45 minutes

NAILIT!

Remember to make notes while you're re-reading your chosen text – these can be in the form of tables, annotations, drawings and key quotes. This will help to keep your mind active.

When you have found the questions about your play/novel they will look like the ones below. Remember, you only have to choose one question to answer.

JB Priestley: *An Inspector Calls*

EITHER

How does Priestley use Eva Smith in *An Inspector Calls* to explore ideas about social responsibility?

Write about:

- how Priestley uses Eva Smith to present characters' actions and attitudes
- how Priestley uses Eva Smith to explore ideas about social responsibility.

[30 marks]

AO4 [4 marks]

OR

How does Priestley present the importance of respectability in *An Inspector Calls*?

Write about:

- how Priestley presents characters' efforts to achieve respectability
- how Priestley presents ideas about respectability by the way he writes.

[30 marks]

AO4 [4 marks]

Assessment objectives

The exam marker will use these assessment objectives to mark your work. Therefore, you need to cover these areas in your written answer.

AO1

Read, understand and respond to texts. Students should be able to:

- maintain a critical style and develop an informed personal response
- use textual references, including quotations, to support and illustrate interpretations.

AO2

Analyse the language, form and structure used by a writer to create meanings and effects, using relevant subject terminology where appropriate.

AO3

Show understanding of the relationships between texts and the contexts in which they were written.

AO4

Use a range of vocabulary and sentence structures for clarity, purpose and effect, with accurate spelling and punctuation.

Although you won't be asked a question directly about the plot, it is important to know what happens. You will need to be able to recall different events and sequences from the novel or play and to write about them in some detail.

DOIT!

1 Give yourself ten minutes to draw a storyboard of the main events in the novel. Stick people will do! A storyboard is a collection of drawings based on the main events of the novel.
2 When you have finished, reduce the play/novel to the ten most important quotations. Write them on sticky notes and stick them on the wall in the order they happen.
3 Look at the storyboard and quotes regularly, and familiarise yourself with them over a number of days.

Here is the start of a list of quotations for *Lord of the Flies*:

WORKIT!

- 'Within the diamond haze of the beach something dark was fumbling along.'
- 'Startled, Ralph realized that the boys were falling still and silent, feeling the beginnings of awe at the power set free below them. The knowledge and awe made him savage.'

SNAPIT!

Make profiles for **four of the main** characters in your play or novel. Start by making a quick sketch, paying attention to facial expressions and clothing. Then annotate the sketch with seven things you know about the character. Add at least one quotation to each character profile. You can then take a picture of these profiles so that you can revisit them easily, wherever you are!
Here is an unfinished example of a profile for Mr Birling from *An Inspector Calls*.

At start of play he is pompous and arrogant.

He thinks he will be given a knighthood.

He calls Eva Smith 'a wretched girl' and is not interested in her suicide.

He believes it would be impossible to be responsible for all our actions.

DOIT!

Choose one of the characters and write down four questions you would ask them to probe their attitudes. Find someone to work with and role play the character. Alternatively, write answers to the questions in the first person (as if you are the character).

DOIT!

Make a themes grid for the modern text you have studied, like the one below, and complete it.

Themes: using *An Inspector Calls* as an example

A theme is a set of ideas, which the writer examines in their work. They return to the theme at different moments. For example, in *The Curious Incident of the Dog in the Night-Time*, Simon Stephens explores themes of isolation, fear, love and identity amongst others. In *An Inspector Calls*, Priestley explores themes of social responsibility, hypocrisy and snobbery.

WORKIT!

An Inspector Calls			
Theme	**Event**	**Supporting quotation**	**How this refers to the theme**
Lies and secrecy	Gerald says he saved Eva at the palace bar from Alderman Joe Meggarty.	'The girl... gave me a glance that was nothing less than a cry for help.'	He hasn't told Sheila anything about his relationship with Eva until now.
Differences between generations			
Social class and snobbery			
Social responsibility			

The exam question below could easily be adapted to suit the modern text you have studied. Think about how you might plan an answer for your own text.

> Write about how [name of author/playwright] explores the theme of [name of theme] in [name of play/novel].

Language

The language the writer uses is vitally important in conveying the meaning in their text. The author's voice might be complex or straightforward. They may be honest with their reader or writing to confuse or trick them. They may be serious or comical.

A writer will often choose to tell a particular part of the story from the point of view of a particular character. Here is an extract from *Lord of the Flies*:

Although Golding is writing about Ralph in the third person, he is clearly looking at Ralph's feelings and exploring these ideas from Ralph's point of view.

> Ralph wept for the end of innocence, the darkness of man's heart, and the fall through the air of a true, wise friend called Piggy.

A writer will use language to create the mood and atmosphere. For example, one student wrote:

WORKIT!

In Chapter 12 of 'Lord of the Flies', when 'Ralph launched himself like a cat; stabbed, snarling, with the spear, and the savage doubled up', the quick, sharp language creates the sense of a chase. The alliteration of the 's' sounds and the frequent use of commas make the atmosphere fast, exciting and breathless.

> This student has focused on language and analyses the way the author creates the atmosphere by examining some of the methods Golding uses.

Of course, the dialogue the characters use and the way they say it reveals much about them.

When questioned by the Inspector in *An Inspector Calls*, Mrs Birling says:

" 'And if you'd take some steps to find this young man and then make sure that he's compelled to confess in public his responsibility – instead of staying here asking quite unnecessary questions – then you really would be doing your duty.' "

> She assumes the higher status and tells the inspector how to do his job. Her choice of language reveals her arrogant attitude and shows how out of touch she is with events.

The language of a play

If you are studying a play you will need to remember that the form means the writer has to use slightly different tools. They cannot use long passages of narration to get across their message. However, they can use stage directions. These are chosen precisely and often reveal important aspects of character.

Below is what one student wrote about the stage directions at the beginning of *An Inspector Calls*.

WORKIT!

The stage directions at the start of 'An Inspector Calls' tell us that Arthur Birling is in 'evening dress' and 'white tie'. This suggests to the audience that he is wealthy. Priestley says that he is 'provincial in his speech' suggesting that Birling has risen to wealth from a modest background.

> Here, the student identifies what the playwright says but goes on to explain the meaning behind it.

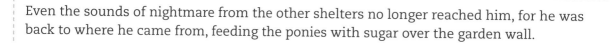

DOIT!

When analysing language you need to look at short quotations in detail. Choose three quotations from the beginning, the middle and end of the modern prose or drama you have studied. Write them down. Make notes on each under these headings:

- Author's voice
- Point of view
- Mood and atmosphere
- Attitude
- Stage directions (if you have studied a play)

Here is an example of a quote that a student picked from Chapter 6 of *Lord of the Flies* and their notes about it.

WORKIT!

> Even the sounds of nightmare from the other shelters no longer reached him, for he was back to where he came from, feeding the ponies with sugar over the garden wall.

- Author's voice – straightforward and authoritative, like the narrator of a boys' adventure story.
- Point of view – Ralph.
- Mood and atmosphere – words like nightmare at the start of the sentence tell us how horrible the situation is but this is juxtaposed with the sweetness of 'sugar' and the pleasant, safe and peaceful image of the garden.
- Attitude – Ralph seems to be showing a strong attitude where he can detach himself from the horrors of the island.

Remember to write about individual words or sentence structure and their effects (what they make the reader think of, and how they make them feel).

For example, look at this student's answer about *The Curious Incident of the Dog in the Night-Time*:

WORKIT!

> I do not like people shouting at me. It makes me scared that they are goin to hit me or touch me and I do not know what is going to happen.

Christopher uses simple sentences with no commas. He repeats 'do not' making it very clear what he thinks.

Setting

The setting of a play or novel refers to the time and place of the story. The writer uses setting to establish the background, mood and atmosphere of the action. Here is an example of a student writing about the setting at the beginning of *An Inspector Calls*:

WORKIT!

> It has good solid furniture of the period. The general effect is substantial and heavily comfortable, but not cosy and homelike.

At the opening of the play the audience sees the dining room of a large suburban house. Immediately, we know that this is a well-off family who seem apparently comfortable and content. Priestley presents carefully chosen details to suggest that the family is awkward and there will be difficulties ahead. For example:

DO IT!

Choose one setting from your modern play/prose and draw a map or plan of it. Use quotations and supporting evidence from your chosen text to annotate it. Then choose four details from your map or plan and write a paragraph about each explaining what this detail tells the audience/reader. Include a key quote for each one.

Context

A novel or play may have many contexts. Any line or sentence fits into the context of the whole work. The work is influenced by the context in which it was written. Understanding the context gives you greater understanding and insight. As an English Literature student, you will be expected to show some of these insights in the exam.

DO IT!

Answer these questions to help you think about the context of your modern text:

- When was it written?
- Who was the original audience?
- What ideas and issues do you think the writer was trying to explore in the play/novel?
- What would the reader/audience have thought about these ideas?
- What does the novel/play have to say to us today and why is this relevant?

Quotations

Quotations can be an important and useful form of evidence to back up your ideas. They show that you have a good in-depth knowledge of your modern text. It is worth choosing some key quotations and learning them.

Here are two useful quotations from *Lord of the Flies*:

- Jack and Ralph look at each other 'baffled, in love and hate'.
- Simon suddenly gets in his mind a 'picture of a human at once heroic and sick'.

Now look at how these quotations have been used in two different student answers:

WORKIT!

Student answer A

The tragedy of the boys' time on the island is that it could have turned out differently. Jack and Ralph are the key characters and they have mixed feeling about each other: early on they were 'baffled, in love and hate'. This shows that they could have worked very closely together under different circumstances. Simon too recognises the contradictions in people – how they can be very good or very bad. He suddenly gets a mental 'picture of a human at once heroic and sick'. In other words, we have the potential for evil or goodness.

Student answer B

'Baffled, in love and hate', Jack and Ralph nearly become close friends and collaborators for the good of all the boys, but, unfortunately, through a combination of circumstances, mutual misunderstanding leads to mutual hatred and then tragedy is inevitable. Simon recognises this tragic contradiction when he suddenly realises that humans are both 'heroic and sick' at the same time. The word 'sick' implies that humans aren't really to blame: they can't control themselves and stay good and rational.

Both of these answers are very good. However, the student in version B integrates quotations with their arguments, and integrating quotations gives their arguments fluency, and – more importantly – satisfies the mark scheme descriptors for the highest grades.

Preparing for the exam

Now that you have revised what you know about your novel/play, you need to practise applying these skills and knowledge under pressure. Detailed essay plans, timed essay plans and timed essays are the best way to do this.

You can make up your own exam-style questions by adapting the ones below.

Do you think [name of character] is an important character in [name of modern play/novel]? Write about:

- how [name of writer] presents the character
- how [name of writer] uses [name of character] to present ideas about people and society.

If you were studying *Lord of the Flies*, this question would become:

Do you think Piggy is an important character in *Lord of the Flies*? Write about:

- how Golding presents the character of Piggy
- how Golding uses Piggy to present ideas about people and society.

How and why does [name of character] change in [name of modern play/novel]?

Write about:

- how [name of character] responds to other characters
- how [name of writer] presents [name of character] by the way they write.

How does [name of writer] explore [theme] in [name of modern play/novel]?

Write about:

- the ideas about [name of theme] in [name of modern play/novel]
- how [name of writer] presents these ideas in the way they write.

Detailed essay plans can be notes, lists or spider diagrams. Detailed essay plans allow you to think around the subject without worrying too much about writing at this stage in your revision.

In the exam, you will only have about five minutes to make your essay plan. It is very important that you get quick and efficient at this. You'll find that the more you do, the better you get. You can often recycle ideas from one plan to another.

DO IT!

1 Decide on five or more key quotations in your play/novel. Try to limit your choice to quotations of no more than seven words. Think about the different ways that you can use the quotations. It may be possible to use the same quotation to make a point about character, setting or language.
2 Write the quotations on separate cards. Carry them around with you and learn them over a period of time.
3 Test yourself on whether you can remember the quotations without looking at them.
4 Try writing about your modern text, using the quotations.

 STRETCH IT!

Try to integrate quotations into your points sometimes if you are going for the highest grades.

Mark scheme

The exam marker will be using a mark scheme like this to help grade your work:

 SNAPIT!

Descriptors	Band 2	Band 3	Band 4	Band 5	Band 6
	The student's answer...	The student's answer...	The student's answer...	The student's answer...	The student's answer...
AO1 Read, understand and respond	• is relevant and backs up ideas with references to the text	• often explains the text in relation to the task	• clearly explains the text in relation to the task	• thoughtfully explains the text in relation to the task	• critically explains the text in relation to the task
Use evidence	• makes some comments about these references	• uses references to support a range of relevant comments	• uses references effectively to support explanations	• uses references which are integrated into the answer	• uses references which are judiciously integrated into the answer
AO2 Language, form and structure	• identifies the writer's methods	• comments on the writer's methods, and the effects these have on the reader	• clearly explains the writer's methods, and the effects these have on the reader	• effectively explains the writer's methods, and the effects these have on the reader	• judiciously explains the writer's methods, and the effects these have on the reader
Subject terminology	• makes some reference to subject terminology	• uses some relevant terminology	• makes apt use of relevant terminology	• makes effective use of relevant terminology	• makes judicious use of relevant terminology
AO3 Contexts	• has some awareness of ideas and contexts.	• shows some understanding of the significance of contexts.	• shows a clear understanding of the significance of specific contexts.	• shows a thoughtful consideration of the significance of specific contexts.	• shows a critical consideration of the significance of specific contexts.

The best answers will explore and evaluate what happens in the play/novel and the writer's purpose. They will use relevant quotations to analyse language, structure and the writer's meaning, using subject specific terminology. They will show a detailed understanding of the context of the play and they will use a range of vocabulary with good spelling and punctuation.

Weaker answers will tend to retell what happens and use no evidence to back up their ideas. They will have little understanding of the context of the play/novel and will show little understanding that this is a story made up and crafted by a writer.

CHECKIT!

1 Choose one of the questions you have adapted and spend 15 to 20 minutes writing a detailed essay plan. Remember, this is for revision only. In the exam you should spend only five minutes on your plan.

2 When you have finished the essay plan, write answers to these questions about your novel or play:

  • What do you know about the characters, events, ideas, themes and structure? (AO1)

  • What can you say about how the writer uses language and structure to get across their meaning? (AO2)

  • What do you understand about the context of the play/novel and how this is relevant? (AO3)

  • Which examples and quotations can you use as evidence?

3 Choose another one of your adapted questions and give yourself five minutes to do an exam-style essay plan.

Paper 2 Section B: Poetry

- Paper 2
- Section B: Poetry
- Marks: 30
- Time: 40 minutes

Introduction and advice

This is how the question on the poetry anthology fits into Paper 2 of the English Literature exam.

You will have studied one of the clusters of poems in the anthology, either 'Love and relationships' or 'Power and conflict'. Each of the clusters has 15 poems. They are from different times in history.

The question will ask you to compare two poems, only one of which will be printed on the paper. You will have to choose the other poem from your memory of a relevant poem in the cluster.

Love and relationships	
Lord Byron	When We Two Parted
Percy Bysshe Shelley	Love's Philosophy
Robert Browning	Porphyria's Lover
Elizabeth Barrett Browning	Sonnet 29 – 'I think of thee!'
Thomas Hardy	Neutral Tones
Charlotte Mew	The Farmer's Bride
C Day Lewis	Walking Away
Maura Dooley	Letters From Yorkshire
Charles Causley	Eden Rock
Seamus Heaney	Follower
Simon Armitage	Mother, any distance
Carol Ann Duffy	Before You Were Mine
Owen Sheers	Winter Swans
Daljit Nagra	Singh Song!
Andrew Waterhouse	Climbing My Grandfather

Power and conflict	
Percy Bysshe Shelley	Ozymandias
William Blake	London
William Wordsworth	The Prelude: stealing the boat
Robert Browning	My Last Duchess
Alfred Lord Tennyson	The Charge of the Light Brigade
Wilfred Owen	Exposure
Seamus Heaney	Storm on the Island
Ted Hughes	Bayonet Charge
Simon Armitage	Remains
Jane Weir	Poppies
Carol Ann Duffy	War Photographer
Imtiaz Dharker	Tissue
Carol Rumens	The Émigree
Beatrice Garland	Kamikaze
John Agard	Checking Out Me History

DO IT!

Make a list of all the poems in the cluster you have studied. Give each poem a star rating where:

*** means you feel very confident about the poem

** means you feel reasonably clear about the poem

* means you feel very unsure about the poem.

You need to know all the poems in your cluster very well, so start by revising the poems you have marked as one star. It is helpful to remind yourself of the following categories.

Meaning: making sense of the poems

As you re-read each poem, underline any words or phrases that you don't understand. If you are able, discuss them with someone else; otherwise look them up. Write two sentences to summarise your understanding of the poem.

For example, one student wrote:

WORKIT!

'Ozymandias'

Shelley retells the story of a traveller who saw a fallen statue, lying broken in the sand. It leads him to think about how all our great ideas and endeavours come to ruin.

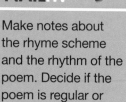

NAILIT!

Make notes about the rhyme scheme and the rhythm of the poem. Decide if the poem is regular or irregular or perhaps a mixture of both.

DOIT!

1 Write down the number of stanzas (verses). Count the number of lines in each stanza and work out the line lengths by quickly counting syllables. Make a note of your results.
2 Write a paragraph interpreting the structure in one of the poems you have worked on.

DOIT!

Write a paragraph explaining the imagery used in one of the poems you are revising.

Structure

Look at the way the poem is built and gather some information about structure.

All these things are helpful to know, but on their own they won't get you any credit. You need to interpret these structural devices and explain **why** the poet might have chosen to use them in this way. For example:

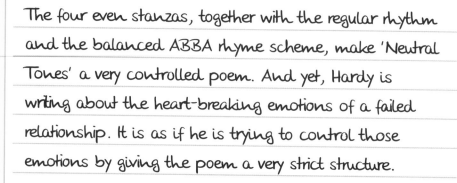

WORKIT!

'Neutral Tones'

The four even stanzas, together with the regular rhythm and the balanced ABBA rhyme scheme, make 'Neutral Tones' a very controlled poem. And yet, Hardy is writing about the heart-breaking emotions of a failed relationship. It is as if he is trying to control those emotions by giving the poem a very strict structure.

Imagery

Poetry is about engaging the reader's senses and emotions. Poets often use imagery to do this. Imagery in a poem refers to the techniques the poet uses to spark the senses. The most obvious of these is visual. However, a poem will often also engage the senses of hearing, touch, taste and smell.

When working on your poems, write down or highlight where the poet engages the senses. You could use a different colour to highlight each sense. Add some annotations to explain **why** you think the poet has done this.

Below is an example of a student's paragraph explaining imagery:

WORKIT!

'Storm on the Island'

In 'Storm on the Island', Heaney uses storm imagery to call upon our senses of hearing and touch. 'So that you can listen to the thing you fear/ Forgetting that it pummels your house too.' All of our senses are immersed in the storm, so we are not just readers or observers but experiencing it through the senses of sound and touch.

Language

Writing successfully about language is often about looking at individual words.

WORKIT!

'Exposure'

Owen describes the, 'agonies of men among its brambles'.
The word bramble is harsh and awkward to say, it seems to
echo the pain and torment the men are suffering.

DOIT!

Choose a poem and highlight any interesting or notable words or groups of words. Of course, once you have done this you will need to explain **why** you think the poet chooses to use these particular words.

A poet may use language in specific ways through, for example, simile, metaphor, personification, onomatopoeia and alliteration. As a literature student, it is important to understand how to use this terminology. These techniques are tools that the poet uses in their work (that's a metaphor). By using this terminology, you will show that you know the tricks of the trade (and that's alliteration).

DOIT!

Make a list of the poetic terms you are familiar with and write down what they mean.

WORKIT!

Simile: a comparison that uses 'as' or 'like'.

DOIT!

For three of the terms in your list, write a short paragraph explaining why the poet has used each.

WORKIT!

'Exposure'

Owen uses the metaphor of the 'iced east winds that
knive us'. The verb 'knive' makes the winds hostile,
vicious and violent. Owen makes us experience the war,
danger and death all around the men.

NAILIT!

Take care when using terminology. Many students think it is enough to simply identify the technique but 'Hardy uses a metaphor' will get no credit. You must explain **why** Hardy uses that metaphor – what effect does it have on the reader, and what point about love and relationships was Hardy trying to make?

Themes

A poet will want to explore themes and ideas in the poem: a set of ideas, which they keep returning to. The poems in your cluster will have themes common to many of the poems. You may have grouped them according to theme when you first looked at them in your study.

<table>
<tr><th colspan="3">'Follower' by Seamus Heaney</th></tr>
<tr><th>Theme</th><th>Quotation</th><th>Analysis</th></tr>
<tr><td>Growing up</td><td>'I stumbled in his hob-nailed wake.'</td><td>The child is trying to catch up. The boots seem big and almost threatening because the boy is so small.</td></tr>
<tr><td>Admiration</td><td>'An expert.'</td><td>As a boy, Heaney sees his father as perfect. There is no need for adjectives to describe him. The full stop is enough.</td></tr>
<tr><td>Identity</td><td>'I wanted to grow up and plough.'</td><td>There is a sense of longing and loss. The poet was unable to come up to his father's standards.</td></tr>
</table>

The viewpoint and attitude of the poet

Think about the persona (the character) who is speaking the poem. In 'Exposure', Owen writes as if he is actually at the battlefront. In 'Follower', Heaney is remembering back to his childhood.

DO IT!

Make a themes grid like the one here for four of your three-star poems.

DO IT!

Write down the viewpoint of each of your chosen poems. Write a sentence to explain the attitude in each.

WORKIT!

'War Photographer'

> The reader's eyeballs prick
>
> with tears between the bath and pre-lunch beers.

Carol Anne Duffy writes from the point of view of the war photographer, however, by mentioning the 'pre-lunch beer' she makes the reader aware that she questions the attitudes of the people who will look at his photos in the Sunday newspapers.

Context

Your understanding (and enjoyment) of the poem is greatly improved if you have some understanding of its context. Use these questions to help you think about the context of the poem you are studying.

a What do you know about the poet and their background?

b When was the poem written and how might the social and historical events of the day have influenced the poet?

Don't just mention a text's context. Only mention an aspect of context if it will deepen our understanding of the text. For example, one student wrote:

DOIT!

Write two or three sentences explaining how the context of a poem of your choice might have influenced the poet.

WORKIT!

In 'The Charge of the Light Brigade', Tennyson seems to celebrate the cavalry charge 'into the valley of Death'. However, he makes it clear that they ARE riding to their deaths, and this fact would have been emphasised for Victorian readers because they would have been very familiar with psalm 23 which features 'the valley of the shadow of Death'. This psalm was often read out or sung at church services, but was especially popular in funerals.

NAILIT!

Remember, when you write about the context of your poem you are not giving us a history lesson but helping your reader to understand the poem and what influenced the poet, as well as explaining the point about love and relationships or power and conflict that the poet was trying to make.

Getting to know the poems

Once you feel comfortable that you understand the poems, use these ideas to get to know them. Remember, you will need to be able to write about them from memory.

- Test yourself by making a spider diagram of all you know about a poem. Time yourself for four minutes.

- Draw the poem as a picture or a diagram.

- Record a reading of the poem and listen to it.

- Annotate copies of the poems and display them where you can see them regularly.

- Consider how the poems in your cluster are similar/different. Draw a table or a Venn diagram to show these.

- Make a grid like the one below, putting all your thoughts about the poems in one place.

Poem	Making sense	Structure	Imagery	Language	Themes	Viewpoint and attitude
'When We Two Parted'						

Mark scheme

The exam marker will be using a mark scheme like this to help grade your work:

 SNAP IT!

Descriptors	Band 2	Band 3	Band 4	Band 5	Band 6
AO1 **Read, understand and compare**	The student's answer… • compares texts	The student's answer… • sometimes explains valid comparisons	The student's answer… • makes clear comparisons between texts	The student's answer… • makes thoughtful, detailed comparisons between texts	The student's answer… • critically explores comparisons between texts
Use evidence	• refers to evidence and comments on it	• refers to details in the text to back up points	• uses textual references effectively to back up points	• thoughtfully builds appropriate references into points	• chooses precise textual details to clinch points
AO2 **Language, form and structure**	• mentions some of the writer's methods	• comments on some of the writer's methods and their effects	• clearly explains the writer's key methods, and their effects	• thoughtfully explains the writer's key methods, and their effects	• analyses the writer's key methods, and how these influence the reader
Subject terminology	• uses some subject terminology	• uses some relevant terminology	• helpfully uses varied, relevant terminology	• makes thoughtful use of relevant terminology	• chooses subject terminology to make points precise and convincing
AO3 **Contexts**	• makes some simple inferences and shows some awareness of contexts.	• infers the writer's point of view and the significance of contexts.	• shows a clear appreciation of the writer's point of view and the significance of contexts.	• explores the writer's point of view and the influence of particular contexts.	• makes perceptive and revealing links between the text and relevant contexts.

 DO IT!

Look back over essays you have written about poems during your GCSE course. See if you can find examples of descriptors from the mark scheme in your answers. Set yourself some targets for improvement in your weaker areas. Make sure those targets are led by relevant descriptors in the mark scheme.

Writing about the poems in the exam

The question about the anthology in Section B of Paper 2 will be like this:

> Compare how poets present attitudes towards love in 'Neutral Tones'
> and in **one** other poem from 'Love and relationships'.
>
> ## Neutral Tones
>
> We stood by a pond that winter day,
>
> And the sun was white, as though chidden of God,
>
> And a few leaves lay on the starving sod;
>
> – They had fallen from an ash, and were gray.
>
> 5   Your eyes on me were as eyes that rove
>
> Over tedious riddles of years ago;
>
> And some words played between us to and fro
>
> On which lost the more by our love.
>
> The smile on your mouth was the deadest thing
>
> 10   Alive enough to have strength to die;
>
> And a grin of bitterness swept thereby
>
> Like an ominous bird a-wing...
>
> Since then, keen lessons that love deceives,
>
> And wrings with wrong, have shaped to me
>
> 15   Your face, and the God curst sun, and a tree,
>
> And a pond edged with grayish leaves.
>
> *Thomas Hardy*

NAILIT!

Remember, you are only allowed a copy of the first poem to look at. You must write about your chosen poem from memory.

Approach the poetry anthology question using the following steps:

1. Read through the poem on the question paper. It will be one from the cluster you have studied.

2. Decide on the poem that you will compare it with.

3. Take five minutes to annotate the 'given poem'. You are allowed to write on the question paper. Highlight words and phrases that are relevant to the question.

4. Use the 'Making sense of the poem – structure – imagery – language – themes – viewpoint and attitude' method from your revision to help you.

5. As you annotate, think about the differences and the similarities between the 'given poem' and your 'chosen poem'. Make some quick notes as annotations around the poem.

(6) Spend a minute or so making a very quick and simple plan. This could be a spider diagram, a list or a two-column table.

(7) Use your annotations and plan to answer the question.

(8) Allow yourself some time to check through your answer.

It is generally more straightforward to compare the poems as you go. Don't write everything about the 'given poem' first and then start writing about your 'chosen poem'. Constantly compare the two poems through your essay to examine their similarities and differences.

Show that you can refer to details in the text by quoting from the poem printed on the exam paper. Make sure your quotations are relevant and useful.

DO IT!

1 Use your themes chart (from Do it! on page 140) to help you adapt this question to suit two poems in your chosen cluster.

> Compare how poets present attitudes towards [name of theme] in [name of poem 1] and in one other poem from 'Love and relationships/Power and conflict'.

2 Make a detailed essay plan in answer to your question. Use your revision notes to help you think about:

- making sense of the poem
- its structure
- its imagery
- its language
- its themes
- the poet's viewpoint and attitude.

CHECK IT!

1 How many minutes should you spend on the poetry anthology question?

2 Name one particularly successful focus when writing about language.

3 Name the only good reason for writing about context.

4 How many poems will the question ask you to compare?

Paper 2 Section C: Unseen poetry

Introduction and advice

Use the skills you have developed when studying the anthology (see pages 136–44) to analyse the unseen poems. Much of the revision in the previous section of this guide, Poetry anthology, will help you prepare for writing about the unseen poems.

Section C will ask you two questions. You should spend 35 minutes on the first question and only 15 minutes on the second question. You should answer both questions.

The first question will be on a poem printed on the exam paper. The second question will ask you to write about another poem printed on the paper, and to compare it briefly with the first poem.

It is not possible to predict which poems the exam board will choose.

- ☞ Paper 2
- ☞ Section C: Unseen poetry
- ☞ Marks: 32
- ☞ Time: 50 minutes

DOIT!

Make a list of all the skills you have learned to help you analyse a poem.

Revising for the first unseen poem

It is unlikely that you will have seen the poem on the exam paper before. Revision for this section is about practising the skills you have learned and using them quickly and accurately. In this section of your revision you will look at the first poem only. It is worth 24 marks and you should spend about 35 minutes on this.

Catrin

I can remember you, child,
As I stood in a hot, white
Room at the window watching
The people and cars taking
5 Turn at the traffic lights.
I can remember you, our first
Fierce confrontation, the tight
Red rope of love which we both
Fought over. It was a square
10 Environmental blank, disinfected
Of paintings or toys. I wrote
All over the walls with my
Words, coloured the clean squares
With the wild, tender circles
15 Of our struggle to become
Separate. We want, we shouted,
To be two, to be ourselves.

Neither won nor lost the struggle
In the glass tank clouded with feelings
20 Which changed us both. Still I am fighting
You off, as you stand there
With your straight, strong, long
Brown hair and your rosy,
Defiant glare, bringing up
25 From the heart's pool that old rope,
Tightening about my life,
Trailing love and conflict,
As you ask may you skate
In the dark, for one more hour.

Gillian Clarke

In 'Catrin', how does the poet present the speaker's relationship with her daughter?

[24 marks]

Making sense of the poem

DO IT!

1 Read Gillian Clarke's poem 'Catrin' and get a general understanding of the poem.
2 Once you have a general understanding of the poem, re-read it. This time make notes and annotations according to the question.
3 Underline any words or phrases that you don't understand.

WORKIT!

'Environmental blank' – at first glance, this might be an unusual phrase. However, when we look at the words in context, we can see they describe the hospital room in which Catrin was born. We can guess that the room was bare and clean. Surprisingly, there is little emotion involved.

Structure

Look at the way the poem is built and gather some information about structure.

- Write down the number of stanzas.

- Count the number of lines in each stanza and work out one or two line lengths by counting syllables. This will help you to think about rhythm.

- Does the poem rhyme?

- Remember, you need to explain **why** the poet has chosen to use this structural device. For example:

WORKIT!

'Catrin' is made up of a series of short lines. The poem seems to have a stuttering rhythm. The broken rhythm seems to echo the conflict in the relationship. However, each short line leads into the next, suggesting the bond between mother and child.

Imagery

You should think about how the poet uses:

- sight
- sound
- smell
- touch.

Are these images grouped around a particular idea or theme?

For example:

> Red rope of love which we both
> Fought over

Here, the poet is asking us to feel the rope which both are fighting over. It is a sensory detail which makes the relationship vivid.

Language

Highlight any interesting words or groups of words. Think about **why** the poet has decided to use the words you have highlighted. For example:

WORKIT!

> In the glass tank clouded by feelings

...makes it seem as if the mother and the child are surrounded and maybe trapped by their relationship.

Terminology

Look for any poetic techniques that the poet might use, such as:

- Simile: this is a comparison where the poet uses 'as' or 'like'. For example, 'The man was as old as the hills'.

- Metaphor: this makes a strong image in the reader's head. When a poet uses a metaphor, they are saying that a person, place, animal or thing *is* something else. For example, 'The man was a mountain'.

- Personification: a poet might give human attributes to inanimate objects. Objects are given feelings and thoughts. For example, 'The mountain looked out across the country with the wisdom of an old man'.

- Alliteration: when a poet repeats the same sounds they are using alliteration. 'Miraculously the mountain managed to mangle its face into that of a moody man.'

- Onomatopoeia: words which sound like the thing they describe can be very effective in poetry. There are obvious examples like 'bang' and 'crash', but also a word like 'rock' could be said to have a hard and brittle sound like the qualities of the object it describes.

- Repetition: poets sometimes use repetition for emphasis. For example, 'His lonely words echo around the hard and tough, the hard and rough mountain'.

It's not enough to spot techniques: you need to explain why the poet has used these techniques. For example:

WORKIT!

'Catrin' uses one powerful extended metaphor. The rope is an image of the bond that ties mother and daughter. It is powerful because it can represent both safety and restraint.

Themes

Make a list of two or three themes in the poem. For example:

WORKIT!

> A central theme in 'Catrin' is the relationship between mother and daughter.

The viewpoint and attitude of the poet

You should think about the persona (the character) of the mother.

- What is her attitude towards her daughter?
- Does she consider the attitude of her daughter in return?
- Do you think the poet and the mother are the same person?
- What does the poet have to say about the relationship between mother and daughter?
- Does the viewpoint of the poet change through the poem?

DOIT!

Choose three of your annotations and develop them into fully written paragraphs. Make sure you give evidence for your ideas by using a short quotation in each paragraph.

DOIT!

Read the four paragraphs below written by students. Put them into a rank order. Which do you think is the best and why? Imagine you are the teacher; give each student some feedback.

WORKIT!

Student answer A	The poem uses little assonance, even though this is a fascinating and eloquent poetic device. Therefore, structurally, the poem could be said to be irregular. It has the tone perhaps of a ballad but is devoid of simile, onomatopoeia or other poetic artifice. A fascinating and charming evocation of the relationship between a mother and daughter.
Student answer B	It's like the relationship between the mother and the daughter changes during the poem. At the start the language is quite hard, 'Fierce confrontation' is not the way a mother usually talks about the birth of her daughter. By the end of the poem, it seems like the mother has come to accept that the daughter must have her independence. I think this is good parenting.
Student answer C	The mother seems to be very honest about her relationship with the daughter. The rope is a metaphor for the way that their love for each other holds them together. This is a struggle; it stops both of them being independent. The final image, 'As you ask may you skate in the dark, for one more hour' is very powerful. A mother needs to allow her daughter to be separate but she is frightened of what might happen if she lets go.
Student answer D	I can't remember being born, but my dad showed me a photo once of me just after I was born. He let me have it and said he didn't need it. It got smudged with chocolate by my brother.

Mark scheme

The best answers will explore the poem with a critical and well-structured argument. They will use relevant quotations to show insight and develop their own ideas about the poem. They will write in detail about language and structure using the correct terminology.

Weaker answers will tend to retell what happens in the poem. They may provide some reference to the poem and use some examples and quotations. They may use some terminology, but they will tend to identify this and not explain it in any detail.

The exam marker will be using mark schemes to help grade your work. Here is a mark scheme for the first question:

SNAPIT!

Descriptors	Band 2	Band 3	Band 4	Band 5	Band 6
	The student's answer...	The student's answer...	The student's answer...	The student's answer...	The student's answer...
AO1 **Read, understand and respond**	• is relevant and backs up ideas with references to the text	• sometimes explains the text in relation to the task	• clearly explains the text in relation to the task	• thoughtfully explains the text in relation to the task	• critically explores the text in relation to the task
Use evidence	• makes some comments about these references	• refers to details in the text to back up points	• uses textual references effectively to back up points	• thoughtfully builds appropriate references into points	• chooses precise textual details to clinch points
AO2 **Language, form and structure**	• mentions some of the writer's methods	• comments on some of the writer's methods and their effects	• clearly explains the writer's key method, and their effects	• thoughtfully explains the writer's key methods and their effects	• analyses the writer's key methods, and *how* these influence the reader
Subject terminology	• uses some subject terminology.	• uses some relevant terminology.	• helpfully uses varied, relevant terminology.	• makes thoughtful use of relevant terminology.	• chooses subject terminology to make points precise and convincing.

The second question – comparing the unseen poems

In Section C you will be given another unseen poem. You will be asked to compare this with the first poem you have looked at in Section C. This is the second and final question you will be asked. The question is worth eight marks, which means you should spend no more than 15 minutes on it.

DO IT!

Use the same method to look at the second unseen poem. Read, re-read and annotate it thinking about:

- making sense of the poem
- its structure
- its imagery
- its language
- its themes
- the poet's viewpoint and attitude.

A Memory

I remember
The crackle of the palm trees
Over the mooned white roofs of the town...
The shining town...
5   And the tender fumbling of the surf
On the sulphur-yellow beaches
As we sat... a little apart... in the close-pressing night.

The moon hung above us like a golden mango,
And the moist air clung to our faces,
10   Warm and fragrant as the open mouth of a child
And we watched the out-flung sea
Rolling to the purple edge
of the world,
Yet ever back upon itself...
15   As we...

Inadequate night...
And mooned white memory
Of a tropic sea... How softly it comes up
Like an ungathered lily.

Lola Ridge

In both 'Catrin' and 'A Memory' the poets write about relationships. What are the similarities and/or differences between the ways the poets present those relationships?

[8 marks]

In Question 2, you need to **compare** the poem with the first unseen poem you have been given. In this example, you will be thinking about how to compare 'A Memory' with 'Catrin'. As you read the poems, think about their **differences** and the **similarities**. The poems will be chosen so that there is plenty to compare. Time is limited, so you only have three or four minutes to make your annotations before writing.

DO IT!

Give yourself three minutes to make your annotations. The copy of the poem below has some annotations to help you.

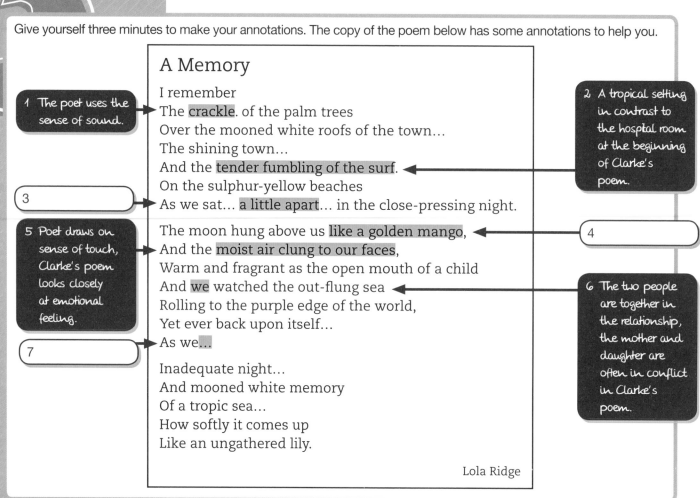

A Memory

I remember
The crackle. of the palm trees
Over the mooned white roofs of the town...
The shining town...
And the tender fumbling of the surf.
On the sulphur-yellow beaches
As we sat... a little apart... in the close-pressing night.

The moon hung above us like a golden mango,
And the moist air clung to our faces,
Warm and fragrant as the open mouth of a child
And we watched the out-flung sea
Rolling to the purple edge of the world,
Yet ever back upon itself...
As we...

Inadequate night...
And mooned white memory
Of a tropic sea...
How softly it comes up
Like an ungathered lily.

Lola Ridge

1 The poet uses the sense of sound.

2 A tropical setting in contrast to the hospital room at the beginning of Clarke's poem.

3

4

5 Poet draws on sense of touch, Clarke's poem looks closely at emotional feeling.

6 The two people are together in the relationship, the mother and daughter are often in conflict in Clarke's poem.

7

Now you need to make comparisons between the two poems. Here is the question again:

> In both 'Catrin' and 'A Memory' the poets write about relationships.
> What are the similarities and/or differences between the ways the poets present those relationships?
>
> **[8 marks]**

Copy and complete the table below, filling it with your ideas about 'Catrin' and 'A Memory'.

When you have completed your table, leave it for a day or two and then re-read it. Add a few more notes.

Poem	Making sense	Structure	Imagery	Language	Themes	Viewpoint and attitude
'Catrin'	Looks at the bond between a mother and daughter		Use of varied and vibrant colours		A mother's need to care for her daughter	At first distant – like viewing an old photo but by the end the mother is concerned with the present
'A Memory'				Lots of physical words: out-flung, clung, crackle		Nostalgia for a perfect past moment

Mark scheme

Here is a mark scheme for the second question:

SNAP IT!

Descriptors	Band 2	Band 3	Band 4	Band 5	Band 6
	The student's answer…	The student's answer…	The student's answer…	The student's answer…	The student's answer…
Comparing	• makes a comparison between poems	• makes a couple of comparisons between the poems' methods and their effects	• makes clear comparisons between the poems in terms of their methods and effects	• makes thoughtful comparisons between the poems in terms of their methods and effects	• explores convincing comparisons between the poems in terms of their methods and effects
Subject terminology	• uses some subject terminology	• uses some relevant terminology.	• uses some relevant subject terminology.	• uses relevant subject terminology effectively to support points.	• uses relevant subject terminology very precisely to support points.

To develop your skills, get used to reading and thinking about poems regularly:

- Read a poem a day.
- Look for poems on the internet.
- Find poems in poetry anthologies in the library.
- Start by searching for poems by a poet you have enjoyed studying.
- Study and analyse song lyrics or rapping – they use similar techniques.
- Read and study poems from the other cluster in the anthology (the one you haven't studied) and treat them as unseen poems. There will be plenty to say about these poems – they have been chosen because they are thematically linked.

Once you have selected some unseen poems, make up your own questions by adapting the ones below:

In [name of poem], how does the poet present the speaker's feelings about [a theme/idea/attitude] in the poem?

[24 marks]

In both [name of poem 1] and [name of poem 2] the speakers describe their [feelings/attitudes/ideas]. What are the similarities and/or differences between the ways the poets present those [feelings/attitudes/ideas]?

[8 marks]

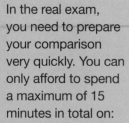

NAILIT!

In the real exam, you need to prepare your comparison very quickly. You can only afford to spend a maximum of 15 minutes in total on:

- reading the poem and annotating it
- preparing your comparison
- writing your answer.

CHECK IT!

1 How many poems must you write about in Section C (unseen poetry)?

2 How many questions will there be in Section C?

3 How long should you allow to do Section C?

4 How many minutes should you spend on the second question?

5 What language technique(s) is used in this line from the poem 'A Memory'?

> " The moon hung above us like a golden mango. "

1 How long is the Shakespeare and 19th-century novel exam paper?

2 How long should you spend on Section A, the Shakespeare question?

3 About how many words will be in the 19th-century novel extract printed on the exam paper?

4 How many bullet points are likely to be below the question on the 19th-century novel?

5 How long is the Modern texts and poetry paper (Paper 2)?

6 What are the three sections of this paper?

7 How many extracts from your modern novel or play will be printed on the exam paper?

8 What is meant by 'an integrated quotation'?

9 How long should you spend writing about your modern novel or play?

10 How long should you spend on Section B, the poetry anthology question?

11 What is a metaphor?

12 What is alliteration?

13 What is meant by 'a theme'?

14 In Section B (the anthology question), how many poems will you be asked to write about?

15 How many of these poems will you be allowed to choose for yourself?

16 In Section C (unseen poetry), what does 'unseen' mean?

17 How many unseen poems will you have to write about?

18 How much time should you spend on the first poem?

19 How many questions will you have to answer in Section C?

20 Which section of Paper 2 – A, B or C – is worth the most marks?

Glossary

adjective A word that describes a noun (for example: a *big* dog; a *good* idea).

adverb A word that modifies the meaning of a verb, an adjective or an other adverb (for example: I run *quickly*; the garden is *quite* pretty; I run *very* quickly).

adverbial A word or phrase that gives more information about a verb. Usually the information is about where, when or how something happened (for example: He looked *under* the bed. She arrived *last week*. They did it *without any fuss*).

alliteration Words starting with the same *sound* that the writer has placed near each other for effect (for example: the **b**ig, **b**lue **b**us; one **k**ick **c**aused **ch**aos).

apostrophe It can be used for two purposes: to show that one or more letters have been missed out (for example: can't, they're, he's); to show possession (for example: Sarah's pen).

argument A point of view that is explained and defended. An argument in an essay can be an exploration of both sides of a point of view.

autobiography Writing about a person's life written by that person. 'Autobiography' is an old Greek word that in direct translation means 'self-life writing'.

biography Writing about someone else's life.

character A person in a play or story: a person created by the writer.

characterisation This is about how a character has been written by the author; how the author presents the character so that we see them in a particular way.

clause See main clause and subordinate clause.

coherence How a whole text is structured and brought together.

cohesion How details in a text join together. For example, through the use of connectives and other cohesive ties.

cohesive tie Another term for a discourse marker.

colloquial language Informal language that is normally used in speech rather than writing (for example: 'They're out' rather than 'They are not at home'; 'yeah' rather than 'yes').

colon (:) A punctuation mark used to introduce a list, a quotation or an explanation of something. Also used in place of the phrase 'that is to say' or 'in other words'.

comma (,) A punctuation mark used as a pause in a sentence to make meaning clear. It is also used to separate words in a list.

complement The complement of a sentence is its *completion*. The complement completes the sense of the sentence or part of it. The complements in these two sentences are in italics: He was *unhappy*. She made *me worried*.

complex sentence A sentence with at least one subordinate clause.

conjunction A word that joins main clauses into one sentence, or joins subordinate clauses to main clauses. Conjunctions include: *when, because, and, but, or, while, although, if, unless*.

connective This word is sometimes used to refer to a conjunction or other discourse marker.

connotation The implied meaning of a word of phrase. For example, the word *mob* means a large group of people, but it *connotes* violence. If someone *dashes* down the road, we know that they are moving quickly, but that choice of word also connotes urgency. A connotation is sometimes called a nuance.

context The context of a poem, play, novel or story is the set of conditions in which it was written. These might include: the writer's life; society, habits and beliefs at the time they wrote; an event that influenced the writing; and the genre of the writing. The context is also seen in terms of influences on the reader, so for example, a modern audience would see a Shakespeare play differently from audiences in his own time, as their life experiences would be different.

deduce To work something out for yourself, using clues.

Glossary

dialogue The words that characters say in plays or in fiction. In fiction, these words are usually shown within inverted commas ('…').

discourse marker Words and phrases used to join ideas or to change topics and move an argument on: 'Despite this…'; 'Finally…'; 'On the other hand…'; 'This belief is also…'.

effect The impact that a writer's words have on a reader: how the words create a mood, feeling or reaction.

emotive language Words chosen to make a reader feel a particular way about something (for example: 'Poor, hungry, little mites' or 'Great, hulking bullies').

enjambement When a line of poetry does not end with punctuation, but instead its sense runs straight into the next line.

evaluate To explain how good (or bad) something is: how well it does something. When we evaluate a text we consider ways in which it is successful (or unsuccessful), and the impact it has on us.

evidence Details or clues that support a point of view. A quotation can be a form of evidence in which a few words are copied from a text to support a point of view.

explicit Explicit information is clearly stated; it's on the surface of a text and should be obvious.

fiction Novels or stories made up by an author.

grammar Grammar is the system and structure of language: how words are put together to make sense and be effective. The 'rules' of grammar can change over time, and so 'conventions' would be a better term than 'rules'. Grammar covers word classes (including verbs, nouns, adjectives) and sentence elements (for example: subject, object, complement, clause, phrase, and so on).

iambic (pentameter) A 'beat' in poetry, when syllables alternate between unstressed and stressed (for example: I **walked** along the **stor**my **shore** with **Jane**). An iambic pentameter is a line with five of these unstressed/stressed patterns in a row (as in the example).

imagery The 'pictures' a writer puts into the reader's mind. Similes and metaphors are particular forms of imagery. We also talk about violent, graphic, religious imagery, and so on.

implicit (imply) Implicit information is only suggested (or implied), it is not stated directly; we have to infer to understand it. The opposite of explicit.

infer (inference) To 'read between the lines'; to work out meaning from clues in the text. See implicit. When we infer, we are making an inference.

interpret To work out meaning, using clues and evidence. The same piece of writing can be interpreted in different ways, but evidence has to support interpretations.

language (choices) The words and the style that a writer chooses in order to have an effect on a reader.

main clause The main part of a sentence, including a verb and often an object (for example: *The cat caught a mouse*). The main clause often makes sense on its own.

metaphor Comparing two things by referring to them as though they are the same thing (for example: His face *was a thunder cloud*. The boy *was an angry bear*).

narrator The person who tells the story. A *first person narrator* tells the story as though it is happening to them personally (for example: '*I* walked slowly down the street'). A *third person narrator* tells the story from someone else's point of view (for example: '*He* walked slowly down the street').

non-fiction Texts that are not made up (for example: textbooks, encyclopaedias, information leaflets, speeches, shopping lists).

noun A word used to identify people, places or things (a common noun – for example: *boy, bridge, train*) or to name a particular one of these (proper noun – *Sophie, Liverpool, Westminster Abbey*).

nuance Implied meaning: see connotation.

object The thing in the sentence that 'receives' the action (the verb). In the following sentences the object is in italics: He poured *the tea*. She ate *her breakfast*.

onomatopoeia A word whose meaning is in its sound (for example: *smash, crash, plop*).

oxymoron Two normally contradictory words next to each other (for example: 'Burning ice'; 'miserable happiness').

157

paragraph A section of writing. A new paragraph is shown by leaving a line space between sentences or by starting a sentence in from the margin. New paragraphs show a change of time, topic, speaker or place.

personification A metaphor that represents a thing as a living creature (for example: the waves were *leaping white horses*. The storm *threatened* the town).

perspective Another term for viewpoint. Our perspective is how we 'see' things.

phrase A group of words that do a job together in a sentence (for example: he looked *under the bed*).

playwright The writer of a play.

plot The plot of a literary text is the *story* – the narrative – or an interrelated series of events as described by the author.

preposition A word that shows the physical relationship between two things (for example: *in*, *through*, *under*, *on*, *between*, *over*).

pronoun A word that stands in place of a noun, a noun phrase or pronoun (for example: *I/me, we/us, he/him, she/her, they/them, it, mine, ours, theirs, myself, themselves, and so on*).

quotation A word, phrase, sentence or passage copied from a text, usually used to support an argument or point of view. A quotation should be surrounded by inverted commas ('…'). It is usually wise to make quotations as short as possible, sometimes just one well-chosen word is enough.

register The style and tone of a text. Registers can range from very formal and technical to highly informal, even insulting. Using the right register is a key skill in English.

rhetorical question A question in a text, or particularly in speech, for which no answer is expected (for example: *How many times do I have to tell you? How many times must we go through this before we see the error of our ways?*)

rhyme Words chosen by a poet because they finish with the same sound (for example: *he/flea; stable/label; laughter/after*).

rhythm The 'beat' in poetry or music.

semicolon (;) A punctuation mark sometimes used instead of a full stop when the two sentences either side of the semicolon explain each other (for example: *He was sad; he cried*). It is often used instead of the word 'because'. A semicolon suggests a slightly longer pause in a sentence than a comma.

sentence A group of words that together can stand on their own and make complete sense. It starts with a capital letter and ends with either a full stop, question mark or exclamation mark. A sentence contains or implies a predicate and a subject. Sentences can be very short, very long, or somewhere in between.

setting The setting is the *time and place* in which a play or story takes place. The setting could also include the social and political circumstances (or context) of the action.

simile Comparing two things using either the word *like* or *as* (for example: The boy was *like an angry bear*. His running was *as loud as thunder*. Her face was *as yellow as custard*).

simple sentence A complete sentence with just one verb (or verb chain). A simple sentence can still be long.

slang Informal language (for example: *kid* rather than child; *grub* rather than food; *guys* rather than people).

soliloquy A speech made by a character in a play to the audience only – not to another character. Soliloquies are rarely used nowadays, but they are common in Shakespeare's plays. They can be a good way of allowing the audience to 'hear' what a character is thinking and feeling.

stanza A verse of a poem.

structural features Features used by a writer to give their writing shape and coherence. These are the features that hold writing together. Structural features include: tone, style, repetitions, extended images, shifts of focus, voice and viewpoint, openings and closings, sequencing of ideas, links between paragraphs and sentences.

structure How a text is organised and held together: all those things that shape a text and make it coherent. See cohesion and coherence.

style Writing styles can vary between writers, or writers may use different styles at different times (for example: they might sometimes write informally with energy, while in other texts they might write formally, creating a style that gives them an air of authority). Style and tone are closely related.

subject   The 'do-er' of a sentence (for example, in the following sentences the subject is in italics: *He* ran quickly. *Jane* saw the accident. *The cat* was bored).

subject terminology   The technical words that are used for a particular subject. All the words in this glossary are subject terminology for English.

subordinate clause   Part of the sentence that cannot stand on its own, but gives more information about the main clause. A subordinate clause always contains a subject and a verb. The subordinate clause is set in italics in the sentence: He walked quickly *because he was late.*

summarise   Reduce the content of a text to its essentials (for example: when you explain to a friend what happened in a film).

synthesise   Bring information together from different sources to make a coherent whole. See coherence.

technique   Another word for method. Writers use different techniques to create different effects.

tense (verb)   See verb. Verbs can be used in various forms (or tenses) to indicate *when* something happened. For example, something that happened in the past, is happening now (present) or will happen (future). Tense shows *when* an action took place. For example, *I run* (present), *I ran* (past), *I will run* (future).

theme   A theme is a central idea in a text. Common themes in novels, films, poems and other literary texts include: loyalty, love, race, betrayal, poverty, good versus evil, and so on.

tone   The mood of a text, or the attitude of the author or narrator towards the topic. Tones can be mocking, affectionate, polite, authoritative, and so on.

verb   A *doing*, *being* or *having* word: for example, *run*, *am*, *have*.

viewpoint   A writer's or character's point of view: their attitudes, beliefs and opinions.

vocabulary   The words a writer chooses to use. They might use a particular sort of vocabulary (for example: formal, simple or shocking).

voice (narrative)   A written account of connected events can be neutral in opinion. Sometimes a writer's attitude and tone is much more noticeable – as though you can 'hear' them. This is the writer's voice.

Answers

ENGLISH LANGUAGE

Paper 1 Section A: Reading

Question 1

Do it! (p.11)

Some important points:

- You will answer questions on a fiction extract written after 1900.
- There will be four questions.
- Read the four questions and then spend at least ten minutes reading the extract carefully, underlining useful details.
- Don't spend more time on a question than is justified by the number of marks available.
- In questions 2–4 you must concentrate on the effects on the reader and how these are created by the writer.

Do it! (p.13)

Answer 2 is wrong because the boy's fair hair is not caused by the heat, and therefore it is not relevant.

Answer 3 is wrong because 'smashed' and 'anger' might often be connected to heat, but they are not necessarily connected here.

Check it! (p.14)

2   a   Four minutes

   b   No – stick to the facts

   c   Four

   d   No. You will find the answers only in the part of the source that is given in the question. Usually this will be the first few lines of the source.

   e   Mark words that might be useful in answering the question, so read the question first.

   f   Finding the information.

Question 2

Do it! (p.16)

Answers could include:

Shorter sentences give a sort of punchline effect. This is most apparent at the end: the final sentence is not even a whole sentence because it has no verb and only means something in the context of the previous sentence. It seems to sum up the narrator's disgust and disappointment in a very direct way.

Do it! (p.17)

Answer	How it compares with the mark scheme descriptors	Mark band
A	The student chooses one relevant quotation and gives a very brief explanation of what it tells us about the narrator, although nothing is said about how it affects the mood of the extract, and not much detail is offered in the explanation. However, there is some understanding of language choice and how this conveys meaning.	2
B	The student's answer is perceptive: they infer intelligently from precise details in the text. The analysis is deft and takes account of nuances, vocabulary and sentence forms. The answer uses a range of relevant terminology – impression, swear word, sentence – to precisely identify methods and their effects on the reader.	4

Do it! (p.18)

Example of a simple sentence:

'Miguel was there already.'

Example of compound sentence:

'I left the 'welcome' desk and dragged my bags angrily for the next half hour up to my room.'

Example of complex sentence:

'There were two flights of steep steps to negotiate before I could reach my assigned hovel on the third storey of the dilapidated building.'

The effect the sentence forms on the reader shows the narrator was unhappy with his new accommodation:

- Sarcastic inverted commas around 'welcome' (to show he did not find the hotel welcoming).
- He is angry.
- He chooses to include the detail of how far up and inconvenient his room is.
- He calls his room a 'hovel'.
- The room is cramped.
- He has a roommate who takes more than his fair share of space in the room.
- His roommate is covering the author's part of the room with germs.

Question 3

Do it! (p.20)

A bike – e.g. chain, two wheels, spokes, handlebars.

A school – e.g. timetable, teachers, rules, lessons.

A film – e.g. characters, plot, climax, shots.

An extract from a novel – e.g. paragraphs, dialogue, descriptions, characters, an event, tone of writing.

Do it! (p.22)

- Briony is controlling and very neat and precise. She leaves nothing to chance. She likes order. She likes to be in charge.
- Lists, long sentences, precise details, very precise adjective choices.
- Smaller structural features help the writer to build that impression of Briony. For example, the linking phrase 'in fact' shows the narrator is going to emphasise something they have already explained – her tidiness 'in fact' links the first and second halves of the paragraphs.

Do it! (p.23)

Answer A: Band 3; Answer B: Band 4; Answer C: Band 2.

Check it! (p.24)

1 See page 21 for a list of structural features.

2 Repetitions, although almost anything could be a structural feature if it is deliberately used to give the text shape and meaning.

3 Any three from: change of topic, place, time or speaker.

4 A man as a duck.

5 Eight marks.

6 The attitude of the writer or narrator to what is being written about: for example, mocking, serious, sympathetic.

7 Eight minutes.

8 The features that hold it together, make it 'work', and make it recognisable as narrative fiction.

Question 4

Do it! (p.26)

Other possible and equally reasonable reactions to the Sons and Lovers extract:

'We really sympathise with Miriam, even though we sense that she is a strong character.'

'Paul and Miriam seem so different from each other: she is very anxious, but he seems to be insensitive.'

Do it! (p.27)

Here is an example of what a student said about the writing:

I get the impression that the narrator is fed up and deflated. The writer's choice of words is effective at giving this impression: he 'drags' his bags up the stairs to what he calls his 'assigned hovel'. He sounds like he is unhappy at having no choice of room, which he chooses to call a 'hovel'. This is his judgement, not presumably the official description of the room. The last sentence is just two words, the second one repeating the word at the end of the previous sentence. It makes him sound like he is very miserable and defeated. The writing is good because mostly it just hints at the narrator's feelings.

I also get the impression that he feels let down...

Stretch it! (p.29)

2 B is closest to Band 4, although a case can be made for C.

4 To improve B, some evidence would need to be explored more fully. For example, the weasel image also suggests deceitfulness and quick changes of direction. This contrasts so strikingly with Miriam's 'brooding' attitude, suggesting she is still, thoughtful, undecided. Paul seems to acting out of quick instinct, while Miriam can only act after long deliberation. Answer C is very strong on genuine reader response, but the analysis needs to be more precise: for example, how does Lawrence seem to shift the narrative perspective to Miriam? Briefly explaining would make the comment more convincing.

Check it! (p.30)

2 B, C, A. However, C could be considered to be at least as good as B, just less conventional in its approach. B chooses a wider range of relevant quotations to justify views. C is much stronger on personal response, and the response is valid and considered. There is no depth to answer A: it does not explain points and evidence,

and it does not consider what is good about the writing. It tries simply to stick to 'facts' in the text.

3 a 50%

b 20 minutes

c • Read and understand the question carefully.

• Think about what impact or influence the writer is trying to have on you, the reader.

• Think about what is good (and perhaps less good) about the writing.

• Don't get carried away with your own feelings about the text: keep your distance.

• Make sure you consider some details in the text to support your thoughts.

• Use the question to explore the text fully enough to get all the 20 marks on offer.

d It is the starting point for your answer, but you don't have to agree with it.

Review it! (p.31–32)

1 15 minutes

2 Read the questions and mark useful, relevant bits of the text as you read it.

3 Whether you can find the information that is actually there in front of you: facts.

4 Four minutes.

5 Any four from:

• Hamid was running.

• He was in too much of a hurry to finish using the toilet.

• He grabbed a weapon (and was ready to kill with it).

• His wife was screeching.

• Rupban has stopped plucking the chicken.

• Mumtaz wouldn't let Hamid stop.

• She gave him an urgent instruction (not a request).

• She is sarcastic and insulting to him to sting him into action.

6 Language use and its effects.

7 Eight minutes

8 Some possibilities include:

• Clipped language ('See', 'perfect everywhere') suggests she is harsh, insensitive.

• Grand metaphor to suggest her own grandness: 'ease her path to this world'.

• Aside – 'she should have strangled them at birth' - reveals her selfish ruthlessness.

• 'Of course' suggests generosity, but her real motives are then revealed, suggesting dishonesty.

9 The effects of the writer's structural choices.

10 Eight minutes.

11 Any ten from:

• Information put into a particular order (sequence).

• Dialogue to reveal character, move the narrative on, and so on.

• Narrative chronology.

• Narrative shifts.

• Repetition – of words, phrases, ideas, images, and so on.

• Changing/developing focus.

- Extended images.
- A particular style, tone or mood.
- Narrative voice and perspective.
- Paragraphs.
- Summaries, introductions, conclusions.

12 Some possibilities include:

- A sequence of events, one leading to the next.
- Dialogue (and implied dialogue) to act as a sort of commentary on the sequence of events.
- Words consistently chosen to communicate physical feelings very clearly – 'slick', 'yowl', 'explosions', 'spittle', 'yelled', named colours.

13 To consider how successful the writer has been in engaging the reader.

14 20 minutes

15 Answers will vary but make sure you can justify your feelings with evidence from the text.

16 Answers should:

- show understanding of the mark scheme
- be clear about how the reader reacts to the scene and the characters
- identify amusing aspects of the text, and how successfully the humour is created
- suggest *how* the writer has tried to affect and engage the reader, by referring to/analysing details in the text.

Paper 1 Section B: Writing

Do it! (p.36)

B – It is narrative fiction because it is written in the past tense (for example, 'caught' – not 'catches') and it contains dramatic action: someone seems to be preparing to attack the hotel in some way. In addition, it is written in the third person (she). If you described a day in your life you would be writing in the first person (I).

Check it! (p.37)

1 40 marks

2 24 marks

3 2

4 By topic

5 Audience, purpose and form

6 Descriptive or narrative

Question type 1: descriptive writing with a visual stimulus

Check it! (p.41)

1 For example:

The castle doesn't care any more. It sticks its tongue out rudely at us, but we know it doesn't really mean it: its face is as serene as the lake that surrounds it. The lake is the castle's very own vanity mirror. The old brickwork squats and waits. It has learned to be patient. It has all the time in the world. Still, it does yearn for the old days when armoured knights, not brightly coloured tourists, streamed through its interior.

simile, **metaphor**, personification.

Question type 2: descriptive writing without a visual stimulus

Do it! (p.44)

Most people (and markers) would probably find answer B better because it is much more engaging: the opening is dramatic and grabs our attention. Answer A spends most of the time explaining what the student *will* write. Answer B just gets on with it. If we look at the mark scheme on p.35 we see that answer B is 'engaging' and chooses vocabulary for 'deliberate effect' on the reader. In fact, this answer is probably heading towards Band 4.

Do it! (p.45)

- The castle is sandy brown in the mid-afternoon light.
- Its drawbridge is like an outstretched tongue.

Check it! (p.46)

1 Annotating the question means marking up the question with notes to make sure you understand and do exactly what it is telling you to do. It also helps you to remember your ideas.

2 Planning involves thinking through the structure, the content and the language for your writing.

3 The opening of your writing should engage your reader effectively and in an appropriate way.

4 A is the better opening because it is less factual and more interesting. The description is creative and uses ambitious language.

5 c and e

Question type 3: narrative with a visual stimulus

Check it! (p.49)

1 'Thinking outside the box' for this question could mean asking yourself:

- What might be (happening) just outside the picture?
- What could explain what is in the picture?
- What people in the picture might be thinking and feeling.

2 Characters

Question type 4: narrative – writing the opening to a story

Do it! (p.52)

A sets the mood and atmosphere.

B addresses the reader directly.

C starts with dialogue before setting a dramatic mood.

Do it! (p.52)

Red-faced and grunting, Harry stamped his foot on the accelerator, revving the engine, but only spinning his wheels hopelessly in the sticky mud.

He lay scrunched by the rock that had tripped him, a red pool forming by his outstretched hand.

The dog barked and spun in this strange white world.

Check it! (p.52)

1 **a** Setting mood and atmosphere; raises questions about who she is and what she is up to; description of setting.

b A hook that causes the reader to raise questions or surprises the reader.

c A hook that addresses the reader directly.

2 For example: He stumbled over the kerb.

3 Many elements could be used, including the seven narrative hooks.

Question type 5: narrative – writing a complete story

Do it! (p.55)

1 Normality: the beginning of the story.

Disruption/problem: drinking.

Climax/crisis: setting off the fireworks and going back to one that did not go off.

Return to normality/result: life-changing injuries/beginning to adjust to a new normality.

2 **a** In the middle of Band 3.

b The writing is fairly 'clear, effective and engaging' and chooses language 'for effect'. However, the register becomes too loose and that damages the tension, and there are few examples of careful crafting of language.

Check it! (p.55)

1 You will write more convincingly about situations you know or understand.

2 Normality

Disruption/problem

Climax/crisis

Return to normality/result

3 Too much dialogue and a clichéd ending such as, 'I woke up and it was all a dream.'

Review it! (p.56)

1 Two

2 Descriptive and narrative

3 40%

4 By topic

5 Any of: past tense, characters, action, fiction

6 45 minutes

7 5–10 minutes

8 Any of: metaphor, simile, personification, image

9 A man as a train

10 Turning it into narrative writing.

11 Describing an event.

12 A: the complete version would read, 'I smelt a delicious aroma of chocolate.'

13 Engage the reader (in an appropriate way).

14 Any of the following:

- A hook that sets the mood and atmosphere.

- A hook that causes the reader to raise questions or surprises the reader.

- A hook that focuses on a character.

- A hook that starts with a key event or action.

- A hook which addresses the reader directly.

- A hook that begins with dialogue.

- A hook that describes the setting.

15 Showing allows readers to work something out for themselves, which is what we have to do in real life.

16 For example:

She smiled at Zanira. 'I know you want the last piece of pizza, but I'm afraid it's got my name written all over it, and my need is greater than yours.'

17 Normality, Disruption/problem, Climax/crisis, Return to normality/result

18 Thinking about what might be just outside the picture on the exam paper.

Paper 2 Section A: Reading

Question 1

Do it! (p.59)

1 In answers E and F, the only aspect of inference is that we have to realise that 'insane' and 'mad', and 'unnecessary' and 'no need' are synonyms.

Check it! (p.59)

1 Any three or four of the following:

- Try to do the question in only four minutes.

- The question will be based on only one of the two texts.

- You need to choose the statements that are true.

- Sometimes you have to work out (infer) whether a statement is true.

- You will get one mark for each true statement.

- Don't choose more statements than are asked for.

2 Some true statements that could be used by exam markers for the extract about 'Let it Go':

- Children like 'Let it Go'.

- Very young children like the song a lot.

- The writer cannot remember another song that has been adopted so enthusiastically by very young children.

- The writer thinks that pop music makes lovers seem fickle.

Question 2

Do it! (p.62)

Answer C is wrong because we don't know which of the two sources is being referred to, and in neither source are crocodiles described as always being asleep.

Answer E is wrong because the crocodiles in source A are not always calm. The writer should have referred to how they are presented in the first half of the extract.

Check it! (p.64)

1 Any of:
- Eight minutes to do the question.
- The question focuses on finding and interpreting details.
- Comparing details in different texts.
- You need to infer to find some information.
- Don't analyse language.
- Use short quotations as evidence.
- Making a summary means concentrating on the essential information being asked for, and putting it into your own words.
- Use a systematic approach, possibly in four steps.
- There are two ways of answering the question – merged, or linked paragraphs.
- Appropriate connectives and sentence starters are useful aids.
- You cannot get beyond Band 2 in the mark scheme if you only write about one of the two texts.

2 We have to infer. Just possibly, he could be sweating for a different reason; we are 'best guessing' on the basis of evidence and our common sense.

3 Band 2

4 For example: whereas, while, by comparison.

Question 3

Do it! (p.67)

1 Here is the opening of one student's answer to this question:

For most of us family is very important, and presumably Chief Seattle expects family to be important to the president, so he presents parts of the environment he wants to save as family members: for example,...

Check it! (p.68)

1 Four or five from:
- Explain your views, and use some evidence.
- Use some subject terminology.
- Analyse the effect of the writer's choice of language.
- Take only 12 minutes to do answer the question.
- You will be asked about only one of the texts.
- The focus is on how the writer uses language to influence us.

2 The main focus is the writer's use of language and its effects on the reader.

3 For example: repetitions, echoing of words and phrases, clear, poetic noun phrases.

4 For example:
- Repetitions are for emphasis and to make his letter sound like a rhetorical speech: '<u>Every</u> part of this earth is sacred to my people. <u>Every</u> shining pine needle, <u>every</u> humming insect.'
- Echoing of words and phrases. This also creates a hypnotic rhythm for the letter: 'We know the sap which <u>courses</u> through the trees as we know the blood that <u>courses</u> through our veins. We are <u>part</u> of the earth and it is <u>part</u> of us.'
- Clear, poetic noun phrases that inspire the reader: 'the freshness of the air'; 'the sparkle of the water'; 'the clear waters of the lakes'.

Question 4

Do it! (p.70)

1 Student's own answer

2 Notice the different styles of the titles and the different feelings they give us about cauliflowers. Use this in your answer.

3 Look carefully at the bullet points below the question.

Check it! (p.76)

1 Two

2 Question 4 asks you to compare writers' perspectives, and how they use language to convey their ideas.

3 About four detailed paragraphs.

4 Paragraph 2: nature and people.

Paragraph 3: family and ancestors.

Paragraph 4: land is sacred.

Paragraph 5: mother earth.

Paragraph 6: we depend on the Earth.

Paragraph 7: you depend on the Earth.

Paragraph 8: keep our spirit.

Paragraph 9: we are dependent on the earth and on one another: we are all deeply interconnected.

Review it! (p.78)

1 1 hour

2 1

3 b

4 c

5 Four

6 8

7 You shouldn't analyse the writer's use of language at all.

8 A summary means concentrating on the essential information being asked for, and putting it into your own words

9 b

10 Suitable words and phrases include:

On the one hand…

Whereas

While

Similarly

In the same way

Different

By contrast

By comparison

However

But.

11 1

12 d

13 The quotations from the text are an example of evidence from the text. 'A sequence of personal pronouns' is an example of subject terminology.

14 16 minutes

15 The focus of Question 4 is to compare writers' perspectives, and how they use language to convey their ideas.

16 Communicate or send.

17 c

18 Rhetorical questions. They lead the reader to agree automatically with the writer because only one answer is possible. The rhetorical question tries to stop the reader from thinking about other perspectives on the problem.

Paper 2 Section B: writing

Do it! (p.80)

Audience: readers of a broadsheet newspaper.

Purpose: to explain (your point of view).

Form: an article (for a broadsheet newspaper).

Check it! (p.80)

1 40 marks

2 16 marks

3 There will be just one task. In other words, you will have no choice.

4 By topic

5 explain, instruct/advise, argue, persuade

6 story

Do it! (p.81)

1 Getting the style right for a head teacher:

My friends and I are given a lot of homework. We object to this because it makes us stressed. We already have enough work to do in school. I feel strongly about this. We are asking that teachers should stop setting homework.

Do it! (p.82)

- Relationship: connection (to), interconnection, how we treat…

- Belong: possess, own, property, ours

Do it! (p.82)

1 Preparing the question:

Topic of letter

'School uniform is important because it allows students to focus on their work rather than on fashion.'

    What sort of person might think this?

    Showing off, self-expression, creativity

    Distract, concentrate

Write a letter to the governors at your school, arguing for or against this statement.

    For or against – not both

    Other useful key words:

    persuade

    case

    point

    view(point)

2 Audience: (my school's) governors

Purpose: arguing (for or against)

Form: (formal) letter

Check it! (p.82)

1 Formal English used in official situations.

2 About one minute.

3 Synonyms are different words that mean roughly the same thing. It is useful to have synonyms for key words in the question so that you don't have to keep repeating them. Thinking about synonyms helps you to understand the key words.

Do it! (p.84)

1 Healthy options.

Do it! (p.85)

From best to worst: C, B, A.

A is far too informal and is therefore both inappropriate and ineffective.

Version C might seem a bit long-winded, but it is polite and respectful. By the end of the paragraph, the governors will be willing to read the rest of the letter and give it careful consideration. That is why the opening is effective.

Do it! (p.86)

An exam marker comments:

This letter is well-organised and uses a style and tone that are appropriate for a respectable group like school governors who have to make carefully considered decisions. Perhaps the rather outdated word 'attire' is going too far, and perhaps implying that the governors may be 'patronising' so early in the letter might irritate them unnecessarily. However, the construction of the first main paragraph is a very cunning piece of reader manipulation: it turns governors' supposed opposition to fashion against them: the final sentence implies that it is the governors – not students – who are victims of (old) fashion.

Check it! (p.86)

1 5–10 minutes.

2 Planning means you know what the **content** of your writing and its order will be before you start writing. This allows you to concentrate on how you express yourself.

Do it! (p.89)

a Persuade;   **b** Advise;   **c** Explain;   **d** Argue.

Do it! (p.90)

The point is made forcefully – even rudely here. The language choices are dramatic and emotive: 'crazy', 'terrible', 'just wrong', 'hate'.

The language needs to be more carefully matched to the readers: school governors. The word choices and arguments need to be more sophisticated.

Check it! (p.92)

1 **a** False

    b True

c False

d False

e True: an introduction can be helpful for the reader.

f False. 'Dear Sir' or 'Dear Madam' should sign off with 'Yours faithfully…'.

2 Here are some examples of openings.

a A letter to your head teacher/principal explaining why you need a week off school/college:

Dear Mrs Jones,

I know that the school has a firm policy of not allowing students to take time off during the term. However,…

b A leaflet advising old people on how to stay fit and active:

They say you are never too old to be fit, and there is a great deal of truth in this.

c An article in a free magazine persuading visitors of the advantages of your local area:

Where could you go that is a romantic as Paris, as picturesque as Rome and as reasonably priced as Bournemouth? Well, Bournemouth, of course!

Review it! (p.92–94)

1 Question 5

2 45 minutes

3 Five minutes

4 Audience, purpose, form

5 To state and develop a point of view.

6 To explain; to instruct or advise; to argue; to persuade

7 Formal letter, article, leaflet, speech, essay

8 Purpose: to advise. Form: a leaflet.

9 Organisation and technical accuracy

10 A is more formal. It uses formal language and structure. B uses slang terms such as 'safe as anything', 'kids' and 'ok'.

11 Identify the key words; jot down useful synonyms; identify the audience, purpose and form; jot down first thoughts; make sure you understand the requirements o the question.

12 Audience: readers, listeners

Purpose: aim, what it's for, reason for writing

Form: format, genre, type, style, category

13 None

14 To reject it; or to show you have considered it; or to sound reasonable.

15 Two from:

- To collect your ideas together.
- To plan a structure for your writing.
- To leave you free to concentrate on style and expression as you write.

16 Lively opening that sounds reassuring. However, it doesn't sound as confident as it might. The use of the word 'you' is wrong, as the audience is teachers of the visitors, while 'you' presumably refers to the students themselves.

17 You need to grab the reader's interest, be clear, and make sure that tone, style and vocabulary are appropriate for the task's given context.

18 The seven key elements are:

- clear and effective style
- appropriate language choices

- effective vocabulary
- a range of linguistic devices used well
- detailed and well-connected ideas
- well-organised paragraphs
- effective use of varied structural features.

19 The cool consideration of alternatives, and the lack of dramatic language suggests that this writing is *arguing* a topic. However, this might well be part of an *advice* text.

20 b and e are probably rhetorical questions as they are not genuinely seeking information: instead they are making a point, and no reply is expected.

Writing: Technical accuracy

Sentence demarcation

Do it! (p.95)

We cannot go on spoiling the planet we live on. **I**n just a few decades we have dug up and burnt the fossil fuels that nature took millions of years to create. **H**ow much longer will we be able to carry on doing this? **W**e must stop it now! **O**ur children and grandchildren will not thank us for using up all the planet's resources before they are even born.

Do it! (p.96)

Novel extract: **J**avad stretched and yawned. **H**e could hardly keep his eyes open. **H**ow would he ever stay awake until morning and the safety of daylight? **H**e had promised to keep watch, but now his will was weakening. **H**e edged a few inches away from the fire. **P**erhaps coldness would fight tiredness. **H**e knew that he and James would both rather be cold than dead! *(or .)*

Advertisement extract: **C**ome alive with **Z**ingo **F**izz! **Z**ingo **F**izz is the tingling new soft drink that will make you glad to be young. *(or !)* **I**f you're not young, then **Z**ingo will make you think you are. *(or !)* **W**hat could be wrong with that? **D**rink **Z**ingo. *(or !)* **I**t's good to be young, even if you're not. *(or !)*

Punctuation

Do it! (p.97)

1 Dashes used instead of brackets for non-essential text that adds extra detail; Comma used to make the reader pause so that a detail can be emphasised; Full stop (Jenny B.) to indicate that letters are missing; Full stop to indicate the end of a sentence; Semicolon which stands before an explanation; Comma used to separate words in a list; Comma used to make meaning clearer.

Do it! (p.97)

1 To make the reader pause so that a detail can be emphasised.

2 To separate words in a list.

3 To make meaning clearer.

Do it! (p.98)

a is incorrectly punctuated. The comma should be a full stop.

b is correct.

c is correct.

d is incorrectly punctuated. The comma should be a full stop.

Do it! (p.99)

a We can't go to Nelum's party because we promised we'd visit our nan's house.

b It's important to eat lots of vegetables.

c The students' ideas for raising money were very imaginative.

d Chanelle's idea for raising money was the most popular.

Check it! (p.100)

1 Punctuation can be used to guide and control the reader's reaction or to emphasise certain details for meaning and effect.

2 The three purposes of a comma are to separate words in a list; to make the reader pause so that a detail can be emphasised; to make meaning clearer.

3 a - Leaping in the air, Sadia neatly caught the ball. The comma is needed to mark the end of a non-finite clause at the beginning of a sentence.

4 a He got up late; he missed the bus.

The semicolon here means 'and therefore'. The two statements explain each other.

b There was a reason he missed the bus: he got up late.

Here the colon is used instead of 'and that was...'

5 I was shocked when I saw his parents' car.

The apostrophe comes straight after the owner or – here – owners.

6 Breathing heavily, I came to a stop outside my destination: the station. I gasped for air; my lungs were bursting. Although I had hardly got my breath back, I forced my legs to take me onto the platform. The train was coming in.

Sentences

Do it! (p.101)

For example: Running quickly, he finally reached the safety of the big rock. He looked back for his pursuers. He couldn't see them. Relieved, he drank some water.

Standard English

Do it! (p.103)

Sentences b, d, e and f use informal English. See below for corrected versions:

b Standard English: John and I went to the beach.

d Standard English: She doesn't like curry.

e Standard English: He was sitting on the wall.

f Standard English: We did it so badly.

Check it (p.104)

1 For effect and impact, and to get higher marks.

2 For example: I was hungry so I put two samosas in the oven; I was hungry. Therefore I put two samosas in the oven; I was hungry because I put two samosas in the oven; I was hungry when I put two samosas in the oven.

3 A: Band 3; B: Band 4; C: Band 2

Spelling, vocabulary and mark scheme

Check it! (p.106–7)

1 Homophones are words that sound the same but have different meanings and spellings.

2 a – disappear

3 This is the suggested best version: She lay beneath the tree in **agony**, blood **oozing** from the deep **gash** and soaking into the earth around her.

4 a • Correct layout for formal letter: address, date, starts correctly with 'Dear'.

• The opening uses Standard English: After reading about your proposed review of the school's uniform policy, I am writing to share my viewpoint...

• Ambitious vocabulary is correctly spelled: attire; patronising; Conversely.

• Sentence structure is used for effect: Although some might argue; Despite many adults' concerns; Moreover.

• A wide range of punctuation is used: semicolons – Comfort is an essential requirement when focusing on our work; ... Colons – companies have relaxed the need for such clothing in the workplace: ...

b Here are some important aspects of the mark scheme that apply to this letter:

• Appropriate Standard English with control and flexibility.

• Spells almost all words correctly.

• Wide and adventurous vocabulary.

Review it! (p.109)

1 40%

2 No. It is also about making effective choices of vocabulary, sentences, punctuation.

3 The six aspects are: sentence demarcation, punctuation, sentences, Standard English, spelling, vocabulary

4 Full stop, exclamation mark, question mark

5 Any seven from: full stop, comma, dash, brackets, semicolon, colon, speech marks, apostrophe, exclamation mark, question mark, ellipsis (…)

6 To make content clear, to guide and control the reader's reaction, and to emphasise certain details for meaning and effect.

7 Sentences b and d use a comma incorrectly.

8 a – The semicolon should be a full stop. *He woke up while it was still dark. He went downstairs.*

9 To introduce some information – usually some sort of list; to mean 'that is to say' or 'in other words'.

10 Every sentence uses at least one apostrophe wrongly. Here is how they should have been written:

a Sadiq's uncle bought some potatoes.

b It's hot today.

c The children's teacher couldn't be found anywhere.

d I picked up the kettle by its handle.

e The river's flow wasn't fast enough.

11 Sentence variety is about varying the types of your sentence and the order of their parts to get the best effect and to keep your reader's interest.

12 **This** tiredness stayed with Errol all week. **He** didn't seem to be able to get out of bed. **Even when** Hayley knocked on the door **and** called through the letter box, he just couldn't stir himself. Nights and days slowly passed through his stuffy room like silent visitors. **They** didn't trouble him though. His eyes were closed **and** he was elsewhere in his head. **Because** of his fever, he often didn't really know where he was.

13 c – It should read: *We weren't speaking to each other.*

Note: a is correct. Many people wrongly say '*She waved to John and I.*' This does not make sense because you couldn't say '*She waved to I.*' This is not Standard English.

14 independant should be independent; hopefull should be hopeful; neccessary should be necessary; dissappear should be disappear.

ENGLISH LITERATURE

Paper 1 Section A: Shakespeare

Do it! (p.116)

Response 2 is better because it offers contextual information that is useful: it improves our understanding of the play.

Check it! (p.118)

1 Four
2 The second task asks you to write about other parts of the play.
3 Character and theme

Paper 1 Section B: The 19th-century novel

Check it! (p.124)

1 50 (check style) minutes
2 About 400 words
3 The theme is the central idea in the text: for example, poverty, injustice, marriage, men and women, and so on.

Paper 2 Section A: Modern texts

All answers will be personal responses.

Paper 2 Section B: Poetry

Check it! (p.144)

1 40 minutes
2 Individual words
3 Helping your reader to understand the poem.
4 2 poems

Paper 2 Section C: Unseen poetry

Do it! (p.145)

Other skills and focuses include:
- Analysing the effects of language.
- Quoting to support and clarify your views.
- Spotting key themes.
- Commenting on patterns in the poem – rhyme, rhythm, extended metaphors, etc.

Do it! (p.149)

Rank order from best to worst: C, B, A, C.

Student D: This answer sounds good, but says nothing about the poem, except what it hasn't got!

Student C: Interesting points but nothing is examined precisely: the points are a little vague.

Student C: This answer is more precise and uses evidence to make a clear point.

Student D: This is a charming answer, but completely irrelevant to the question.

Check it! (p.154)

1 Two poems
2 Two questions
3 50 minutes
4 15 minutes
5 Simile

Review it! (p.155)

1 1 hour 45 minutes
2 55 minutes
3 About 400 words
4 Two
5 2 hours 15 minutes.
6 A: The modern text, B: Poetry anthology, C: Unseen poetry.
7 None. The question will not focus on one part of the text.
8 One which you build into your own sentence. For example, Macbeth concludes that life is 'a tale told by an idiot.'
9 45 minutes
10 40 minutes
11 Comparing two things by saying they *are* the same: e.g. His face was a big plate.
12 Words near to each other that have been chosen because they start with the same sound: for example, the <u>ph</u>one was <u>f</u>lat and <u>f</u>unky.
13 A central idea or belief that a text explores.
14 Two
15 One
16 You won't know in advance what the poems are, and so you will probably not have read them before.
17 Two
18 35 minutes
19 Two
20 Section A, the modern text, which is worth 34 marks including 4 marks for spelling, punctuation and grammar.

Index

ENGLISH LANGUAGE

KNOWIT!

There are two English Language papers:

☞ Paper 1: Explorations in creative reading and writing lasts 1 hour 45 minutes, and is worth 50 per cent of the GCSE.

☞ Paper 2: Writers' viewpoints and perspectives lasts 1 hour 45 minutes, and is worth 50 per cent of the GCSE.

This is how the English Language papers will be organised in the exam.

Exam	Section A: Reading	Section B: Writing
Paper 1: Explorations in creative reading and writing • 1 hour 45 minutes • 80 marks • 50% of GCSE	Answer four questions on part of a 20th/21st century literary fiction text. • 40 marks • 25% of GCSE	Write a description or a narrative (story). • 40 marks • 25% of GCSE
Paper 2: Writers' viewpoints and perspectives • 1 hour 45 minutes • 80 marks • 50% of GCSE	Answer four questions on two linked non-fiction texts. • 40 marks • 25% of GCSE	Write to present a viewpoint. • 40 marks • 25% of GCSE

When the examiners mark your answers, they refer to **mark schemes**. These mark schemes are made up of 'band descriptors'. Below are some simplified mark schemes for the two English Language papers. You will need to refer to these as you work through the book.

Paper 1 Section A: Reading

Question 2 mark scheme

Band 2 descriptors (Roughly GCSE grades 2–3)	Band 3 descriptors (Roughly GCSE grades 4–6)	Band 4 descriptors (Roughly GCSE grades 7–9)
The student's answer...	The student's answer...	The student's answer...
• shows some appreciation of language choices	• shows clear appreciation of language choices	• examines language choices with insight and precision
• comments on the effects of language choices	• explains the effects of some language choices	• closely analyses the effects of language choices
• uses some relevant evidence, including quotations	• uses relevant evidence (including quotations) from different parts of the text	• carefully chooses a variety of evidence, including quotations
• tries to use some subject terminology.	• uses helpful, relevant subject terminology.	• uses a range of precise and helpful subject terminology.

Question 3 mark scheme

The mark scheme for Question 3 is similar to the mark scheme for Question 2, except that the focus is on **structural features** rather than **language choices**. The answer must give evidence – not necessarily quotations – and use subject terminology accurately.

Band 2 descriptors (Roughly GCSE grades 2–3)	Band 3 descriptors (Roughly GCSE grades 4–6)	Band 4 descriptors (Roughly GCSE grades 7–9)
The student's answer...	The student's answer...	The student's answer...
• shows some appreciation of structural features • comments on the effects of structural features • uses some relevant evidence • tries to use some subject terminology.	• shows clear appreciation of relevant structural features • explains the effects of some relevant structural features • uses different forms of relevant evidence • uses helpful, relevant subject terminology.	• examines relevant structural features with insight and precision • closely analyses the effects of relevant structural features • carefully chooses a variety of evidence • uses a range of precise and helpful subject terminology.

Question 4 mark scheme

Here are the sort of descriptors that exam markers will use when they mark Question 4.

Band 2 descriptors (Roughly GCSE grades 2–3)	Band 3 descriptors (Roughly GCSE grades 4–6)	Band 4 descriptors (Roughly GCSE grades 7–9)
The student's answer...	The student's answer...	The student's answer...
• tries to make some comments that evaluate the text • refers to a relevant example from the text • refers to some of the writer's techniques • uses a couple of helpful quotations.	• includes a clear evaluation • gives examples that support and clarify points • helpfully explains the effects of some of the writer's techniques • uses helpful quotations from different parts of the text.	• critically evaluates the text in a detailed way • gives examples from the text to explain views convincingly • analyses effects of a range of the writer's choices • justifies points with relevant quotations from different parts of the text.

Paper 1 Section B: Writing

Whatever category the writing task belongs to, it is meant to help you to write creatively. The skills required by the task are always the same, and every task will be marked against the same mark scheme.

Here are the sort of descriptors that exam markers will use when they mark your writing.

Band 2 descriptors (Roughly GCSE grades 2–3)	Band 3 descriptors (Roughly GCSE grades 4–6)	Band 4 descriptors (Roughly GCSE grades 7–9)
Content The student's answer… • is mainly clear in expression • keeps trying to match register to purpose, form and audience • chooses words with some care • uses some linguistic devices.	**Content** The student's answer… • is clear, effective and engaging throughout • mainly matches register to purpose, form and audience • precisely chooses words and phrases for deliberate effect • uses varied linguistic devices for impact.	**Content** The student's answer… • wins the reader over and holds their interest throughout • precisely matches register to purpose, form and audience • uses a wide and adventurous vocabulary • carefully chooses linguistic devices for effect throughout.
Organisation The student's answer… • uses suitable ideas that have some variety and sometimes link together • uses some paragraphs and discourse markers • uses some other structural features (for example, deliberate repetition, topic sentences).	**Organisation** The student's answer… • uses varied ideas, linking them well • carefully organises paragraphs around well-chosen discourse markers • uses structural features for deliberate impact.	**Organisation** The student's answer… • is highly structured and developed around a range of dynamic and complex ideas • is highly coherent and fluent in organisation, incorporating discourse markers in a natural way • uses a range of structural features skilfully and creatively.

Paper 2 Section A: Reading

Question 2 mark scheme

Band 2 descriptors (Roughly GCSE grades 2–3)	Band 3 descriptors (Roughly GCSE grades 4–6)	Band 4 descriptors (Roughly GCSE grades 7–9)
The student writes about...	The student writes about...	The student writes about...
... at least one of the texts, and: • interprets • tries to infer • chooses some appropriate detail • points out some relevant similarities and/or difference(s).	... both texts, and: • clearly synthesises and interprets • makes clear inferences • chooses clear, relevant details • points out clear, relevant similarities and/or differences between texts.	... both texts, and: • perceptively synthesises and interprets • makes perceptive inferences • chooses very precise, relevant details • explores perceptive, relevant similarities and/or differences between texts.

Question 3 mark scheme

Band 2 descriptors (Roughly GCSE grades 2–3)	Band 3 descriptors (Roughly GCSE grades 4–6)	Band 4 descriptors (Roughly GCSE grades 7–9)
The student's answer...	The student's answer...	The student's answer...
• shows some understanding of language • attempts to comment on the effect of language • uses some appropriate textual detail • makes some use of subject terminology, mainly appropriately.	• shows clear understanding of language • explains clearly the effects of the writer's choices of language • uses a range of relevant textual detail • makes clear and accurate use of subject terminology.	• shows clear understanding of language • explains clearly the effects of the writer's choices of language • uses a range of relevant textual detail • makes clear and accurate use of subject terminology.

Question 4 mark scheme

Band 2 descriptors (Roughly GCSE grades 2–3)	Band 3 descriptors (Roughly GCSE grades 4–6)	Band 4 descriptors (Roughly GCSE grades 7–9)
The student's answer...	The student's answer...	The student's answer...
• tries to compare ideas and perspectives • makes some comments on how writers' methods are used • chooses some appropriate textual detail/references, not always supporting from one or both texts • identifies some different ideas and perspectives.	• compares ideas and perspectives in a clear and relevant way • explains clearly how writers' methods are used • selects relevant detail to support from both texts • shows a clear understanding of the different ideas and perspectives in both texts.	• compares ideas and perspectives in a perceptive way • analyses how writers' methods are used • selects a range of judicious supporting detail from both texts • shows a detailed understanding of the different ideas and perspectives in both texts.

Paper 2 Section B: Writing

The mark scheme for Paper 2 Section B: Writing is the same as the mark scheme for Paper 1 Section B: Writing on page 174.

Technical accuracy

The mark scheme for technical accuracy is the same for the writing tasks in both English Language papers. (There are no technical accuracy marks to be won or lost when you are answering the reading questions.)

Aspect	Band 2 descriptors (Roughly GCSE grades 2–3)	Band 3 descriptors (Roughly GCSE grades 4–6)	Band 4 descriptors (Roughly GCSE grades 7–9)
	The student's answer…	The student's answer…	The student's answer…
Sentence demarcation	• marks the beginnings and ends of most sentences	• marks the beginnings and ends of almost all sentences	• correctly marks the beginnings and ends of sentences
Punctuation	• often uses basic punctuation well	• uses a range of punctuation usually correctly	• uses a wide range of punctuation almost always correctly
Sentences	• tries out different sentence structures and types	• varies sentences for effect	• uses a wide range of sentence structures confidently and effectively
Standard English	• sometimes uses Standard English, perhaps with some mistakes over agreement or tense endings	• mainly uses Standard English with good control and flexibility	• uses appropriate Standard English with control and flexibility throughout
Spelling	• sometimes spells more complex words correctly (such as, height, definite)	• makes few spelling mistakes – even complex and irregular words (such as accommodation, rhythmic, parallel)	• spells almost all words correctly, including adventurous vocabulary (such as combustible, opprobrium, machination)
Vocabulary	• varies vocabulary.	• chooses some precise and sophisticated vocabulary.	• uses a wide and adventurous vocabulary.

Paper 1 Section A: Reading
Introduction and advice

Here is the sort of text you will get in Paper 1:

Source A
This extract is from early in a novel by Andrea Levy. In this section, Hortense has arrived in London to join her husband after a long journey by sea from Jamaica. She arrives at the address her husband has given her.
Small Island

The door was answered by an Englishwoman. A blonde-haired, pink-cheeked Englishwoman with eyes so blue they were the brightest thing in the street. She looked on my face, parted her slender lips and said, 'Yes?'

5 'Is this the household of Mr Gilbert Joseph?'

'I beg your pardon?'

'Gilbert Joseph?' I said, a little slower.

'Oh, Gilbert. Who are you?' She pronounced Gilbert so strangely that for a moment I was anxious that I would be delivered to
10 the wrong man.

'Mr Gilbert Joseph is my husband – I am his wife.'

The woman's face looked puzzled and pleased all at one time. She looked back into the house, lifting her head as she did. Then she turned to me and said, 'Didn't he come to meet you?'

15 'I have not seen Gilbert,' I told her, then went on to ask, 'but this is perchance where he is aboding?'

At which this Englishwoman said, 'What?' She frowned and looked over my shoulder at the trunk, which was resting by the kerbside where it had been placed by the driver of the taxi
20 vehicle. 'Is that yours?' she enquired.

'It is.'

'It's the size of the Isle of Wight. How did you get it here?' She laughed a little. A gentle giggle that played round her eyes and mouth.

25 I laughed too, so as not to give her the notion that I did not know what she was talking about as regards this 'white island'. I said, 'I came in a taxicab and the driver assured me that this was the right address. Is this the house of Gilbert Joseph?'

The woman stood for a little while before answering by saying,
30 'Hang on here. I'll see if he's in his room.' She then shut the door in my face.

And I wondered how could a person only five feet six inches tall (five feet seven if I was wearing my wedding-shoe heels), how could such a person get to the top of this tall house? Ropes
35 and pulleys was all I could conceive. Ropes and pulleys to hoist me up. We had stairs in Jamaica. Even in our single-storey houses we had stairs that lifted visitors on to the veranda and another that took them into the kitchen. There were stairs at my college, up to the dormitories that housed the pupils on
40 two separate floors. I was very familiar with stairs. But all my mind could conjure as I looked up at this tall, tall house was ropes and pulleys. It was obvious that I had been on a ship for too long.

You will need to refer to this extract when you look at the pages that follow on **questions 1–4**.

Question 1

Here is an example Question 1:

Read again the first part of the Source from **lines 1 to 7**.

List **four** facts from this part of the text about the Englishwoman's appearance.

[4 marks]

DOIT!

Now answer the question you have just prepared in the space below.

1 ....

....

2 ....

....

3 ....

....

4 ....

....

Here is an example Question 2:

Look in detail at this extract from **lines 15 to 31** of the Source:

15 'I have not seen Gilbert,' I told her, then went on to ask, 'but this is perchance where he is aboding?'	
At which this Englishwoman said, 'What?' She frowned and looked over my shoulder at the trunk, which was resting by the kerbside where it had been placed by the driver of the taxi 20 vehicle. 'Is that yours?' she enquired.	
'It is.'	
'It's the size of the Isle of Wight. How did you get it here?' She laughed a little. A gentle giggle that played round her eyes and mouth.	
25 I laughed too, so as not to give her the notion that I did not know what she was talking about as regards this 'white island'. I said, 'I came in a taxicab and the driver assured me that this was the right address. Is this the house of Gilbert Joseph?'	
The woman stood for a little while before answering by saying, 30 'Hang on here. I'll see if he's in his room.' She then shut the door in my face.	

How does the writer use language here to suggest how Hortense and the Englishwoman misunderstand each other?

You could include the writer's choice of:

• words and phrases

• language features and techniques

• sentence forms.

[8 marks]

WORKIT!

Here is the first half of a student's answer to the question on page 181:

> Everything about the choice of language emphasises the two women's misunderstanding of each other. Presumably, Hortense feels intimidated by the Englishwoman and so she tries to use very impressive words - 'perchance' and 'aboding'. However, Hortense does not realise that the Englishwoman is a very ordinary person - not posh at all - who will not understand complex words. The woman's ordinariness is clearly signalled to the reader by her response with the direct, even rude question, 'What?'. There is a cultural misunderstanding between the two women which comes across in the form of language. For example, when the woman makes a joke about Hortense's luggage being as large as the Isle of Wight, Hortense takes this as meaning a 'white island'.

Use the mark scheme for Question 2 on page 172 to write the second half of this student's answer. Comment on the sorts of sentences the writer uses, and the effect this has on her description of the scene.

The writer has used simple sentences to...

DO IT!

Here are two more example questions for you to answer. They both use the extract on page 181. Use the space provided to write your answer and continue on your own paper.

How does the writer use language here to show the two women's thoughts and feelings?

You could include the writer's choice of:

- words and phrases
- language features and techniques
- sentence forms.

[8 marks]

....

....

....

....

....

....

....

....

....

....

....

....

....

....

....

....

....

....

....

....

DO IT!

How does the writer use language here to create a contrast between the two women?

You could include the writer's choice of:

- words and phrases

- language features and techniques

- sentence forms.

[8 marks]

Question 3

☞ Question 3 will always be about how the writer has **structured** (organised) the whole extract to have an **effect** on the reader.

☞ You will need to use relevant subject terminology to support your views.

☞ You should spend 8 minutes on this question.

☞ It is worth 8 marks.

Here is a example Question 3:

> You now need to think about the **whole** of the **Source**.
>
> This text represents a dramatic and amusing episode early in the novel.
>
> How has the writer structured the text to interest you as a reader?
>
> You could write about:
>
> • what the writer focuses your attention on at the beginning
>
> • how and why the writer changes this focus as the Source develops
>
> • any other structural features that interest you.
>
> **[8 marks]**

PREPAREIT!
Prepare the question by underlining the key words and annotating it with your initial thoughts and ideas. Mark up the extract on pages 178–79 with the question in mind.

WORKIT!

Below is what one student wrote for the example Question 3 you were shown on page 185. The exam marker has made a few comments in the margin:

> This opening has a strong impact. The Englishwoman who opens the door is so simply described that we can 'see' her face in our minds straight away and we are intrigued by who she might be. (Although we might know her well if we had read the whole novel.) The first paragraph contains a strong piece of characterisation – a woman who is very self-confident and perhaps direct and impatient. It is as though we have been delivered straight into the scene and we are standing on the doorstep with Hortense. The next few lines are dialogue between the two women, and this keeps us – the reader – 'in the moment'. We are not being given narrative to explain the situation and we seem to share the astonishment of the two women. Our confusion keeps growing with the women's puzzlement: What does the woman mean by 'I beg your pardon' – is she puzzled, offended, aggressive perhaps? We are left wondering what the relationship between these two women could be – especially as one seems to be living with the other one's husband!
>
> The next section is based around a series of misunderstandings – the two women are using mismatching language, and the joke that one of them makes is completely misunderstood by the other – possibly as a racist attack on her (assuming she is a black Jamaican). The final part of the source changes from dialogue and confusion to one character thinking about her situation, and this attempt to make sense of her feelings and her circumstances is sort of shared by the reader. At the very end of the source the narrator comes to a sort of interim conclusion: perhaps she was disorientated by her long voyage when she was living on a ship.

Margin comments: Opening/intriguing reader · Subject terminology · Dialogue as structural feature · Unfolding detail · Leading the reader through the text via their curiosity · Commentary/conclusion

This is what an exam marker says about the student's answer:

> This answer shows a clear understanding of a number of structural features – opening, how detail is provided gradually to inform and intrigue and the use of dialogue. Some of this is perceptive, but mainly features are described and explained, without their effects being analysed. This would have involved exploring the use and effects of at least one main structural feature. There is a good attention to details and some specific examples are mentioned to support points. Terminology used is helpful (characterisation, paragraph, dialogue) but often quite limited. Terminology could have been more precise (e.g. 'language register'). This answer is in the upper half of Band 3.

Use the exam marker's comments and the mark scheme on page 173 to rewrite the student's answer in order to improve it. Use the space below and then continue on your own paper.

DO IT!

Now have a go at the question below. Use the space provided to write your answer and continue on your own paper if necessary.

You need to think about the **whole** of the **Source**.

This text is from early in the novel. How has the writer structured the text to suggest the conflicts and confusion in Hortense's mind? You could write about:

- what the writer focuses your attention on at the beginning

- how and why the writer changes this focus as the Source develops

- any other structural features that interest you.

[8 marks]

KNOWIT!

☞ Question 4 will ask you to consider how well the writer **engages** the **reader's interest**.

☞ You need to give a thoughtful **personal response,** and you must choose **evidence** from the text to support your response.

☞ You should spend 20 minutes on this question.

☞ It is worth 20 marks.

Here is an example Question 4:

Focus this part of your answer on the second part of the Source from **line 17 to the end**.

When the book was published, a critic said: 'At this point in the novel the reader gets a very clear sense of Hortense's personality and her values.'

To what extent do you agree?

In your response, you could:

• consider your own impressions of Hortense in this part of the novel

• evaluate how the writer creates the reader's response to Hortense

• support your opinions with references to the text.

[20 marks]

PREPAREIT!

Annotate the question in preparation for answering it.

PLANIT!

Look at the question that you prepared on your sense of Hortense's personality and her values. Make a quick plan for your answer.

PLANIT!

DOIT!

Write your answer to Question 4 you have been preparing and planning (on pages 188 and 189) about your sense of Hortense's personality and her values.

....

....

....

....

....

....

....

....

....

....

....

....

....

....

....

....

....

....

....

....

....

....

....

....

DO IT!

Here is another Question 4 for you to answer. Use the space below to answer the question and continue on your own paper if necessary.

Focus this part of your answer on the second part of the Source from **line 15 to the end**.

One reader, having read this section of the text said: 'Even though Hortense makes obvious mistakes that make her look foolish, we find ourselves warming to her.'

To what extent do you agree?

In your response, you could:

- consider your own impressions of Hortense
- evaluate how the writer conveys Hortense's thoughts and feelings
- support your opinions with references to the text.

[20 marks]

Paper 1 Section B: Writing
Introduction and advice

KNOWIT!

☞ Question 5 of Paper 1 Section B: Writing will ask you to write **creatively**, inspired by a topic linked to the texts in the reading section of Paper 1.

☞ There will only be two tasks and you must choose **one** of them.

☞ You should spend 45 minutes on the planning and writing.

☞ There are 40 marks for the writing task.

- 24 of the marks are for content – your ideas and information and organisation – how you organise the content

- 16 of the marks are for technical accuracy – spelling, punctuation and grammar.

☞ The question (the task) will give you a context for your writing: an audience (reader), purpose and form. This context will apply to both writing tasks. The purpose will be to describe or to narrate.

☞ The stimulus for one of the two questions will be a picture.

NAILIT!

Spend 45 minutes on planning, writing and checking your work:

- 5 minutes preparing and planning
- 35 minutes writing
- 5 minutes checking and correcti[ng]

There are five possible sorts of task that can be set on this paper:

Question type 1: descriptive writing with a visual stimulus

An environmental organisation is planning a booklet of writing by young people under the title: 'When nature hits back'.

Entries for the booklet will be chosen by four senior civil servants in the government's Environment Agency.

Write a description suggested by the picture.

Question type 2: descriptive writing without a visual stimulus

Describe an occasion when you had to make a difficult decision.

Focus on the thoughts and feelings you had at that time.

Question type 3: narrative with a visual stimulus

Write a story set during a flood as suggested by the picture.

Question type 4: narrative – writing the opening to a story

Write the opening part of a story about an unusual journey.

Question type 5: narrative – writing a complete story

Write a story about a misunderstanding.

Question type 1: descriptive writing with a visual stimulus

Here is an example question:

A charity is running a creative writing competition under the title: 'Street life'.

Entries for the competition will be judged by a panel of leaders of large companies.

Write a description suggested by this picture:

(24 marks for content and organisation
16 marks for technical accuracy)
[40 marks]

PREPAREIT!

Prepare the question by underlining the key words and annotating it with your initial thoughts and ideas. Annotate the image with some notes about what you can see.

PLANIT!

Use the four boxes below to plan your answer.

Paragraph 1:

Paragraph 2:

Paragraph 3:

Paragraph 4:

DOIT!

Use the space below to write an opening paragraph for the 'Street life' competition task. Then use your own paper to write the rest of your description.

....

....

....

....

....

....

DOIT!

Now have a go at answering the *descriptive writing with a visual stimulus* question on page 192. Use your own paper to prepare and plan your answer as you have done above.

Question type 2: descriptive writing without a visual stimulus

Here is an example question:

Describe an occasion when something exciting happened. Focus on the thoughts and feelings you had at that time.

(24 marks for content and organisation
16 marks for technical accuracy)

[40 marks]

PREPAREIT!

Underline the key words in the question, so that you are sure what the question is asking you to do. Jot down some of your first thoughts and ideas.

NAILIT!

Make sure you **describe**. Don't just tell a story.

PLANIT!

Use the four boxes below to plan your answer. A few ideas on how to organise the question have been suggested, but you don't have to use them.

Paragraph 1: anticipation of the event or what life was like before if the event was unexpected. Describe mood, feelings.

Paragraph 2: start of event. Describe details, especially sights, sounds, and so on.

Paragraph 3: during the event/event develops.

Paragraph 4: after the event/results of the event. Feelings now.

DO IT!

Use the space below to answer the question. Continue on your own paper.

....

....

....

....

....

....

....

....

....

....

....

....

....

....

....

....

....

....

....

DO IT!

Now have a go at answering the *descriptive writing without a visual stimulus* question on page 192. Use your own paper to prepare, plan and answer your question.

NAILIT!

Check through your writing. Make sure you have:

- used an appropriate style, tone and vocabulary
- not made any careless mistakes.

Question type 3: narrative with a visual stimulus

Here is an example question:

You are going to enter a creative writing competition.

Your entry will be judged by a panel of people of your own age.

Write a story suggested by this picture:

(24 marks for content and organisation
16 marks for technical accuracy)
[40 marks]

PREPAREIT!

Prepare the question by underlining the key words and annotating it with your initial thoughts and ideas. Annotate the image with some notes about what you can see.

PLANIT!

Use the boxes below to gather your thoughts and ideas and plan your answer.

NAILIT!

Before you write the opener to your story, you should ask yourself the following questions:

- How can I use language that is clear and creative?
- How will I engage my reader straight away?

DOIT!

Write the opening of the story in the space provided.

DO IT!

Use the space below to continue your story suggested by the balloon picture. Continue on your own paper if necessary.

....

....

....

....

....

....

....

....

....

....

....

....

....

....

....

....

....

....

....

....

....

DO IT!

Now have a go at answering the *narrative with a visual stimulus* question on page 192. Use your own paper to prepare, plan and answer your question.

Question type 4: narrative – writing the opening to a story

Here is an example question:

> Write the opening of a story called 'Getting away'.
>
> (24 marks for content and organisation
> 16 marks for technical accuracy)
> **[40 marks]**

PREPAREIT!

Prepare the question by underlining the key words and annotating it with your initial thoughts and ideas.

WORKIT!

Here is the beginning of one student's opening to their 'Getting away' story:

> At last Tessa was ready. The oars were neatly stacked in the boat along with all the water and food and equipment and everything she might need on her journey. She pushed hard and finally the boat began to scrunch along the sand until it got into the water. She could feel her injured arm aching with every movement, but she pushed and pushed until the boat was floating about. Now she felt a lot of joy because she was getting away. Suddenly her enthusiasm changed to worry because of how long would she be on her own on the sea? Could she survive long enough? She didn't know.

Look at the mark scheme on page 174. Decide whether the writing currently fits most closely into Band 2 or Band 3. Now rewrite the beginning of the opening so that you improve it. Use the mark scheme descriptors to guide your improvements.

PLANIT!

Plan your own opening of a story called 'Getting away' in the space below.

DOIT!

Write the opening of your story called 'Getting away' in the space provided and continue on your own paper.

DO IT!

Now try this question using the space below. Continue on your own paper if necessary. Remember to prepare and plan!

An accident prevention charity is planning to publish a series of stories about risks for children during school holidays. You have been invited to do some creative writing for the series.

Write the opening of a story called 'The dare'.

(24 marks for content and organisation
16 marks for technical accuracy)
[40 marks]

DO IT!

Have a go at answering the *narrative – writing the opening to a story* question on page 192. Use your own paper to prepare, plan and answer your question.

Question type 5: narrative – writing a complete story

Here is an example question:

You have been invited to produce a piece of creative writing set in one place.

Write a story about something that happens in an empty building.

(24 marks for content and organisation
16 marks for technical accuracy)
[40 marks]

PREPAREIT!

Underline the key words in the question, so that you are sure what the question is asking you to do. Jot down some of your first thoughts and ideas.

WORKIT!

Here is part of one student's answer. Notice how the student is trying to develop the story at this point.

... became less confident. His behaviour became less joky and carefree. He too was beginning to think about what might happen next.

Omran had lost his confidence long ago. He hated cobwebs and dark, damp places, but he pushed on until he could no longer hear the others wimpering and whining. He could not see anything now and so he held out his hands and tried to feel what was ahead. He stumbled occasionally as he went forward and he had to reach out to find something to help him keep his balance so that he wouldn't just fall flat on his face into something nasty. Then he reached something solid that he couldn't get past.

Look at the mark scheme on page 174. Decide whether the writing currently fits most closely into Band 2 or Band 3. Rewrite this part of the story so that you improve it in the space provided below. Use the mark scheme descriptors to guide your improvements.

....

....

....

....

....

....

....

Write the rest of the 'empty building' story on a separate piece of paper.

DO IT!

Now try this question. Remember to prepare and plan! Use the space below and continue on your own paper if necessary.

You are going to enter a creative writing competition.

Your entry will be judged by a panel of people of your own age.

Write a story about two teenagers who get lost together.

(24 marks for content and organisation
16 marks for technical accuracy)
[40 marks]

....

....

....

....

....

....

....

....

....

....

....

....

....

....

....

....

DO IT!

Have a go at answering the *narrative – writing a complete story* question on page 192. Use your own paper to prepare, plan and answer your question.

Paper 2 Section A: Reading
Introduction and advice

KNOWIT!

There are two sections in Paper 2. Section A: Reading comes first.

You will be given two linked sources from different time periods and genres in order to consider how each presents a perspective or viewpoint to influence the reader. The sources will be non-fiction and literary non-fiction texts. They will be drawn from the 19th century, and either the 20th or 21st century. The texts may include:

☞ articles

☞ reports

☞ essays

☞ articles

☞ letters

☞ diaries.

Here is a rough guide to how you should allocate your time:

☞ Spend 15 minutes reading the two texts and the four questions you are given.

☞ Spend 40 minutes answering the four questions.

☞ Leave 5 minutes at the end to check your answers.

The questions have different focuses and are worth different amounts of marks. Here are the focuses, mark allocations and how long you should spend answering each question:

☞ Question 1: identify and interpret explicit and implicit information and ideas (4 marks/4 minutes).

☞ Question 2: select and synthesise evidence from different texts (8 marks/8 minutes).

☞ Question 3: how writers use language to achieve effects and influence readers (12 marks/12 minutes).

☞ Question 4: compare writers' ideas and perspectives, and how these are conveyed (16 marks/16 minutes).

On pages 206 and 207 are examples of the sorts of text you will get in Paper 2 Section A.

Source A – 21st century non-fiction

From 'A beginner's guide to wild camping gear'

Wild camping will obviously mean carrying everything you need with you, so with everything you take, consider the weight.

You'll be needing:

Shelter: Most likely a tent, but that's not the end of the story.

5 **Sleeping bag and mat**: Your bed for the night: do not underestimate the importance of a good night's sleep!

Food, drink & some way of cooking it: You need fuel for your body and fuel to cook it with. We'll check out a few different approaches.

Clothing: General outdoor wear, naturally, but we'll examine how to
10 give it a wild camping slant.

Rucksack: Simply put – big enough but not too big; comfortable to carry.

A few choice extras to make it all more comfortable.

Let's start with shelter…

Tent

15 You'll notice we said 'shelter' just then. Well, by and large, this will mean a tent, but there are other options. In fact, those other options would be regarded by some as the very essence of wild camping, but we'll come to those ideas later.

If you're intending to wild camp, you should try to avoid brightly
20 coloured tents. That needn't mean obsessively searching out something with a camo-print flysheet, but if you're trying to blend in discreetly and not be noticed, vibrant orange isn't very sensible.

The 'best' tent is the one which offers the best trade-off between comfort when you're in it and comfort when you're carrying it. Where that balance
25 should be struck is different for everyone, so you'll have to make that judgement for yourself. Bear in mind though, this is not really a luxury activity, and you're likely to be somewhere remote… which means carrying it a fair old way. You don't want to be cursing the weight on your back with every overloaded step you take. Most of your time inside the
30 tent will be spent sleeping, most of the time carrying it you'll be awake! For that reason, for the sake of being unobtrusive, and because big tents don't fit easily into small spaces, small and light is a good bet…

Other shelters that are not tents

If you really want to go simple, discreet and light, then look into bivi-bags.
35 Essentially a waterproof cover for a sleeping bag – with maybe enough room for your rucksack too – they certainly tick the 'small and light' box. Some are exactly as I've just described: when you zip it closed, you'll have a face full of cloth. Some are a bit more structured, with one or two short hoops to lift the fabric clear of you, making something akin to a sleeping-
40 bag-sized tunnel tent. Not everybody's cup of tea, but if you're happy to sacrifice living space of any description, bivis definitely have the advantage over tents. They're light, tiny, frequently made in murky colours, and however severe the wind may be, it's pretty difficult to flatten something that's already flat on the floor!

Source B – 19th century literary non-fiction

From *Travels with a Donkey in the Cévennes* by Robert Louis Stevenson, published in 1879. Here Stevenson explains how he prepared to set out on a long hike on his own.

It was already hard upon October before I was ready to set forth, and at the high altitudes over which my road lay there was no Indian summer to be looked for. A traveller of my sort was a thing hitherto unheard of in that district.

5 I was looked upon with contempt, like a man who should project a journey to the moon. I was determined to have the means of camping out in my possession; for there is nothing more harassing to an easy mind than the necessity of reaching shelter by dusk, and the hospitality

10 of a village inn is not always to be reckoned sure by those who trudge on foot. A tent is troublesome to pitch, and troublesome to strike again. A sleeping-sack, on the other hand, is always ready—you have only to get into it; it serves a double purpose—a bed by night, a portmanteau

15 by day; and it does not advertise your intention of camping out to every curious passer-by. This is a huge point. If a camp is not secret, it is but a troubled resting-place; you become a public character; the convivial rustic visits your bedside after an early supper; and you must sleep with

20 one eye open, and be up before the day. I decided on a sleeping-sack.

This child of my invention was nearly six feet square, exclusive of two triangular flaps to serve as a pillow by night and as the top and bottom of the sack by day. I call it

25 'the sack,' but it was never a sack by more than courtesy: only a sort of long roll or sausage, green waterproof cart-cloth without and blue sheep's fur within. I could bury myself in it up to the neck; for my head I trusted to a fur cap, with a hood to fold down over my ears and a band to

30 pass under my nose like a respirator; and in case of heavy rain I proposed to make myself a little tent, or tentlet, with my waterproof coat, three stones, and a bent branch.

It will readily be conceived that I could not carry this huge package on my own, merely human, shoulders. It

35 remained to choose a beast of burden. What I required was something cheap and small and hardy, and of a stolid and peaceful temper; and all these requisites pointed to a donkey.

Question 1

Here is an example Question 1:

Read again **Source A** from **lines 23 to 32**.

Choose **four** statements below which are TRUE.

- Shade the boxes of the ones that you think are true.
- Choose a maximum of four statements.

[4 marks]

A	Always choose a tent that will be very comfortable to be inside.	
B	The best tent is one that is fairly comfortable to carry and to lie in.	
C	Some people think it is more important for a tent to be comfortable to carry than comfortable to sleep in.	
D	You won't have to carry your tent a long way.	
E	You don't need to worry about how heavy your tent is because most of the time you will be sleeping in it.	
F	Sometimes you will be hiking asleep.	
G	It is important not to draw attention to yourself when you are camping.	
H	A tent that is big and light is a good choice.	

PREPAREIT!

Look at the text extract below, also on the subject of outdoor activities. In the table that follows are some pieces of information we get from the text. Explain how we have to infer information in order to know that the statement is true. One statement is already explained to guide you.

Solo backpacking can be a thrilling experience. However, when planning a trip, throwing caution to the wind is not wise. Attention to detail will keep you safe and happy, and will avoid the misery of humping 25 kilos of unnecessary weight through a mosquito-infested marsh at night.

True statement	Inferred from
Backpacking on your own can be a great experience.	Solo is a synonym for 'on your own'. We need to know that, in order to say the statement is true.
It is wise to plan carefully.	
Your safety and happiness will depend on good planning.	
Poor planning will lead to avoidable miseries.	

WORKIT!

Here is another example Question 1. A student has chosen one statement that is true.

Read again **Source A** from **lines 1 to 22**.

Choose **four** statements below which are TRUE.

- Shade the boxes of the statements that you think are true.
- Choose a maximum of four statements.   **[4 marks]**

Statement A is true. Here are the words from Source A that prove the statement: '... that's not the end of the story'. You have to interpret a colloquial expression to realise that you are being told that there is more to shelter than just tents.

A	There is more to shelter than a tent.	
B	There is no need to worry about the weight of items you take with you.	
C	Sleep is not very important when you are wild camping.	
D	There are different ways of cooking food when you are wild camping.	
E	Your rucksack should only be as big as absolutely necessary.	
F	All wild campers think tents are essential.	
G	Tents should be a colour that makes them noticeable.	
H	Wild camping tents should not be orange.	

Find and shade the box next to the remaining three true statements. Underline the words in **Source A** which provide the best evidence for the statement.

NAILIT!

Read carefully, inferring information where necessary. Only mark the number of boxes you are asked to – the ones next to the true statements.

Read again **Source A** from **lines 23 to 32**.

Choose **four** statements below which are TRUE.

- Shade the boxes of the ones that you think are true.
- Choose a maximum of four statements.   **[4 marks]**

A	Always choose a tent that will be very comfortable to be inside.	
B	The best tent is one that is fairly comfortable to carry and to lie in.	
C	Some people think it is more important for a tent to be comfortable to carry than comfortable to sleep in.	
D	You won't have to carry your tent a long way.	
E	You don't need to worry about how heavy your tent is because most of the time you will be sleeping in it.	
F	Sometimes you will be hiking asleep.	
G	It is important not to draw attention to yourself when you are camping.	
H	A tent that is big and light is a good choice.	

Question 2

Here is an example Question 2:

You need to refer to **Source A** and **Source B** for this question.

Use details from **both** Sources. Write a summary of the similarities between the preparations for sleeping outdoors advised in Source A and described in Source B.

[8 marks]

PREPAREIT!

What **two** things are you asked to write about? Tick two boxes.

Similarities ☐

Differences ☐

Similarities and differences ☐

Preparations for sleeping outdoors ☐

The best time to go camping ☐

NAILIT!

In the exam you will be asked about similarities **or** differences **or** a combination of the two.

Find and underline details in both Source A and Source B that relate to these two things.

PLANIT!

Use the table below to identify **similar** information from the two sources. The table is partly filled in for you.

Aspect of preparation	Source A	Source B	What's similar? What can I infer?
Shelter	Some are opposed to tents.		
Carrying equipment			
Being discreet	'blend in'; 'not be noticed'; 'unobtrusive'	'secret' camp; not carrying a tent 'does not advertise your intention of camping'	Neither of them wants the camp to be noticed by others.
Sleeping without a tent			

DOIT!

Now have a go at answering the question in full. Use the space provided below and then continue on your own writing paper.

....

....

....

....

....

....

....

....

....

....

....

....

....

....

....

....

....

....

....

....

....

....

NAILIT!

In this exam a 'summary' means a simple and accurate explanation in your own words (but perhaps with some very brief quotations). Use appropriate connecting words and phrases to point out similarities or differences: for example, however, whereas, just as, like, in the same way, and so on.

DOIT!

Here is another example question for you to answer. It uses the two sources you have been working on.

Write your answer in the space below and continue on your own paper.

You need to refer to **Source A** and **Source B** for this question.

There are both similarities and differences in the sources' attitudes towards wild camping. Use details from **both** sources to write a summary of the similarities and differences.

[8 marks]

....

....

....

....

....

....

....

....

....

....

....

....

....

....

....

....

....

NAILIT!

- Underline the key words in the question. Then in the two sources of information, underline information relating to the key words.
- Use a simple table to bring relevant information together.
- Write about both sources together, or write about one, then the other.

KNOWIT!

☞ This question will always be about how the writer of one source uses language to influence the reader. You will need to use relevant subject terminology and details from the text to support your views.

☞ You should spend 12 minutes on this question.

☞ It is worth 12 marks.

Here is an example question:

> You now need to refer **only** to **Source B**, from **line 16** ('This is a huge...') **to the end**.
>
> How does Stevenson use language to convince us that he has prepared well?
>
> **[12 marks]**

PREPAREIT!

You need to be clear about the difference between content and language: in other words, the difference between *what* is said and *how* it is said. Here are six statements that might be used in an answer to the question above. However, two of the statements are only about *content*, not *language*. Shade those two statements:

A	He gives a lot of reasons why you must not let people know you will be camping.	A
B	He uses a sudden short sentence in order to sound decisive and as though he knows what he is talking about.	
C	He uses metaphors to make his descriptions more appealing.	
D	He uses lists of details that build in momentum, making it sound like he has everything covered.	
E	He mentions lots of ways to sleep warmly and comfortably.	
F	He uses a semicolon to separate a problem and his solution, thus creating suspense before the solution, so that it surprises us and makes it sound clever and original.	

NAILIT!

Writing about language means mentioning some specific techniques and commenting on their **effect**.

NAILIT!

Write only about the part of the source that is given in the question.

PLANIT!

Use the table below to analyse some language techniques you find in Source B. Some of the table has been filled in to help you.

Language feature	Example	Effect
Sudden short sentence	'I decided on a sleeping-sack.'	Coming at the end of a long sentence full of problems, the shortness of this sentence sounds decisive and as though he knows what he is talking about.
Metaphor		

DO IT!

Now have a go at writing the answer to the question. Continue on your own paper.

....

....

....

....

....

....

....

....

....

....

DO IT!

Here is another example Question 3 for you to answer. Use the space below and continue on your own paper.

You now need to refer **only** to **Source B,** from the **beginning to line 21**.

How does Stevenson use language to show his feelings about the trip he is planning?

[12 marks]

Question 4

Here is an example Question 4:

For this question, you need to refer to the **whole of Source A,** together with **Source B**.

Compare how the two writers convey their different views and experiences of camping and hiking.

In your answer, you could:

- compare their different views and experiences

- compare the methods they use to convey those views and experiences

- support your ideas with references to both texts.

[16 marks]

PLANIT!

After you have prepared the question for one minute, you should plan your answer. Here is a plan started by another student. Add further evidence supporting **different** views and experiences.

	Source A	Source B
Views	Confident, friendly and humorous	Sounds a bit resentful
Experiences	Sounds very experienced	Has had experience it seems
Details/evidence	Often informal ('a good bet')	Uses present tense to shift into advice rather than narrative: 'A tent is...' Shows wisdom of experience

NAILIT!

Plan your answer either by using a comparison and evidence chart, or – more informally – by annotating the source itself, underlining details and writing notes in the margin.

DO IT!

Write your answer to the question about how the two writers convey their different views and experiences of camping and hiking. Continue on your own paper.

....

....

....

....

....

....

....

....

....

....

....

....

....

....

....

....

....

....

....

....

....

....

....

....

DO IT!

Here is another question for you to answer. Use the space below and continue on your own paper.

For this question, you need to refer to the **whole of Source A**, together with **Source B**.

Compare how the two writers convey their different attitudes to wild camping.

In your answer, you could:

- compare their attitudes
- compare the methods they use to convey those attitudes
- support your ideas with references to both texts.

[16 marks]

Paper 2 Section B: Writing
Introduction and advice

KNOWIT!

☞ The exam question will ask you to express your own **personal viewpoint** on a topic that is linked to the texts in the reading section of Paper 2.

☞ There will be just one writing task: you will **not** have a choice.

☞ You should spend 45 minutes on the planning and writing.

☞ There are 40 marks for the writing task.

  • 24 of the marks are for content and organisation.

  • 16 of the marks are for technical accuracy – spelling, vocabulary, punctuation and grammar (see page 225).

☞ The question (the task) will give you a specific audience (reader). For example, you might be asked to write to parents, a school governor or the readers of a local newspaper.

☞ The question will also state a purpose and a form from the following lists:

Purposes	Forms
• to explain (a point of view)	• a letter
• to instruct or advise	• an article (such as, for a newspaper)
• to argue	• the text for a leaflet
• to persuade	• a speech

Here are some examples of a Question 5:

'The internet can be a very unsafe place for children. Parents should supervise their children's use of computers and smart phones.'

Write the text for a leaflet advising parents on how they can help to protect their children's safety online.

(24 marks for content and organisation
16 marks for technical accuracy)
[40 marks]

'The government must control the amount of fat and sugar young people eat and drink. Obesity is too big an issue to be left to individuals to make their own decisions.'

Write a speech for a debating competition judged by teachers, arguing for or against this statement.

(24 marks for content and organisation
16 marks for technical accuracy)
[40 marks]

NAILIT!

Aim to spend your time as follows:

- 5 minutes preparing and planning
- 35 minutes writing
- 5 minutes checking and correcting.

NAILIT!

Make sure you:

- identify the audience, purpose and form
- make sense of the statement
- are clear about exactly what you must do.

WORKIT!

Here is an example of how a student has 'marked up' a question to prepare it.

> Statement to stir up my opinion: youth, rights, futures (emotive words)

'The age for voting in elections should be lowered to 16. Young people should have the right to vote on the issues that will influence their future lives.'

Purpose

Write an article for your local newspaper in which you explain your point of view on this statement.

Form

Audience

> I need to explain my views on whether the voting age should go down to 16. Keep it formal.

The student has read the statement carefully and has identified the audience, purpose and form in the question. The student has made a clear note about what they have to do, to avoid misreading the question.

PREPAREIT!

Choose one of the examples of a Question 5 and think about the following carefully.

Who is the audience? _____

What is the subject matter? _____

What form is needed? _____

What is the purpose? _____

DOIT!

Now annotate the Question 5 that you have chosen with some ideas.

PLANIT!

Below is a student's quick six-paragraph plan in answer to the question about lowering the voting age. Note that the plan includes ideas as well as notes on suitable language and tone.

Introduction: Say I'm in favour. Show that I've thought it through and have a number of reasons. Sound reasonable/thoughtful. Each reason will be a paragraph (below). After a great deal of thought/although I realise that... Mention a recent national vote.
Point 1: Responsibility and pressures – GCSE, education. We must be mature enough.
Point 2: How can we take responsibility if we are not allowed to take part in the decisions that will determine our futures? (but be respectful to older people and their judgement)
Point 3: They had vote at 16 in the Scottish referendum. Need to be consistent. Wasn't a disaster.
Point 4: It's our future. Result of vote will have even more impact on our young lives. (Acknowledge other side to show I've thought it through: 'While some people will say that...' However... Despite that... If it's really true that... then.) Don't be too pushy.
Conclusion: The most important point... Maturity? Responsibility? Strong 'sign off'. Refer back to first paragraph for neatness.

Now create your a plan for your chosen question in the space provided below.

WORKIT!

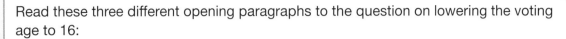

Read these three different opening paragraphs to the question on lowering the voting age to 16:

A

People who read this newspaper are very interested in politics and they were probably also very interested when they were young so they would probably have wanted to be allowed to vote when they were as young as 16. Nowadays, we have to wait until we are 18 to vote, but why? I am going to explain why I believe that the voting age should be reduced to 16 so that people can get involved in politics from an early age. We need more people to be involved because there are less and less people voting in elections – it's like it's going out of fashion. Getting the voting age down to 16 will create a new zest for the political process and an energised electorate.

B

I would like to see the voting age lowered to 16. 18-year-olds can vote at the moment but there isn't much difference between an 18-year-old and a 16-year-old. They are really almost the same age. Some 16-year-olds are much more mature than some 18-year-olds even so why can't 16-year-olds have the vote? Give us the vote!

C

In the recent Scottish referendum on independence, the voting franchise was extended to 16-year-olds. At the time, many older people complained that this would create havoc because young people could not be expected to understand the complex issues involved, and to cast their vote sensibly. However, I would like to argue that far from provoking chaos, extending the vote to younger people has been a great success: it generated excitement around a very important referendum, and it enthused young people about the political process in a way that can only be good for our democracy.

Look at the mark scheme on page 174 and then rank the three paragraphs in order of effectiveness.

NAILIT!

The first paragraph of your writing is crucial. In that opening you need to reassure the exam marker that you can get the right style, tone and vocabulary for the task you have been given.

In the opening you must think carefully about:

- audience
- purpose
- form.

WORKIT!

Here is one paragraph from a student's answer to the question on lowering the voting age. Read the paragraph and the exam marker's notes and comments.

> Rather vague vocab - 'old days', 'got'

> I/you – engaging, but perhaps too informal

> 'lower' is clumsy used like this

In the old days almost no one had the vote. More and more people were given the vote during Victorian times and just after. At first men got the vote, and then women above thirty got the vote, and then everyone over twenty-one got the vote. Eventually - I think in the 1970s - the voting age for everyone was lowered to 18. You can see how more and more people and younger and younger people have been given the vote. I think it's inevitable that the voting age will lower to sixteen. If sixteen is not right now, then why was eighteen right many years ago?

This is clearly expressed and the paragraph is effectively organised so that it leads logically to its conclusion. Perhaps the central point - inevitability - should have been at the start though? The language and tone is mainly suitable, although it could be more formal and precise. It could have more authority. Repetition and the final rhetorical question give some force to the argument, but the paragraph is better on persuasion than explanation. This paragraph suggests the answer will just reach into Band 3.

How could you improve this student's answer? Use the space below to rewrite the paragraph so that it is firmly in Band 4.

....
....
....
....
....
....
....
....
....
....
....
....

Writing: Technical accuracy

KNOW IT!

☞ The mark scheme for content and organisation covers 24 of the 40 marks for the Paper 2 Section B: writing question.

☞ The other 16 marks are for technical accuracy: **spelling**, **punctuation**, **vocabulary** and **grammar**. You can find the mark scheme for technical accuracy on page 177.

WORK IT!

Below is one paragraph from a student's answer to the question on lowering the voting age. Read the paragraph and the exam marker's comment at the end.

Keep referring back to the mark scheme on page 177.

> The most important thing to consider is not how old a voater is, but how machure they are, some people are old and immachure and some people are young and very machure, instead of giving anyone a voat when they reach a curtain age it might be better to give them a test to find out how sensable they are. Some voaters mite find they fale this test in later life; they woud have to hand back there voat as well as there driving license so there mite be some voaters who are 16 and other ex-voaters who are 75.

The exam marker says:

```
The student sometimes uses a comma when they should be ending a
sentence with a full stop. However, sentences are well constructed
and are often effective: they make the point with force and
originality. The semi-colon usefully introduces a connected
thought. There is some range of punctuation. The vocabulary hints
at some sophistication (voter, sensible, immature) but these more
ambitious words are almost always misspelt. For technical accuracy
this answer is in Band 2.
```

In this piece of writing:

- there are 18 spelling mistakes (including some words spelled incorrectly more than once)
- two commas have been used instead of a full stop and a colon
- at least one comma has been missed out.

Use the space below and your own paper if necessary to rewrite the student's paragraph so that it is firmly in Band 4. Look again at the band descriptors, the exam marker's comment and the list of mistakes, and use them to guide your writing. Don't just correct the writing: improve it.

DO IT!

Now write your own opening paragraph below for the question that you prepared and planned on pages 221 and 222.

....

....

....

....

....

....

....

....

....

....

....

....

....

....

....

....

....

....

....

....

....

....

NAILIT!

Before you write your paragraph, ask yourself the following questions:

- Have I prepared and planned the question?
- Am I ready to use formal language?
- How will I engage my reader in an appropriate way?
- Am I aware of the mark schemes and how these might help me?

WORKIT!

When you plan your writing, decide the topic of each paragraph, and the best order for these paragraphs.

Here are the second and third paragraphs of a student's writing about lowering the voting age. Next to the writing are some comments by an exam marker:

It would be very arrogant for a young person like me to lecture readers on this subject. After all, I have only been alive for 16 years, so what do I know about the sort of responsibility that probably comes with having children, finding jobs and paying a mortgage? However, what teenagers lack in experience they more than make up for in enthusiasm and determination. When we study for our GCSEs we learn to handle pressure and we learn to make mature decisions that will potentially influence the rest of our lives.

This maturity does not arrive all at once: it comes bit-by-painful bit as we get ourselves ready for the real world of qualifications and careers and we prove ourselves to be worthy of responsibility. But we can only prove ourselves if we are given opportunities. One valuable opportunity is taking a full part in decisions that determine our future, a future which – if we are as lucky as many of you – will stretch into decades ahead. Taking part in elections is a perfect way to become fully responsible citizens. I am convinced – and I hope you will agree – that being trusted with something as important as the vote, will make us more trustworthy people.

- Acknowledges opposite view.
- Long, well-controlled, flowing sentence for impressive effect.
- Contrasting shorter sentence for effect.
- Learn… learn: student often uses repetition for effect and to connect ideas.
- 'This maturity' makes neat link with previous paragraph, and shows development of argument.
- Gives central example of an opportunity.
- Logical sequencing/ conclusion of ideas makes it hard for the reader to disagree.

This writing targets purpose, form and audience very successfully, as well as meeting requirements for technical accuracy. It is an answer at the top of Band 4.

Now on a separate piece of paper, write your own second and third paragraphs for the question you have been preparing.

DO IT!

Below is another example exam question for you to work on. Use the space below and continue on your own paper.

'The internet has greatly improved our lives. It's hard to imagine how we ever lived without it.'

Write a magazine article in which you explain your point of view on this statement.

(24 marks for content and organisation

16 marks for technical accuracy)

[40 marks]

....

....

....

....

....

....

....

....

....

....

....

....

....

....

....

....

....

....

....

....

NAIL IT!

Make sure you:

- prepare the question
- plan your answer
- write your answer with a good opening and linked paragraphs
- check for technical accuracy.

ENGLISH LITERATURE

KNOWIT!

There are two English Literature papers:

☞ Paper 1: Shakespeare and the 19th-century novel lasts 1 hour 45 minutes, and is worth 40 per cent of the GCSE.

☞ Paper 2: Modern texts and poetry lasts 2 hours 15 minutes, and is worth 60 per cent of the GCSE.

Here is a simplified mark scheme for the papers:

Descriptors	Band 3	Band 4	Band 5	Band 6
	The student answer…	The student answer…	The student answer…	The student answer…
AO1 Read, understand and respond Use evidence	• often explains the text in relation to the task • uses references to support a range of relevant comments.	• clearly explains the text in relation to the task • uses references to support explanations effectively.	• thoughtfully explains the text in relation to the task • integrates apt references into the answer.	• critically explains the text in relation to the task • integrates references into the answer very precisely.
AO2 Language, form and structure Subject terminology	• comments on the writer's methods, and the effects these have on the reader • uses some relevant terminology.	• clearly explains the writer's methods, and the effects these have on the reader • uses relevant terminology appropriately.	• effectively explains the writer's methods, and the effects these have on the reader • uses relevant terminology effectively.	• precisely explains the writer's methods, and the effects these have on the reader • uses relevant terminology precisely.
AO3 Contexts (**not** relevant to the unseen poetry question)	• shows some understanding of the significance of context.	• shows a clear understanding of the significance of specific contexts.	• shows a thoughtful consideration of the significance of specific contexts.	• shows a critical consideration of the significance of specific contexts.

Contexts

AO3 (Contexts) is worth far fewer marks than AO1 or AO2, but it is important. You will find some advice on writing about contexts on the following pages.

Spelling, punctuation and grammar (SPaG)

Two questions have four additional marks available for spelling, punctuation and grammar (AO4). To get these marks you must take care to express yourself clearly and accurately.

The two questions tested for SPaG are the Shakespeare question on Paper 1, and the modern texts question on Paper 2.

Paper 1 Section A: Shakespeare

KNOWIT!

☞ You will answer the question on the Shakespeare play that you have studied, either: *Macbeth, Romeo and Juliet, Much Ado About Nothing, The Merchant of Venice, The Tempest* or *Julius Caesar.*

☞ You will be given an extract from the play, and you will be asked to write about the extract and the whole play.

☞ You should spend 55 minutes on this section.

☞ There are 34 marks available – 30 are for the content of your answer and 4 are for spelling, punctuation and grammar.

Questions will follow the format below. This question is about *Macbeth:*

Read the following extract from Act 5 Scene 5 of *Macbeth* and then answer the question that follows.

At this point in the play Macbeth is reacting to his wife's death.

MACBETH
I have almost forgot the taste of fears;
The time has been, my senses would have cool'd
To hear a night-shriek; and my fell of hair
5   Would at a dismal treatise rouse and stir
As life were in't: I have supp'd full with horrors;
Direness, familiar to my slaughterous thoughts
Cannot once start me.

Re-enter SEYTON

10   Wherefore was that cry?

SEYTON
The queen, my lord, is dead.

MACBETH
She should have died hereafter;
15   There would have been a time for such a word.
To-morrow, and to-morrow, and to-morrow,
Creeps in this petty pace from day to day
To the last syllable of recorded time,
And all our yesterdays have lighted fools
20   The way to dusty death. Out, out, brief candle!
Life's but a walking shadow, a poor player
That struts and frets his hour upon the stage
And then is heard no more: it is a tale
Told by an idiot, full of sound and fury,
25   Signifying nothing.

Starting with this moment in the play, do you think Shakespeare presents Macbeth as a thoughtful character?

Write about:

• what Macbeth's thoughts are at this point

• how Shakespeare presents Macbeth's thoughts in the play as a whole.

[30 marks]

AO4 [4 marks]

All of the questions in this section will follow this format and you should use the bullet points to guide you when you write your answer.

Below are some example questions and extract references for all of the Shakespeare plays covered in this section.

Macbeth Act 3 Scene 1 Lines 1–10	Starting with this extract, how does Shakespeare present suspicions about Macbeth? Write about: • how Shakespeare presents Banquo's suspicions in this speech • how Shakespeare presents suspicions about Macbeth in the play as a whole.
Romeo and Juliet Act 1 Scene 5 Line 92 ('If I profane…') to Line 109 ('… my sin again')	Starting with this extract, explain how Shakespeare presents the relationship between Romeo and Juliet. Write about: • how Shakespeare presents the relationship between Romeo and Juliet in this conversation • how Shakespeare presents their relationship in the play as a whole.
Much Ado About Nothing Act 2 Scene 1 Line 50 ('Well niece…') to Line 65 ('… in my kindred')	Starting with this extract, explain how far you think Shakespeare presents Beatrice as a confident and witty woman. Write about: • how Shakespeare presents Beatrice in this conversation • how Shakespeare presents Beatrice in the play as a whole.
The Merchant of Venice Act 1 Scene 2 Line 53 ('God made…') to Line 72 ('… behaviour everywhere')	Starting with this extract, explain how far you think Shakespeare presents Portia as an independent woman. Write about: • how Shakespeare presents Portia in this conversation • how Shakespeare presents Portia in the play as a whole.
The Tempest Act 4 Scene 1 Line 147 (Be cheerful…) to Line 169 (… brain is troubled)	Starting with this extract, explore how Shakespeare presents the limits of Prospero's power. Write about: • how Shakespeare presents Prospero's powers in this speech • how Shakespeare presents Prospero's powers in the play as a whole.
Julius Caesar Act 1 Scene 3 Line 19 ('Besides…') to Line 32 ('… they point upon')	Starting with this extract, write about how Shakespeare explores fate in *Julius Caesar*. Write about: • how Shakespeare presents attitudes towards fate in this speech • how Shakespeare presents the role of fate in the play as a whole.

NAILIT!

• Read the question **before** you read the extract to give you a clear focus for your reading.

• Go back to the extract and spend at least five minutes reading it carefully and making some notes that are likely to be relevant to the question.

• Don't ignore the bullet points in the question. They are there to help you be relevant.

WORKIT!

It is important that you really understand the question and what it is asking you to do. You should 'prepare' the question.

Here is how one student prepared the question on *Macbeth*. Notice how they have underlined key words and made some notes about their first thoughts. This will help them to keep their answer sharp and relevant.

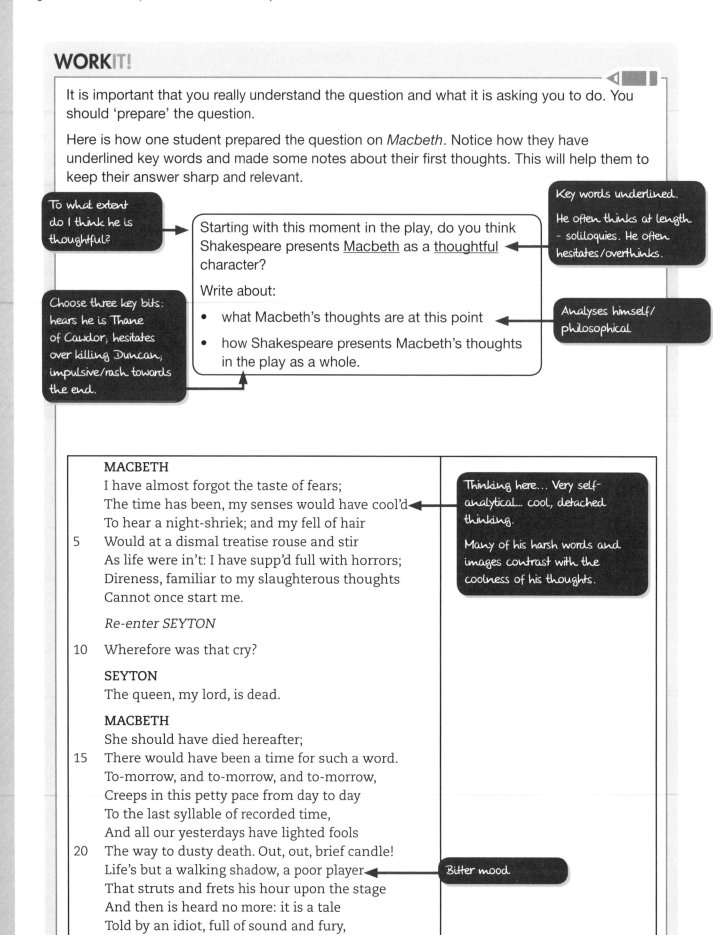

To what extent do I think he is thoughtful?

Key words underlined.
He often thinks at length – soliloquies. He often hesitates/overthinks.

Starting with this moment in the play, do you think Shakespeare presents Macbeth as a thoughtful character?

Write about:

- what Macbeth's thoughts are at this point

- how Shakespeare presents Macbeth's thoughts in the play as a whole.

Analyses himself/philosophical

Choose three key bits: hears he is Thane of Cawdor; hesitates over killing Duncan; impulsive/rash towards the end.

MACBETH
I have almost forgot the taste of fears;
The time has been, my senses would have cool'd
To hear a night-shriek; and my fell of hair
5   Would at a dismal treatise rouse and stir
As life were in't: I have supp'd full with horrors;
Direness, familiar to my slaughterous thoughts
Cannot once start me.

Re-enter SEYTON

10   Wherefore was that cry?

SEYTON
The queen, my lord, is dead.

MACBETH
She should have died hereafter;
15   There would have been a time for such a word.
To-morrow, and to-morrow, and to-morrow,
Creeps in this petty pace from day to day
To the last syllable of recorded time,
And all our yesterdays have lighted fools
20   The way to dusty death. Out, out, brief candle!
Life's but a walking shadow, a poor player
That struts and frets his hour upon the stage
And then is heard no more: it is a tale
Told by an idiot, full of sound and fury,
25   Signifying nothing.

Thinking here... Very self-analytical... cool, detached thinking.

Many of his harsh words and images contrast with the coolness of his thoughts.

Bitter mood

PREPAREIT!

Select a question from page 231 and make some notes to prepare it, as shown in the example on page 232. You can either base your answer on the extract suggested, or select a different passage from the play, which you can use to give evidence in support of your ideas.

Use the space below to prepare your question.

PREPAREIT!

PLANIT!

Once you have prepared the question, you should spend a few minutes planning the outline of your answer. This plan should be about:

- key ideas to include
- the content of each paragraph
- the order of the paragraphs.

Don't forget to:

- take note of the bullet points in the question
- compare the extract with two or three other relevant points in the text
- use evidence and subject terminology.

Below on the left is one student's plan for their answer to the question about Macbeth as a thoughtful character.

Paragraph 1
Write about the extract: Macbeth's thinking/state of mind here.
Paragraph 2
Vivid words/images; repetition; extended metaphor of 'player'.
Paragraph 3
Early in play when he reacts to news about promotion: "Look how our partner's rapt" (Banquo).
Paragraph 4
Decides not to kill Duncan: 'If it were done...' speech. His conscience.
Paragraph 5
Decision to slaughter Macduff and family 'before this purpose cool'.

Now use the boxes below to plan an answer to the question you have been preparing for *your* Shakespeare text.

Paragraph 1
Paragraph 2
Paragraph 3
Paragraph 4
Paragraph 5

WORKIT!

Here is part of one student's answer to the question about Macbeth as a thoughtful character. In the margin you will find a few notes made by an exam marker.

> **Very obvious, but good point!**

> **But what sort of thinker?**

> **Effective choices of quotation, well integrated, but could investigate how at least one of them works on the audience: what are the word's connotations?**

> **Quick consideration of significance of context – audiences in different eras.**

> **Good precise summary of Macbeth's state of mind at this point.**

...Shakespeare gives Macbeth soliloquies when he is speaking to himself, so he must be very thoughtful because no one is listening. In this speech, he uses many words to show the strength of his thoughts about how much he has changed: he knows he has 'supped full of horrors'. Putting supping (eating) and horrors together is shocking for the audience, and 'direness' and 'slaughterous' are equally vivid and emotive words that add to the shock for the audience, who have to know that this man is a deep thinker. It's like his mind is possessed. Of course audiences then might have been even more impressed then than they are now because a belief in the supernatural was probably even stronger. They might have concluded that he was literally possessed by the devil.

We shouldn't be surprised by Macbeth's thoughtfulness because even at the start of the play – when he is surprised by news of his promotion – we discover that he is not just a man of violent action, but also the sort of person who can be paralysed by his thinking. Banquo comments on, 'look how our partner's rapt.' He means that Macbeth has gone into a sort of trance of thinking...

Look at the checklist on page 236 and the mark scheme on page 229.

- Add to the comments the marker has already made.

- Write some advice in the space below for this student about what they have done well and how they might make their answer even better. Continue on your own paper.

....

....

....

....

....

....

....

....

....

....

....

DO IT!

Now using all the tools you have learned, write your own answer to the question you have prepared and planned on the play you have been studying. Try to spend only 40 minutes on your writing. Aim to write at least 500 words. You will need to use your own paper for this.

NAILIT!

Here is a checklist to make your answer as good as possible:

- Prepare and plan.
- Be aware of the mark scheme for literature (see page 229).
- Make clear, relevant points.
- Back up your points with examples, short quotations and other references to the text.
- Make sure you concentrate on *how* Shakespeare puts over his ideas.
- Make a *useful*, relevant point about context.
- Don't forget the marks for spelling, punctuation and grammar.
- When you finish your writing, spend between three and five minutes checking it over. Check that your answer makes sense and that you have not made any careless mistakes with spelling, punctuation and grammar.
- Check that you have used appropriate vocabulary, including subject terminology.

DO IT!

Try constructing your own questions for the play you have studied, based on the list of themes below. Then prepare, plan and answer your questions.

Play	Possible themes
Romeo and Juliet	Love, marriage, conflict, youth and age, reconciliation
The Tempest	Revenge, forgiveness, love, power, fatherhood, justice
The Merchant of Venice	Justice, mercy, race, fatherhood, deception
Julius Caesar	Power, loyalty, plotting, ambition
Macbeth	Evil, power, kingship, heroism, guilt, bravery, the supernatural
Much Ado About Nothing	Jealousy, men and women, love, law and order, loyalty

Paper 1 Section B: The 19th-century novel

Here is an example of the sort of extract and question you might be given. It is from *A Christmas Carol* by Charles Dickens.

Read the following extract from Stave 3 and then answer the question that follows.

In this extract, the second ghost has taken Scrooge to see the shops on Christmas morning.

> The people who were shovelling away on the house-tops were jovial and full of glee; calling out to one another from the parapets, and now and then exchanging a facetious snow-ball—better-natured missile far than many a wordy jest—laughing heartily if it went right, and not less
> 5 heartily if it went wrong. The poulterers' shops were still half open, and the fruiterers were radiant in their glory. There were great, round, pot-bellied baskets of chestnuts, shaped like the waistcoats of jolly old gentlemen, lolling at the doors, and tumbling out into the street in their apoplectic opulence. There were ruddy, brown-faced, broad-girthed
> 10 Spanish onions, shining in the fatness of their growth like Spanish friars, and winking from their shelves in wanton slyness at the girls as they went by, and glanced demurely at the hung-up mistletoe. There were pears and apples clustered high in blooming pyramids; there were bunches of grapes, made, in the shop-keepers' benevolence, to dangle
> 15 from conspicuous hooks, that people's mouths might water gratis as they passed; there were piles of filberts, mossy and brown, recalling, in their fragrance, ancient walks among the woods, and pleasant shufflings ankle-deep through withered leaves; there were Norfolk Biffins, squab and swarthy, setting off the yellow of the oranges and
> 20 lemons, and, in the great compactness of their juicy persons, urgently entreating and beseeching to be carried home in paper bags and eaten after dinner. The very gold and silver fish, set forth among these choice fruits in a bowl, though members of a dull and stagnant-blooded race, appeared to know that there was something going on; and, to a fish, went gasping
> 25 round and round their little world in slow and passionless excitement.

Starting with this extract, write about how Dickens presents excitement about Christmas.

Write about:

- how Dickens presents Christmas in this extract

- how Dickens presents excitement about Christmas in the novel as a whole.

[30 marks]

All of the questions in this section will follow this format and you should use the bullet points to guide you when you write your answer.

Below are some example questions for all of the 19th-century novels in this section.

Novel	Example question
The Strange Case of Dr Jekyll and Mr Hyde by Robert Louis Stevenson	Read the ending of the novel from 'About a week has passed' to the end. How does Stevenson present Dr Jekyll as a man in torment? Write about: • how Stevenson presents Dr Jekyll in this extract • how Stevenson presents Dr Jekyll's torment and internal conflict in the novel as a whole.
Jane Eyre by Charlotte Brontë	Read Chapter 2 from 'All John Reed's violent tyrannies' to 'general opprobrium.' To what extent does Brontë present Jane as a victim? Write about: • how Brontë presents Jane in this extract • how Brontë presents Jane as a victim in the novel as a whole.
Pride and Prejudice by Jane Austin	Read Chapter 56 from 'Not so hasty' to 'contempt of the world'. How does Austen present attitudes towards social status in *Pride and Prejudice*. Write about: • how Austen presents attitudes towards social status in this extract • how Austen presents attitudes towards social status in the novel as a whole.
A Christmas Carol by Charles Dickens	Read from Stave 2: The First of the Three Spirits when Scrooge's sister comes to bring him home from 'It opened; and a little girl' to 'accompanied her.' Explain how Dickens explores the importance of family in *A Christmas Carol*. Write about: • how Dickens explores the importance of family in this extract • how Dickens explores the importance of family in the novel as a whole.
Great Expectations by Charles Dickens	Read Chapter 27 when Pip is waiting for Joe's arrival from 'Not with pleasure' to 'quite so brisk about it'. How does Dickens present the importance of appearances and respectability in *Great Expectations*? Write about: • how Dickens present the importance of appearances and respectability in this extract • how Dickens present the importance of appearances and respectability in the novel as a whole
Frankenstein by Mary Shelley	Read The Third Victim from 'Or were they rude to every stranger?' to 'took place last night'. How does Shelley present the effects of prejudice in *Frankenstein*? Write about: • how Shelley present the effects of prejudice in this extract • how Shelley present the effects of prejudice in the novel as a whole.
The Sign of Four by Sir Arthur Conan Doyle	Read Chapter 10 from 'We were fairly after her now' to 'rounding the Isle of Dogs'. Explore how Conan Doyle creates a sense of tension in *The Sign of Four*. Write about: • how Conan Doyle creates a sense of tension in this extract • how Conan Doyle creates a sense of tension in the novel as a whole.

PREPAREIT!

Before you begin answering the question, make sure that you really understand what it is asking you to do. This will help you to keep your answer sharp and relevant.

Here is how one student began preparing the question on *A Christmas Carol*:

> The people who were shovelling away on the house-tops were jovial and full of glee; calling out to one another from the parapets, and now and then exchanging a facetious snow-ball—better-natured missile far than many a wordy jest—laughing heartily if it went right, and not less
> 5 heartily if it went wrong. The poulterers' shops were still half open, and the fruiterers were radiant in their glory. There were great, round, pot-bellied baskets of chestnuts, shaped like the waistcoats of jolly old gentlemen, lolling at the doors, and tumbling out into the street in their apoplectic opulence. There were ruddy, brown-faced, broad-girthed
> 10 Spanish onions, shining in the fatness of their growth like Spanish friars, and winking from their shelves in wanton slyness at the girls as they went by, and glanced demurely at the hung-up mistletoe. There were pears and apples clustered high in blooming pyramids; there were bunches of grapes, made, in the shop- keepers' benevolence, to dangle
> 15 from conspicuous hooks, that people's mouths might water gratis as they passed; there were piles of filberts, mossy and brown, recalling, in their fragrance, ancient walks among the woods, and pleasant shufflings ankle-deep through withered leaves ; there were Norfolk Biffins, squab and swarthy, setting off the yellow of the oranges and
> 20 lemons, and, in the great compactness of their juicy persons, urgently entreating and beseeching to be carried home in paper bags and eaten after dinner. The very gold and silver fish, set forth among these choice fruits in a bowl, though members of a dull and stagnant-blooded race, appeared to know that there was something going on; and, to a fish,
> 25 went gasping round and round their little world in slow and passionless excitement.

Annotation (top): All these 'ing' verbs make the fun sound continuous and very active

Annotation (middle): So many images suggest fatness, which suggests plenty and ripeness - 'pot bellied', 'broad-girthed', 'fatness', and so on.

Annotation (bottom): Excitement, but why does he choose 'passionless'?

Choose the question for the 19th-century novel you are studying from the table on page 238 and 'prepare' the question in the space below.

PLANIT!

Once you have prepared the question on the novel you have studied, spend a few minutes planning the outline of your answer using the boxes below. (You do not have to stick to this number of paragraphs.) This plan should be about:

- key ideas to include
- the content of each paragraph
- the order of the paragraphs.

Paragraph 1

Paragraph 2

Paragraph 3

Paragraph 4

Paragraph 5

Paragraph 6

NAILIT!

Don't forget to:

- take note of the bullet points in the question – they are there to guide you
- compare the extract with two or three other relevant points in the text
- use evidence and subject terminology.

WORKIT!

Here is part of what one student wrote for the question on *A Christmas Carol* with some notes from an exam marker.

> One way Dickens makes the Christmas preparations sound exciting is by making a big list of stuff and starting lots of actions with 'ing' words: for example, 'shovelling', 'exchanging', 'laughing'. It makes the action very breathless and full of action. Also there are so many details listed that the reader can hardly keep up. For example, all the different foods are mentioned and described. So there are chestnuts, onions, pears, apples, grapes and other stuff and it's like we are rushing from one to the other and we can't help ourselves.

Lists – good point.

Evidence followed by some explanation. Good.

No mention of how these are described.

Here is what one exam marker wrote about this part of the student's answer.

> The answer is quite well organised: it makes good points, provides evidence and points out the effect on the reader. However, the student's own language is too vague and repetitive for the explanations to be very clear. Comments made about effects are useful and sometimes even perceptive (for example, the use of the word 'breathless'), but are too brief: nothing is explored. The answer will probably not get above Band 3.

Use the space below to make more notes about the writing. Pick out words or phrases from the text to back up your points. Refer to the mark scheme on page 229 to guide you.

....

....

....

....

....

....

....

....

....

....

....

....

....

DO IT!

Now have a go at answering the question you have been preparing and planning. You should spend 35–40 minutes on your writing and aim to write at least 500 words. Use the space provided below and continue on your own paper.

....

....

....

....

....

....

....

....

....

....

....

....

....

....

....

....

DO IT!

Try constructing your own questions for the novel you have studied, based on this list of themes.

Novel	Some themes
The Strange Case of Dr Jekyll and Mr Hyde	Evil, science, morality, horror, self-awareness
A Christmas Carol	Family, Christmas, greed, social responsibility, kindness, learning
Great Expectations	Love, ambition, self-improvement, social class, guilt, innocence
Jane Eyre	Love, independence, the position of women, marriage, education, justice, class
Frankenstein	Science, horror, mankind, nature, evil, prejudice
Pride and Prejudice	Social class, marriage, women, love, ambition, respectability
The Sign of Four	Evil, fear, empire, justice

Paper 2 Section A: Modern texts

KNOWIT!

☞ You will answer one essay question from a choice of two on your studied modern prose or drama text.

☞ You will have studied one of the following texts:

JB Priestley	*An Inspector Calls*
Willy Russell	*Blood Brothers*
Alan Bennett	*The History Boys*
Dennis Kelly	*DNA*
Simon Stephens	*The Curious Incident of the Dog in the Night-Time*
Shelagh Delaney	*A Taste of Honey*
William Golding	*Lord of the Flies*
AQA Anthology	*Telling Tales*
George Orwell	*Animal Farm*
Kazuo Ishiguro	*Never Let Me Go*
Meera Syal	*Anita and Me*
Stephen Kelman	*Pigeon English*

☞ You should spend 45 minutes on this section.

☞ The question is worth 30 marks.

☞ There are four additional marks for AO4: use a range of vocabulary and sentence structures for clarity, purpose and effect, with accurate spelling and punctuation.

Questions will follow the format below. This question is about *An Inspector Calls*.

In *An Inspector Calls,* Mr Birling says: 'a man... has to look after himself'. How does Priestley use the character of Mr Birling to explore ideas about the individual in society?

Write about:

• how Priestley presents the character of Mr Birling

• how Priestley uses Mr Birling to explore ideas about individuals in society.

[30 marks]

AO4 [4 marks]

All of the questions in this section will follow this format and you should use the bullet points to guide you when you write your answer.

Below are some example questions for all of the modern texts in this section.

JB Priestley *An Inspector Calls*	To what extent is Gerald changed by the events of *An Inspector Calls?* Write about: • how Gerald reacts to the inspector's visit • how Priestley presents Gerald by the way he writes.
Willy Russell *Blood Brothers*	How does Russell present freedom in *Blood Brothers*? Write about: • the ways particular characters struggle for freedom • how Russell presents freedom by the way he writes.
Alan Bennett *The History Boys*	How does Bennett present different ideas about education in *The History Boys?* Write about: • the different attitudes towards education in the play • how Bennett uses these different attitudes to explore ideas about education in *The History Boys.*
Dennis Kelly *DNA*	How does Kelly present the power of speech in *DNA?* Write about: • how characters use talk to have a strong effect on other characters • how Kelly uses these characters to explore ideas about the power of speech.
Simon Stephens *The Curious Incident of the Dog in the Night-Time*	How does the relationship between Christopher and his father change and develop in *The Curious Incident of the Dog in the Night-Time?* Write about: • how Christopher reacts to his father • how Stephens presents the relationship between Christopher and his father by the way he writes.
Shelagh Delaney *A Taste of Honey*	How does Delaney explore responsibility in *A Taste of Honey?* Write about: • ideas about responsibility in *A Taste of Honey* • how Delaney presents these ideas by the way she writes.
William Golding *Lord of the Flies*	How does the relationship between Ralph and Jack change in *Lord of the Flies?* Write about: • how Ralph and Jack react to each other at first • how and why their relationship changes during the rest of the novel.

AQA Anthology *Telling Tales*	In *The Darkness Out There*, the boy realises, 'you could get people wrong'. How do writers present 'getting people wrong' in *The Darkness Out There* and in one other story from *Telling Tales?* Write about: • some of the ideas about misjudging people presented in the two stories • how the writers present these ideas by the way they write.
George Orwell *Animal Farm*	How do the pigs gain and strengthen their control over the other animals in *Animal Farm*? Write about: • the pigs' actions at some key moments in the novel • how Orwell presents the pigs' control methods by the way he writes.
Kazuo Ishiguro *Never Let Me Go*	How does Ishiguro use the relationship between Kathy and Ruth to explore the importance of friendship in *Never Let Me Go*? Write about: • how Ishiguro presents the relationship between Kathy and Ruth • how Ishiguro uses this relationship to explore ideas about friendship.
Meera Syal *Anita and Me*	How does Syal present ideas about tolerance and kindness in *Anita and Me*? Write about: • how Syal presents examples of tolerance and kindness • how Syal presents ideas about tolerance and kindness by the way she writes.
Stephen Kelman *Pigeon English*	How does Kelman present the importance of decisions in *Pigeon English?* Write about: • decisions and choices that Harri makes • how Kelman presents the importance of decisions by the way he writes.

PREPARE**IT!**

Make sure that you really understand the question and what it is asking you to do. Choose the question for the modern text you are studying from the tables on pages 244–45 and 'prepare' the question in the space below. You should underline the key words and make a few notes to yourself, pointing out the key aspects of the question.

Here is how one student prepared the question on *An Inspector Calls* by JB Priestley.

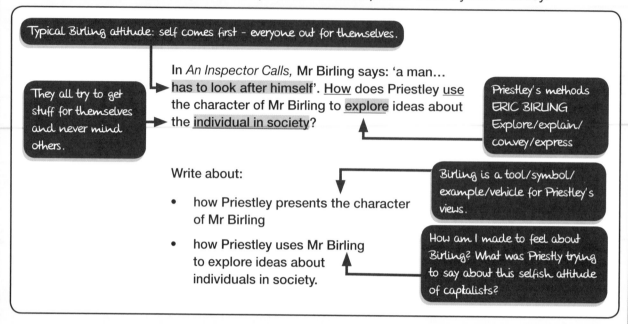

Typical Birling attitude: self comes first – everyone out for themselves.

They all try to get stuff for themselves and never mind others.

In *An Inspector Calls,* Mr Birling says: 'a man… has to look after himself'. <u>How</u> does Priestley <u>use</u> the character of Mr Birling to <u>explore</u> ideas about the <u>individual in society</u>?

Priestley's methods
ERIC BIRLING
Explore/explain/ convey/express

Write about:

- how Priestley presents the character of Mr Birling
- how Priestley uses Mr Birling to explore ideas about individuals in society.

Birling is a tool/symbol/ example/vehicle for Priestley's views.

How am I made to feel about Birling? What was Priestly trying to say about this selfish attitude of capitalists?

Use the space below to prepare your question:

PLANIT!

Once you have prepared your question, you should spend a few minutes planning the outline of your answer.

Below on the left is one student's plan for their answer to the question about how Priestley uses Birling to explore ideas about the individual in society. Use the boxes on the right hand side to plan your own answer to the question that you prepared on page 246.

Intro. Key ideas – Birling is selfish and proud of it. Himself and own family. Others all selfish. He doesn't really change in the play. Contrast with Sheila and Eric.	
How presented – bigot, selfish, destructive. How we feel about how he behaves/what he says. Use of inspector to guide how we react to Birling 'cranks' 'community and all that nonsense' 'a man has to mind his own business'.	
How Birling is used by Priestley. We don't believe/agree with him. He is a bigot. His views are contrasted directly with the inspector. He is made to look stupid, arrogant and dishonest.	
Are there some key methods Priestley uses? Juxtaposition/contrast? Dramatic irony? Birling being set up by Priestley?	
What is the Priestley trying to highlight about people's attitudes towards individuals? Why was this a key concern at that time?	

NAILIT!

- Your plan should be about the content of each paragraph, the order of the paragraphs, evidence to support your points and key ideas to include.
- You need to get quick and efficient at planning.
- Spend only 7–10 minutes on preparing the question and planning the answer.

WORKIT!

Here is part of one student's answer to the question about how Priestley uses Birling to explore ideas about the individual in society.

> Mr Birling's 'look after himself' speech echoes right through the play, almost drumming it into us, making us dislike Birling more every time he opens his mouth. When the inspector says a completely different speech as he leaves them all – 'we are responsible for each other' – this contradicts what Mr Birling said and makes us side against him even more. Priestley makes us agree that not only must a man 'look after himself and his own' but also treat others as friends, just like you would want others to treat you.
>
> Towards the end of the play, the inspector tells the family that if they haven't learned any lessons tonight then they would be 'taught it in fire and blood and anguish'. Basically, Priestley is saying they will have to learn the hard way, watching family go through the same torture that Eva Smith went through. Also the words 'fire and blood and anguish' relate to the horrors of the First World War that the characters didn't know was about to start. The play was written much later than it is set so the audience knows that the inspector's horrible prediction is right, even though Birling earlier called this prediction 'fiddlesticks'. This dramatic irony helped us to see Birling as blind and stupid.

Look at the mark scheme on page 229. Write some advice for this student about what they have done well and how they might make their answer even better.

....

....

....

....

....

....

....

....

....

....

....

....

....

....

NAILIT!

Here is a checklist for making your answer as developed as possible:
- Prepare and plan your answer.
- Be aware of the mark schemes for English Literature (see page 229 for a simplified mark scheme).
- Make clear, relevant points.
- Support your points with examples, quotations and other references to the text.
- Make sure you concentrate on *how* the writer puts across their ideas.
- Make a thoughtful, relevant point about context for each point.
- When you have finished your writing, spend at least 5 minutes checking that your answer makes sense and that there are no careless mistakes with spelling, punctuation and grammar.
- Check that you have used appropriate vocabulary, including subject terminology.

DOIT!

Now write your own answer to the question you prepared and planned earlier. Spend only 35 minutes on your writing, so that you do not steal time from sections B and C. Aim to write three to four detailed paragraphs, with an introduction and conclusion. Use the space provided below and continue on your own paper.

....

....

....

....

....

....

....

....

....

....

....

....

....

....

....

....

....

....

Paper 2 Section B: Poetry

KNOWIT!

You should answer the question on the cluster that you have studied – **either:**

> Love and relationships
> **or**
> Power and conflict

The question will always name one poem from your cluster and ask you to compare it with another poem of your own choice from the same cluster.

You cannot take your anthology into the exam with you, so you must make sure you know all the poems well.

The named poem will be printed on the exam paper so that you can easily refer to it.

☞ You should spend 40 minutes on this section, including 5–7 minutes of preparation and planning.

☞ The question is worth 30 marks.

Here are some example questions:

Love and relationships

Compare how poets present feelings of sadness in 'When We Two Parted' and in **one** other poem from 'Love and relationships'.

[30 marks]

Power and conflict

Compare how poets present attitudes towards violence in 'War Photographer' and in **one** other poem from 'Power and conflict'.

[30 marks]

PREPAREIT!

Make sure that you really understand the question and what it is asking you to do. Choose the question for the cluster you have been studying and 'prepare' the question in the space below. You should underline the key words and make a few notes to yourself, pointing out the key aspects of the question.

Here is how a student prepared a 'Love and relationships' poetry anthology question.

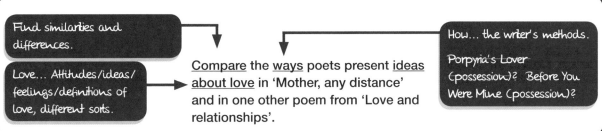

Find similarities and differences.

Love... Attitudes/ideas/feelings/definitions of love, different sorts.

Compare the ways poets present ideas about love in 'Mother, any distance' and in one other poem from 'Love and relationships'.

How... the writer's methods.

Porpyria's Lover (possession)? Before You Were Mine (possession)?

Use the space below to prepare your question. Don't forget to think about the context.

WORKIT!

The named poem will be printed on the exam paper, so do your quick plan on the exam paper. Write the name of your chosen poem next to the printed poem and then make some notes like in the example below:

Mother, any distance greater than a single span

Mother, any distance greater than a single span
requires a second pair of hands.
You come to help me measure windows, pelmets, doors,
the acres of the walls, the prairies of the floors.

5   You at the zero-end, me with the spool of tape, recording
length, reporting metres, centimetres back to base, then
leaving up the stairs, the line still feeding out,
unreeling years between us. Anchor. Kite.

I space-walk through the empty bedrooms, climb
10   the ladder to the loft, to breaking point, where something
has to give;
two floors below your fingertips still pinch
the last one-hundredth of an inch...I reach
towards a hatch that opens on an endless sky
15   to fall or fly.

Simon Armitage

Before You Were Mine also has single word sentence – Marilyn. These might suggest some contempt? Mockery? Not fully engaged?

Is she left with nothing – zero?

'base' – security? Control?

Single word sentences

Ideas about love

- Is love an anchor (restriction) or a kite (freedom) – fall or fly? Mother's love provides the anchor that makes flight/escape/freedom possible?

- Mother – child love: who has the upper hand?

- Child possesses the mother ('mine'). Photos 'capture' the past/the mother.

PLANIT!

Plan the answer to your question in the space provided below:

Named poem	Chosen poem

NAILIT!

Practise planning. However, don't spend more than 5–6 minutes on this in the exam.

WORKIT!

Here is part of the same student's answer with some comments by an exam marker.

In 'Mother, Any Distance' you can feel the way that the speaker feels about his mother; her 'fingertips still pinch the last one-hundredth of an inch' of the tape. This could suggest that she is desperate to hold on to her son but he knows she is losing him. He keeps contrasting her love and the freedom that he reaches towards: she is the 'anchor' to his 'kite', and in the final stanza he reaches upwards towards the 'endless sky'. She is the 'base' and is 'below' while he is reaching out and up. It's as though he almost resents her maternal help and love. And finds it a burden. This theme of tension in mother-child love is also in 'Before You Were Mine'.

> Integrated evidence.
> Evidence explained and explored briefly.

> Accurate subject terminology.

> Relevant subject terminology.

Look at the mark scheme on page 229. Write some advice for this student about what they have done well and how they might make their answer even better.

....

....

....

....

....

....

....

....

....

....

....

....

....

....

....

....

....

DO IT!

Now write an answer to the question you prepared. Start by writing one paragraph in which you use evidence, subject terminology and make a helpful reference to context. Continue on your own paper.

....
....
....
....
....
....
....
....
....
....
....
....
....
....
....
....
....
....
....

DO IT!

Here are two more questions for you to work on:

Compare how poets present ideas about togetherness in 'Love's Philosophy' and in **one** other poem from 'Love and relationships'.

[30 marks]

Compare the ways poets present ideas about violence in 'My Last Duchess' and in **one** other poem from 'Power and conflict'.

[30 marks]

Paper 2 Section C: Unseen poetry

KNOWIT!

☞ You will be given poems that you have not seen before. To prepare for the unseen poetry section of the exam you should read a wide range of poetry in order to develop your ability to closely analyse unseen poems.

☞ You will need to be able to analyse and compare key features such as their content, theme, structure and use of language.

☞ There are two questions and you must answer both of them.

☞ You should spend 50 minutes on this section.

☞ Section C is worth 32 marks.

Question 1

☞ You will be given a poem you have not seen before and you will be asked a question about it.

☞ Spend 35 minutes on this question.

☞ It is worth 24 marks.

☞ Try to write three significant paragraphs.

Here is an example of Question 1:

Your Dad Did What? ◄─────

Speaker must be teacher

Where they have been, if they have been away,
or what they've done at home, if they have not – ◄─────
you make them write about the holiday.
One writes *My Dad did*. What? Your Dad did what?

This list of things sounds weary – teacher done it loads of times?

'make them' sounds bossy and unfeeling

5   That's not a sentence. Never mind the bell.
     We stay behind until the work is done.
     You count their words (you who can count and spell);
     all the assignments are complete bar one

     and though this boy seems bright, that one is his.
10   He says he's finished, doesn't want to add
     anything, hands it in just as it is.
     No change. *My Dad did*. What? What did his Dad?

     You find the 'E' you gave him as you sort
     through reams of what this girl did, what that lad did,
15   and read the line again, just one 'e' short:
     This holiday was horrible. My Dad did.

                                    Sophie Hannah

In 'Your Dad Did What?' how does the poet present the speaker's feelings about the boy?

[24 marks]

256

NAILIT!

The exam question will ask you to consider:

- the theme and meaning of the poem
- the poet's methods
- the poem's mood, feelings and attitude
- how the reader is being made to feel about the topic, the speaker or a theme.

Always read the question before you read the poem. Then you know what to look out for.

PREPAREIT!

Use the space to the right of the poem and the lines below (Your Dad Did What?) to make some notes about the poem and annotate the question.

Use the space below to prepare your question. Don't forget to think about the context.

....
....
....
....
....
....
....
....
....
....
....
....
....
....

WORKIT!

Here is part of one student's answer to the question on page 256:

> In the first two stanzas the speaker (the teacher) sounds fed up and frustrated with the boy. I think this is because some of the lines sound like a teacher being naggy: 'that's not a sentence' and 'never mind the bell'. It's just like a teacher going on, but the boy is supposed to be writing about something sensitive and personal. When it then says 'We stay behind until the work is done' it gets worse because now the teacher is being threatening and the 'we' sounds sarcastic. I think the poem makes the speaker's feelings sound bad and makes us against her, so we are on the boy's side.

Now look at what an exam marker says about what this student has written:

> There are strengths in this answer: the student pays attention to detail in the poem and uses evidence (quotations). Also the student notices the feelings of the speaker, and goes on to consider how the reader is likely to feel about the speaker. The answer could be better organised, with one point being made and explained at a time, and some of the student's own language is too everyday to be clear. For example, 'it's just like a teacher going on' is not entirely clear, so that we can't be sure what the student means.

Rewrite the student's answer to improve it. Take into account:

- what the exam marker wrote
- the mark schemes for English Literature (see page 229 for a simplified mark scheme)
- the notes you made on the poem.

Continue on your own paper if necessary.

....

....

....

....

....

....

....

....

....

....

DO IT!

Here is another example first question on the same poem for you to try. Use the space provided and continue on your own paper.

In 'Your Dad Did What?' how does the poet present the relationship between teachers and students?

[24 marks]

....

....

....

....

....

....

....

....

....

....

....

....

....

....

....

....

....

....

....

....

....

....

....

KNOWIT!
Question 2

☞ You will be given another poem and you will be asked to compare it with the first poem.

☞ It is worth 8 marks.

☞ You should spend 15 minutes on this question.

Here is an example of Question 2:

The Lesson

'Your father's gone,' my bald headmaster said.
His shiny dome and brown tobacco jar
Splintered at once in tears. It wasn't grief.
I cried for knowledge which was bitterer
5 Than any grief. For there and then I knew
That grief has uses – that a father dead
Could bind the bully's fist a week or two;
And then I cried for shame, then for relief.

I was a month past ten when I learnt this:
10 I still remember how the noise was stilled
in school-assembly when my grief came in.
Some goldfish in a bowl quietly sculled
Around their shining prison on its shelf.
They were indifferent. All the other eyes
15 Were turned towards me. Somewhere in myself

Pride, like a goldfish, flashed a sudden fin.

Edward Lucie-Smith

Both 'Your Dad Did What' and 'The Lesson' present students' experiences of school. What are the similarities and/or differences between the ways the poets present those experiences?

[8 marks]

PREPAREIT!

Use the space next to the poem to make some notes that will help you to answer the question.

NAILIT!

Remember: you only have a few minutes for this question, so spend no more than five minutes reading and annotating the poem, and deciding on a couple of **relevant** similarities and/or differences between the two poems.

PLANIT!

Add a few of your own ideas to the chart below:

Your Dad Did What	Both poems	The Lesson

DO IT!

Now write your answer. Aim to write two points of comparison. Continue on your own paper.

DO IT!

Here is another example question for you to practise. Use your own paper.

Both 'Your Dad Did What' and 'The Lesson' present a student's grief and the teacher's response. What are the similarities and/or differences between the ways the poets present those experiences?

[8 marks]

ENGLISH LANGUAGE

Paper 1 Explorations in creative reading and writing
Time allowed: 1 hour 45 minutes

Source A

This extract is from a novel by George Orwell. It was written and set in the 1930s. Dorothy is the daughter of a vicar. In this section she is carrying out her duty of visiting local people (parishioners) in their homes.

A Clergyman's Daughter

It was a little after eleven. The day, which, like some overripe but hopeful widow playing at seventeen, had been putting on unseasonable April airs, had now remembered that it was August and settled down to be boiling hot.

5   Dorothy rode into the hamlet of Fennelwick, a mile out of Knype Hill. She had delivered Mrs Lewin's corn-plaster, and was dropping in to give old Mrs Pither that cutting from the Daily Mail about angelica tea for rheumatism. The sun, burning in the cloudless sky, scorched her back through her gingham frock, and the dusty road quivered in the heat, and the hot, flat meadows, over which even at this time of year numberless larks chirruped tiresomely, were so green that it hurt your eyes to look at them. It was the kind of day that is called 'glorious'
10 by people who don't have to work.

Dorothy leaned her bicycle against the gate of the Pithers' cottage, and took her handkerchief out of her bag and wiped her hands, which were sweating from the handle-bars. In the harsh sunlight her face looked pinched and colourless. She looked her age, and something over, at that hour of the morning. Throughout her day — and in general it was a seventeen-hour day —
15 she had regular, alternating periods of tiredness and energy; the middle of the morning, when she was doing the first instalment of the day's 'visiting', was one of the tired periods.

'Visiting', because of the distances she had to bicycle from house to house, took up nearly half of Dorothy's day. Every day of her life, except on Sundays, she made from half a dozen to a dozen visits at parishioners' cottages. She penetrated into cramped interiors and sat
20 on lumpy, dust-diffusing chairs gossiping with overworked, blowsy housewives; she spent hurried halfhours giving a hand with the mending and the ironing, and read chapters from the Gospels, and readjusted bandages on 'bad legs', and condoled with sufferers from morning-sickness; she played ride-a-cock-horse with sour-smelling children who grimed the bosom of her dress with their sticky little fingers; she gave advice about ailing aspidistras*,
25 and suggested names for babies, and drank 'nice cups of tea' innumerable — for the working women always wanted her to have a 'nice cup of tea', out of the teapot endlessly stewing.

Much of it was profoundly discouraging work. Few, very few, of the women seemed to have even a conception of the Christian life that she was trying to help them to lead. Some of them were shy and suspicious, stood on the defensive, and made excuses when urged to
30 come to Holy Communion⁺; some shammed piety for the sake of the tiny sums they could wheedle out of the church alms box; those who welcomed her coming were for the most part

the talkative ones, who wanted an audience for complaints about the 'goings on' of their husbands, or for endless mortuary tales ('And he had to have glass chubes let into his veins,' etc., etc.) about the revolting diseases their relatives had died of. Quite half the women on
35 her list, Dorothy knew, were at heart atheistical in a vague unreasoning way. She came up against it all day long — that vague, blank disbelief so common in illiterate people, against which all argument is powerless. Do what she would, she could never raise the number of regular communicants to more than a dozen or thereabouts. Women would promise to communicate, keep their promise for a month or two, and then fall away. With the younger
40 women it was especially hopeless. They would not even join the local branches of the church leagues that were run for their benefit — Dorothy was honorary secretary of three such leagues, besides being captain of the Girl Guides. The Band of Hope and the Companionship of Marriage languished almost memberless, and the Mothers' Union only kept going because gossip and unlimited strong tea made the weekly sewing-parties acceptable. Yes, it was
45 discouraging work; so discouraging that at times it would have seemed altogether futile if she had not known the sense of futility for what it is — the subtlest weapon of the Devil.

*An aspidistra is a houseplant that was popular at the time.

⁺ Holy Communion is a church service

Section A: Reading

Answer **all** questions in this section.
You should spend about 45 minutes on this section.

(1) Read again the first part of the Source **lines 1 to 10.**
List **four** things from this part of the text that show that it was summer.

[4 marks]

1 ....

....

2 ....

....

3 ....

....

4 ....

....

(2) Look in detail at this extract from **lines 17 to 26** of the Source:

'Visiting', because of the distances she had to bicycle from house to house, took up nearly half of Dorothy's day. Every day of her life, except on Sundays, she made from half a dozen to a dozen visits at parishioners' cottages. She penetrated into cramped interiors and sat on lumpy, dust-diffusing chairs gossiping with overworked, blowsy housewives; she spent hurried halfhours giving a hand with the mending and the ironing, and read chapters from the Gospels, and readjusted bandages on 'bad legs', and condoled with sufferers from morning-sickness; she played ride-a-cock-horse with sour-smelling children who grimed the bosom of her dress with their sticky little fingers; she gave advice about ailing aspidistras*, and suggested names for babies, and drank 'nice cups of tea' innumerable — for the working women always wanted her to have a 'nice cup of tea', out of the teapot endlessly stewing.

How does the writer use language here to describe Dorothy's visits?

You could include the writer's choice of:

- words and phrases
- language features and techniques
- sentence forms.

[8 marks]

Continue on a separate piece of paper.

(3) You now need to think about the **whole** of the **Source**.

This text is from the beginning of the novel.

How has the writer structured the text to interest you as a reader?

You could write about:

- what the writer focuses your attention on at the beginning
- how and why the writer changes this focus as the source develops
- any other structural features that interest you.

[8 marks]

....

....

....

....

....

....

....

....

....

....

....

....

....

....

....

....

....

....

....

Continue on a separate piece of paper.

(4) Focus this part of your answer on the final paragraph of the Source from **line 27 to the end**.

A student, having read this section of the text, said: 'This part of the text gives me a very clear understanding of Dorothy and her attitudes.'

To what extent do you agree?

In your response, you could:

- consider your own impressions of Dorothy and her attitudes
- evaluate how the writer has created the character of Dorothy
- support your opinions with references to the text.

[20 marks]

Continue on a separate piece of paper.

Section B: Writing

You should spend about 45 minutes on this section.
Write in full sentences.
You should plan your answer.
Make sure you leave enough time to check your work at the end.

5. A hospital is planning a booklet of creative writing under the title 'Just visiting'.

You have been asked to contribute some writing for the booklet, which will be edited by a doctor.

Either:

Write a description suggested by this picture:

Or:

Write a story about a visit to someone either at their home or in hospital.

(24 marks for content and organisation
16 marks for technical accuracy)

[40 marks]

....

....

....

....

....

....

....

Continue on a separate piece of paper.

ENGLISH LANGUAGE

Paper 2 Writers' viewpoints and perspectives
Time allowed: 1 hour 45 minutes

Source A: 21st century non-fiction
> An article called *No Way Out* by Richard Durant.

Source B: 19th century non-fiction
> A transcript from a newspaper article called 'Narrative of a survivor' published in 1882.

Source A – 21st century non-fiction

33 Miners, Buried Alive for 69 Days: This Is Their Remarkable Survival Story

After an explosion, some miners in Chile find themselves trapped underground.

Where there had always been the long tunnel to light and air, there was now a wall of stone. It was obvious there was no way through. Despite their desperate situation, the men knew they had to stay calm. The decisions they took now would be crucial if they were to have any chance of surviving.

5 They split into two groups. One group would explore the mine's complex tunnel network. Perhaps they would discover another route to the surface. In addition to the normal tunnels through which the miners reached their work stations, there were also occasional much steeper and narrower supply shafts that were used as supply routes for air, water and electricity. In an emergency these shafts could also be used as emergency exits, and were supposed to be fitted with ladders bolted securely to the rock face. In reality, the San José Mine owners had cut costs
10 by not maintaining these escape routes. Many of them were not even fitted with ladders. Just before the two groups went their separate ways, a foreman, Florencio Ávalos, advised a senior miner in the explorer group to stop his companions from eating and drinking all their supplies. What was obvious to Avalos – and what he wanted to keep secret from the men – was that their chances of survival were slim. If they didn't ration their provisions then their chances were zero.

15 The second group headed back to the central refuge – the underground safety area. When they got there their worst fears were confirmed: supplies of air, water and electricity had all been cut off. The miners settled down to conserve their energy, and waited. For hours. The only light came from the dim lamps on their helmets. When those ran down the darkness would be complete. Hunger, thirst and fear closed in on them.

20 Elsewhere, the explorer group had found a jumbo lifter and had used it to cut a hole in a tunnel roof near to where an escape shaft was marked on the map. One of the men, Sepúlveda, stood on the lifter platform and put his head through the hole. To his delight the light from his helmet lamp revealed a rough iron ladder clamped to a shaft wall. He grabbed a rung and, followed by another miner, Raúl Bustos, he began to climb. Going was hard: the miners choked on the thick
25 dust that filled the air; the walls were damp and slippery; and the metal rungs were rusty and insecure. One rung broke off and fell into Sepúlveda's upturned face, gashing his mouth. Despite these difficulties, the two men kept climbing.

Finally they reached the top of the shaft and climbed onto a broad and lightly-shelving rock shelf. Their hopes rose: this was clearly a ramp to the surface. An escape route. But why was it
30 still pitch dark? They took a few steps upwards and almost immediately came up against a solid, continuous wall of rock. Simultaneously the two men felt the hope drain from them. At that moment they knew they were going to die.

They forced themselves to retrace their steps, climbing back down the shaft. From there they searched for another way out. Perhaps there was another, better used shaft. For a long time all they
35 found was the smooth, black, unyielding rock face. Then suddenly their groping hands found a gap leading to another passage that turned almost straight upwards, and they trained their weakening lamps on the walls of the shaft. This one didn't even have a ladder. This was not the escape route.

Source B – 19th century non-fiction

A narrative of a survivor

In 1882, an explosion in a mine in the North-East of England killed 29 miners. On 17 February 1882 the local newspaper – *The Durham Advertiser* - reported the account of a survivor.

I heard a report* which appeared to come right to me from the direction of the shaft. I said to my marrow†, 'What's that?' To which he replied, 'I think it'll be a shot.' I said, 'That's no shot,' and as I spoke a boy came running up and shouted, 'Be sharp out-bye; there's a something happened. All the 'overcast' is blown out'.

5   We went off as hard as we could towards the shaft, other men and lads joining us. As we ran, the dust was so dense that it was like to smother us. We reached the shaft, however, and there we found the tubs all blown about, and the 'way' torn up, and the timbering and brattice piled up in a heap. The first thing we saw was the dead body of a young man which we recognised as that of William Jefferson. We lifted him up and placed him by the side of
10   the way. We then tried to get round to the other side of the shaft, but on our way we came upon the body of a man whose head had been blown off, a terribly mutilated body. One of our party succeeded in getting round, and saw a young boy's foot peeping out from beneath a tub. We all cowered about the shaft, and wondered if we should get out; it was then evident that no one but those about us could be saved.

15   When we had waited from between half-an-hour and an hour, we saw the lights of lamps coming towards us from the direction of the Cross-cut Flat. There were about nine men in this party, and one of them, just as they came up to us, dropped down. The men got him and brought him safely to the shaft where we were. The other eight men were all very bad from after-damp, and asked for something to drink, but of course we could give them nothing. We
20   stood about the pit for someone to come to us. No one else was found there whilst I was at the shaft bottom. These nine men told us that in the cross-cut flat, from which they came, all the boys were killed. When the explosion took place Jacob Soulsby, the deputy-overman in charge of that district, said, 'Tell them (the boys) to wait at the 'Rest' a bit.' They delivered this message, but the boys did not do so, and they were all killed by the choke-damp‡.

25   The cage was broken in the shaft, but at length the slings were let down, and we were drawn to bank by them and the 'kibble'. The engineman underground and I got into the slings together. He told me that when the explosion occurred he was blown away from his engine, but he did not appear to be seriously hurt. There were about thirty men and boys drawn up at the bottom of the shaft – gathered up from the various parts of the workings.
30   None of them appeared to be much the worse, although they had all suffered more or less from choke-damp. The engineman and I came to bank in the sidings, but the kibble was afterwards let down and brought the remainder of the men to bank.

*report – loud sound

†marrow – friend

‡choke damp – carbonic acid gas

Section A: Reading

Answer **all** questions in this section.

You should to spend about 45 minutes on this section.

1 Read again the first part of **Source A** from **lines 1 to 14**.

Choose **four** statements below which are TRUE.

- Shade the boxes of the ones that you think are true.
- Choose a maximum of four statements.

[4 marks]

A Only one group of miners looked for an escape route. ☐

B They all hoped to find a window behind the curtains. ☐

C The mining company also made shoes. ☐

D The mining company had saved money by providing fewer ladders. ☐

E Florencio Ávalos didn't expect to be rescued immediately. ☐

F Florencio Ávalos shouted instructions to the other miners. ☐

G Luckily, electricity and air were still flowing into the mine. ☐

H Electricity, air and water usually came through supply shafts. ☐

② You need to refer to **Source A** and **Source B** for this question.

Use details from **both** Sources. Write a summary of the differences between the experience of the miners in England and the miners in Chile.

[8 marks]

....

....

....

....

....

....

....

....

....

....

....

....

....

....

....

....

....

....

....

....

Continue on separate paper.

(3) You now need to refer **only** to **Source A**, the account of the accident in the mine in Chile.

How does the writer use language to try to make the account lively and interesting?

[12 marks]

Continue on separate paper.

④ For this question, you need to refer to the **whole** of **Source B**, together with **Source A**, the account of the accident in the mine in Chile.

Compare how the two accounts convey their different attitudes to the mining disasters.

In your answer, you could:

- compare the different attitudes conveyed
- compare the methods they use to convey their attitudes
- support your ideas with references to both texts.

[16 marks]

Continue on separate paper.

Section B: Writing

You should spend about 45 minutes on this section.

Write in full sentences.

You should plan your answer.

Make sure you leave enough time to check your work at the end.

(5) 'Health and safety in schools and colleges or at work is not taken seriously enough. We need to do something about this urgently.'

Write a letter to your local member of parliament, arguing for or against this statement.

(24 marks for content and organisation

16 marks for technical accuracy)

[40 marks]

....

....

....

....

....

....

....

....

....

....

....

....

....

....

....

....

Continue on separate paper.

Practice papers for English Literature are available online. Visit: www.scholastic.co.uk/gcse

Answers

English Language

You should also refer to the mark schemes for AQA English Language when checking your answers.

Paper 1 Section A: Reading

Question 1

Do it! (page 180)

Things that suggest the Englishwoman is surprised or puzzled:

- Her 'face looked puzzled'.
- She seems surprised that Hortense's husband did not go to meet her.
- She frowns when Hortense uses unfamiliar language and says, 'What?'.
- She asks Hortense if the luggage on the pavement is hers.

Question 2

Work it! (page 182)

Just as the words chosen show misunderstanding and a sort of clash of cultures, the styles of speech and narrative also stress collision between the two women. Hortense tries to give herself authority by speaking in flowing, extended sentences. By contrast, the Englishwoman speaks in short, abrupt sentences: 'What?'; 'It's the size of the Isle of Wight'; 'Hang on here'. The narrative confirms this abruptness too: 'She then shut the door in my face' is factual and direct and complements the way the Englishwoman speaks.

Do it! (page 183)

Answers could explore:

- Hortense's over-formal vocabulary and grammar suggest she is feeling vulnerable and is trying to sound impressive and full of authority.
- The Englishwoman's informal speech suggests she feels relaxed and in control: 'It's', 'he's', 'Hang on'.
- Simple, short sentence, 'She then shut the door in my face', suggests Hortense is surprised/confused/ offended.
- The Englishwoman's colourful hyperbole (exaggeration), 'It's the size of the Isle of Wight', suggests that the woman is feeling playful and humorous.

Do it! (page 184)

Answers could explore:

- The contrast in the two women's registers of language – Hortense is absurdly formal, the Englishwoman is very direct and informal.
- The Englishwoman's use of very direct, short questions.
- The 'white island' pun is used to draw attention to the two women's very different cultural backgrounds.
- Hortense's description of the woman's 'gentle giggle that played...', which tells us how much more relaxed the Englishwoman is than Hortense.

Question 3

Do it! (page 187)

Answers could explore:

- The clear and striking description of the Englishwoman at the beginning, so that we have this as a reference point for the rest of the episode.
- The use of dialogue rather than narrative to reveal the mutual misunderstandings of the two women, so that we share the confusion with Hortense.
- The contrasting patterns of language used by the two women.
- The role of the last paragraph in providing a sort of amazed commentary by Hortense, as she tries to account for her confusion.

Question 4

Do it! (page 190)

Answers could explore:

- To what extent *do* you agree? After all, Hortense's behaviour and confusion might be caused by her sense of vulnerability, so we could wonder if her behaviour is not typical of her.
- What impression of Hortense do you get? Is she a snob? Is she foolish to use language that she clearly cannot control? Is she over-concerned with appearances and with giving an impression of her 'superiority'?
- How do you feel about Hortense? What is your reaction to her? Do you feel sympathy for her?
- Look at some particular details in the text and ask yourself how these affect your reaction to Hortense. For example, explore the effect on you of her imagining that she will need 'ropes and pulleys to hoist me up'. The choice of 'hoist' creates an amusing mental picture.

Do it! (page 191)

Answers could explore:

- To what extent do you agree? Do you find yourself warming to her? If so, why?
- What impression of Hortense do you get? Do you think her mistakes make her look foolish?
- Look at some particular details in the text and ask yourself how these affect your reaction to Hortense.

Paper 1 Section B: Writing

Question type 1

Do it! questions (page 194)

Answers could include:

- A description of the whole scene, followed by a section of the scene, followed by one detail in that section – a sort of 'zooming in' approach.
- What is the mood or feeling of the scene? Try to capture/evoke that mood in words.

- Write in the present tense as though you are there and writing as you look.
- Are there any smells and sounds you could describe, as well as sights?

Question type 2

Do it! (page 196)

The answer could include:

- A lovely surprise, such as being taken to a football match or a theme park.
- Describe how you were feeling just before the surprise.
- Describe your reaction to the exciting thing.
- The use of some similes and metaphors to make your descriptions more original and fresh for the reader.

Do it! (page 196)

The answer could include:

- The difficult decision.
- Describe how you were feeling just before you had to make the decision. Worried, nervous?
- Describe how you were feeling after you had made the decision. Relieved or still worried?
- The use of some similes and metaphors to make your descriptions more original and fresh for the reader.

Question type 3

Do it! questions (pages 197–9)

Answers could:

- Start by setting the scene with an interesting description based on the picture.
- Write in the first person as the narrator describing the scene suggested by the picture.
- Start with a 'teaser' such as, 'As I looked out of my window that morning, how could I possibly have known that this was the last time I would see this familiar scene for a very long time?'
- Start the next section of the opening with someone or something coming into the scene from outside the picture.

Question type 4

Work it! (page 200)

At last Tessa was ready. She had planned carefully and in in secret. In some bushes at the edge of the cove, her boat was waiting for her, its oars stacked neatly. Supplies of food, water and essential equipment were neatly stored under the seats. In the moonlight her groping hands found the stern of the boat and she shoved hard. At first – weighed down with its cargo – the boat resisted her efforts, but suddenly with a scrunching noise the boat released from its hiding place and slid over the sand and into the water with a gentle whoosh. One last agonised push with her injured arm and the boat was floating. Joy pulsed through her body, driving out the pain, as she realised she was nearly free. But then worry nagged at her again: how long would she be on her own out at sea? How long could she survive? She still had no answer to these dreadful doubts.

Do it! (page 201)

The answer could include:

- What you were getting away from.
- What made you decide to get away when you did.
- Your feelings.
- How you prepared.
- The moment/day you got away.

Do it! (page 202)

The answer could include:

- What the dare was.
- How the dare came about.
- Why someone was tempted to do the dare.
- Start the story with the dare taking place, and then jump back in time.

Do it! (page 202)

The answer could include:

- What was unusual about the journey.
- Where you were going.
- Why you were going on the journey.
- How you got there.

Question type 5

Work it! (page 203)

... could feel his confidence draining out of him: he wasn't so jokey and carefree now. He too was overcome with dread about what might happen next.

Omran hated cobwebs and dark, damp places, but he pushed on until he was out of range of the others' whimpering and whining. He could see nothing now and so he stretched his hands forward and felt his way ahead. Occasionally he stumbled as – blind and terrified – he inched his way forward, and he had to reach into the menacing blackness to find something solid by which he could steady himself and stop himself from falling headlong into whatever his overheated imagination could summon up. Then he met something very real. Something solid. Something that there was no way through or around.

Do it! (page 204)

Answers could include:

- They are lost in a forest.
- They are in the forest because they dared each other to go deeply into the forest.
- One of them is injured.
- The situation allows them to learn things about themselves and each other.

Do it! (page 204)

Answers could include:

- What the misunderstanding was.
- Who the misunderstanding was between.
- What the consequences of the misunderstanding were.
- How the misunderstanding was resolved.

Paper 2 Section A: Reading

Question 1

Prepare it! (page 208)

- It is wise to plan carefully. We need to know that 'throwing caution to the wind' means being careless.
- Your safety and happiness will depend on good planning. We need to know that 'attention to detail' means *more than* just attention: it means doing something about it.
- Poor planning will lead to avoidable miseries. We need to realise that 'attention to detail' is another way of saying 'careful planning'.

Work it! (page 209)

A, D, E, H

Do it! (page 209)

B, C, G, H

Question 2

Prepare it! (page 210)

Tick:

Similarities

Preparations for sleeping outdoors

Do it! (page 211)

Answers could include:

- Shelter.
- Something to sleep in.
- Being unobtrusive.
- Carrying your sleeping equipment.

Do it! (page 212)

Some similarities:

- Both are light-hearted (at times).
- Both use informal (colloquial) phrases (e.g 'look into bivi-bags' in Source A; 'This child of my invention' in Source B) to suggest a slightly flippant, jokey attitude.
- Both use precise technical terms to convey authority.

Differences:

- Source A is encouraging and helpful; Source B is a narrative account and does not encourage readers in general to try wild camping.
- Source B suggests a more individual and amateur approach to wild camping – an approach based on improvisation and experiment.

Question 3

Prepare it! (page 213)

A and E are only about content.

Do it! (page 214)

Answers could include:

- Short, factual statements make Stevenson sound authoritative.

- Precisely described details suggest he knows what he is talking about: he is a confident expert.
- The use of the present tense in the early lines suggest that he is able to draw wise conclusions from a lot of personal experience: he is able to generalise from his experience.
- A teasing edge to Stevenson's tone suggests that he is not the fool we might assume he is: he is laughing at us for doubting him.

Do it! (page 215)

Answers should explore Stevenson's choice of language.

Question 4

Do it! (page 218)

Answers could include:

- Source A gives advice, whereas Source B gives an account of his own personal preparations with no attempt to convince readers that these were the best possible preparations.
- Although Source A does use humour, it is very practical and gives clear, professional advice. Source B maintains a personal, entertaining tone throughout, even though useful advice could be extracted from the account.
- Source B sounds as though wild camping must be a solitary activity and that avoiding company is one of its delights. Source A does not imply this, and does not overtly assume that a wild camper will be a solitary camper.
- Source B is clearly literary and rhetorical in tone, making use of a number of literary devices for effect. The main purpose of Source A – by contrast – is to give clear information and advice rather than to entertain.

Do it! (page 219)

Answers should compare the different attitudes of the two writers and compare the methods they use to convey those attitudes. References to both texts should be used to support ideas.

Paper 2 Section B: Writing

Work it! (page 223)

C (Band 4); A (Band 3); B (Band 2)

Work it! (page 224)

The right to vote was won in 1832, but even then very few people were included in the electorate: basically, you had to be rich to be allowed to vote. As time went on, more and more men were given the right to vote. By the end of the 19th century, almost every man had the vote. Women, however, had to wait until 1930 before they all got the vote on equal terms with men. Then, much later in the 20th century, the voting age was lowered from 21 to 18. It does seem that over time, the vote has been going down. In 1930 many people claimed it would cause chaos to give women below 30 the vote. In the 1970s many people claimed it would cause chaos to give the vote to eighteen-year-olds. But chaos did not follow. If we reduce the voting age again to 16, then the same sorts of people will predict chaos and the end of the world as we know it. History tells us that they will be wrong again.

Technical accuracy

Work it! (page 225)

The most important consideration is not how old a voter is, but how mature they are, some people are old and immature, while others are both young and very mature. Instead of giving anyone a vote when they reach a certain age, it might be wiser to give them a test first to find out how sensible they are. Some elderly voters might fail this test; they would have to give up their vote along with their driving licence. This rule might mean that the electorate would include some voters who are as young as 16, but some older people might become ex-voters.

Do it! (page 226)

Answers should take into account the required audience, subject matter, form and purpose.

Do it! (page 228)

Answers could include:

* A series of paragraphs, each containing one developed point, not too assertively presented.
* How life was/would be different without the internet.
* How a couple of specific examples of aspects of the internet have improved life.
* Possible bad effects of some aspects of the internet.

English Literature

Answers will vary according to the material studied. You should refer to the mark schemes for AQA English Literature when checking your answers.

Paper 1 Section A: Shakespeare

Work it! (page 235)

This is a well-organised and relevant response. Well-chosen references effectively support points made. The answer points out some ways Shakespeare's language affects the audience, although none of these are well-developed. Consideration of possible differences in audience reactions over time is useful. 'Emotive language' is correctly and usefully identified. To get into Band 5 the answer needs to more fully explore the effects of Shakespeare's language choices.

Paper 1 Section B: The 19th-century novel

Work it! (page 241)

Other points that could be explored include:

* Unnecessary repetition: e.g. 'breathless' is basically the same as 'can hardly keep up'.

* Many of the foods are described as though they are fat humans so that we get the connection between the foods and their potential to fill bellies that are often empty.
* Foods are sometimes described as though they are begging to be eaten – 'entreating', 'beseeching'
* The very long, 'rolling' sentences seem to envelop the reader as though they are inside the shops among all the ripe foods.

Paper 2 Section A: Modern texts

Work it! (page 248)

This is a thoughtful and generally well-organised response. Precisely chosen quotations are fluently integrated into the answer. The answer points out some ways the writer uses to manipulate the audience to be on the side of the inspector. The reference to the historical context is very relevant and adds to our understanding. 'Dramatic irony' is correctly and usefully pointed out. The answer would be even better if some of the writer's methods were explored more fully, with some analysis of their intended effect on the audience.

Paper 2 Section B: Poetry

Work it! (page 254)

This paragraph deals with the contrast between the mother and son very well, and it roots its analysis in relevant, well-chosen details from the text. Explanations use precise subject terminology which allows the student to make perceptive points quickly and efficiently. The use of hesitant language such as 'this *could* suggest…' and 'it's *as though*…' helps the student to interpret and consider possible explanations rather than treating the poem like something that has definite answers. The answer would be even better if the student occasionally paused and explored the nuances of particular features. For example, what does the word 'pinch' suggest that – say – 'hold' wouldn't? What is so 'endless' about the sky? Why did he choose to emphasise that feature of the sky?

Paper 2 Section C: Unseen poetry

Do it! (page 259)

Answers could include:

* The teacher does not trust the student, and is not sensitive to them.
* A very unequal relationship – no dialogue.
* The account is looking back (even though it is written in the present tense for immediacy), so there is a suggestion that the teacher is ashamed of how he treated the student.
* The unusual use of the word 'you' means that the whole narrative is in the second person. It sounds as though the poet is accusing the teacher, or as though the teacher is trying to distance himself from himself, referring to himself as 'you', not 'I'.

Do it! (page 261)

Answers could include:

- We are sorry for the students – especially because the teachers seem so insensitive.

- The way the teachers speak is harsh and very unkind (although in 'Your Dad Did What?' the teacher's words are only implied.)

- The second poem explores the development over time of the student's experience, whereas the first poem deals only with the experience itself – and its implied effect on the teacher.

- Both poems use rhyme to shape the narratives and give extra force to the lessons that we/the teachers/students should learn from the events.

Answers to the practice papers are available online. Visit: www.scholastic.co.uk/gcse